The Book of
SPELLS,
HEXES, AND
CURSES

The Book of
SPELLS, HEXES, AND CURSES

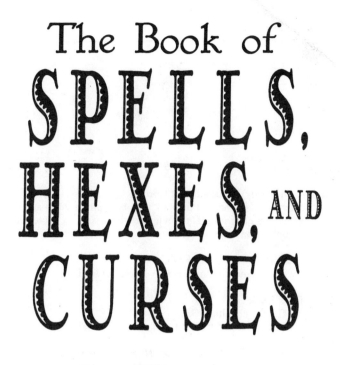

True Tales From Around the World

STUART GORDON

A Citadel Press Book
Published by Carol Publishing Group

Carol Publishing Group Edition, 1995

Previously published as *The Book of Curses*
Published by arrangement with Headline Book Publishing

A Citadel Press Book
Published by Carol Publishing Group
Citadel Press is a registered trademark of Carol Communications, Inc.

Editorial Offices: 600 Madison Avenue, New York, NY 10022
Sales & Distribution Offices: 120 Enterprise Avenue, Secaucus, NJ 07094
In Canada: Canadian Manda Group, One Atlantic Avenue, Suite 105
Toronto, Ontario, M6K 3E7

Queries regarding rights and permissions should be addressed to:
Carol Publishing Group, 600 Madison Avenue, New York, NY 10022

Manufactured in the United States of America
ISBN 0-8065-1675-5

10 9 8 7 6 5 4 3 2 1

Carol Publishing Group books are available at special discounts
for bulk purchases, sales promotions, fund raising, or
educational purposes. Special editions can also be created to
specifications. For details contact: Special Sales Department,
Carol Publishing Group, 120 Enterprise Ave., Secaucus, NJ 07094

The Cataloging-in-Publication Data for this title may be obtained
from the Library of Congress.

The Book of

SPELLS,
HEXES, AND
CURSES

Damn braces. Bless relaxes
  – William Blake, 1793

May you live in interesting times
  – ancient Chinese curse

To Bill Smith of Urquhart

Thanks, Bill,
for suggesting this lovely subject.

You didn't know what you were getting me into.
Neither did I.

Contents

Ancient sorcery: the Witch of Endor, Erichtho, the Crone of Thessaly. The Ides of March. Cursed comets. Scapegoats. Anti-Semitism, from Alexander the Great to Adolf Hitler.

legendary fate in the 1660s. Various accounts of his death and the curse. The last Seaforth and the *cailleach*. The death of his sons as prophesied. The four deformed lairds. Wide knowledge of the curse before its fulfilment. The historical Coinneach.

brother Joe Jr, led to suicide mission in 1944. How JFK became President. His affairs, Mafia connections, death of Marilyn Monroe, assassination. Murder of his brother Bobby in 1968. Chappaquiddick, 1972: shame of third brother Teddy. Troubles of the third generation. Curse of the father's ambition.

Case of 'The Nanny they Called a Witch'. Twenty-year-old Scots girl follows Italian lover to Rome in 1982, works as nanny with two Italian families. In each house inexplicable fires break out in children's beds. Spends seventeen months in jail before trial. Found guilty of arson and deported. Fires remain inexplicable, but parapsychologists speak of 'Recurrent Spontaneous Psycho-kinesis'. Fires subconsciously produced due to emotional misery? Other cases: London, Brazil and Germany. Science cannot comprehend it.

Bad luck attached to inanimate objects; typically cars, ships and jewels, murder or sudden death causing the jinx. Cars in which Franz Ferdinand (1914) and James Dean (1955) died. The *Great Eastern* and *Titanic* and *Titanian*, also the *Scharnhorst*. Leth-bridge: 'ghoul' of Ladram Bay, and death of a 'witch' who cursed cattle. Devastation of Henry James. Occult history of jewels: the Regent, Koh-i-Noor, and Hope diamonds. The 'Diamond Neck-lace Affair' that disgraced Marie Antoinette. The Aztec 'Skull of Doom'.

Curious history of belief that disaster arises from naming or quoting from *Macbeth* in a theatre. Superstition? Enough exam-ples suggest that flouting the belief in a curse has led to unlucky results. Was the curse caused by Shakespeare using actual black magic incantations? True or not, who would want to risk it?

Three million official reports of child sex abuse in USA in 1992 alone. Fantasies taken at face value: innocents jailed. Return of a medieval curse? Edenton, North Carolina; East Olympia, Wash-ington; Christchurch, New Zealand; the Orkney Case. False Memory Syndrome.

Belief that prolonged staring curses. Ancient belief in an 'eye-beam'. The eye of Atum. The eye of Horus. The gaze of the Medusa. Celtic and African beliefs. Italian fear of the *jettatore*.

The evil eye of Pope Pius IX. Talismans and amulets against *malocchio*. Demonic images and shields. The *mano cornuta, mano fica*, 'V-sign', and sign of the cross.

Appendix II: Thought-forms
A theory towards how curses work. The power of mind, whether conscious or otherwise. Edward Russell's theory of 'T-fields'. The claim by Daskalos that any intense emotional brooding creates 'elementals' which can take on a life of their own. Alexandra David-Neel's *tulpa*; Dion Fortune's werewolf; the *egrigor*; 'Philip the Imaginary Ghost'.

1 Introduction

Welcome to *The Book of Curses*!

Herein you will find tales ancient and modern, from all round the world and all said to be true, on the grim subject of curses, malediction, the evil eye, death-prayers and hexes, taboos and magical prohibition.

You may feel that such unpleasant territory is best left unexplored. Certainly, the subject itself seems to be cursed. Compared with the flood of books available on almost every other occult theme, few texts deal with curses. Information on UFOs, earth energies, pet crystals, pyramid power, ghosts, prophecy and astrology crowds bookshop shelves; also darker texts, from hoary old witch-burning manuals like the *Compendium Maleficarum*, to discourses on satanism, demonology, necromancy, serial killing and other such subjects. Millions enjoy gory slash-and-exorcise horror tales or their movie/video versions. Fancy a Coke with Hannibal the Cannibal, or popcorn at a late-nite double bill of old *Dracula* movies?

Yet the curse (preferably cast millennia ago by Egyptian magicians or wild-eyed druids), while a stock-in-trade of B-grade horror found in the video/book store next to Clive Barker's latest, gets no respect. It is not regarded as a subject fit for serious treatment.

This is understandable. Cursing is not pleasant. But neither is vampirism nor mass murder, which does not keep Stephen King off the best-seller lists. And how many of us get through our lives without cursing something or someone – late trains, bad weather, the car that will not start, an unfaithful lover? Even so, most of our curses are casual, made in the heat of the moment, without deliberation or real belief in their effect.

Cursing on the grand scale is as rare today in the West as is belief in the power of prayer or blessing. Today, to admit belief in the actuality of hex or death-prayer is to risk being laughed at. Few of us, driving our car into a wall if distracted by a neighbour shouting angrily, will claim that the neighbour, an amateur black magician, made us crash having cursed us because we would not lend him the lawn-mower. Maybe so, but who could prove it? Even if he put a note through the door: *May you drive your car into a wall, you mean sod*, no court of law would accept that it was his curse that did it.

Yet in parts of Northern Europe three hundred years ago, hundreds of thousands of women were judicially killed (burned at the stake, usually after torture) on the basis of similar accusations. *She put the evil eye on my cow, and now the milk is curdled. She's a witch! Burn her!*

It is no great loss that today, by and large, we are too sophisticated to believe in the efficacy of curses; or that we dismiss them by insisting that their power is entirely psychological, accepting only that, if you believe in curses and the shaman points the bone at you, you die because you know you will. Especially if everyone else behaves as if you're already dead.

Mostly, our scepticism is positive. Not to believe in something is to deny it power, and as curses are usually malign (even if or when deserved), then is it not sensible to deny the power of the evil will?

However, to be consistent, we must also then deny the power of blessing and prayer. Both, after all, involve the consciously directed magical will, if to different ends. The malign effect of a curse is as hard to prove or disprove as is the benign effect of a blessing. In each case, the invisible active agent, willed intention, cannot be weighed or measured. In each case, the active agent is the human *mind* (aided, some say, by undetermined 'higher forces') . . . and though some behavioural psychologists have tried to deny the existence of this ghost in their machine, they can do so only because they have a mind with which to deny mind.

But that is another kind of curse. It is called dogmatic stupidity.

So, what *is* a curse?

From the Anglo-Saxon word *cursien* (etymology unknown), meaning 'to invoke harm or evil upon', a curse is a malediction spoken or written to make an enemy or malefactor suffer or die, or to punish the breaking of taboo, or to prophesy harm to evil-doers or their kin. The latter type, typically cast by the poor on the mighty, and often the last resort of those treated unjustly, assumes the existence of a universal moral or karmic balance. The crime will be punished, though perhaps not for generations. Thus cases like (in Scotland) the Seaforth Doom, and (in England) the Cowdray Curse.

The prohibitive curse is designed to prevent action through fear of the consequences. Rob a pharaoh's tomb, and be struck down. Touch the king's head, and die. Ignore a Papal Bull, and be anathematised. Eat pork, and be cursed. Sleep around, and go to hell (ancient) or get AIDS (modern)!

This type of curse or taboo is primarily a social, not a magical act, though supernatural power may be invoked to add weight to it, in the belief that the workings of divine law will realise the prophesied retribution.

Curses may be cast in secret; by open evil look and pointed finger; by spoken or written word (anathema); by sending the victim an object charged with the curse, or by magic ritual, as by burning or stabbing an image of the victim. Traditionally, such images are wax or wood dolls incorporating the victim's nail-parings, hair or spit. Today, it may be enough to place seven black candles on a photograph of the victim, and burn them for seven minutes on seven successive days – a technique still popular in New Orleans.

The principle here is that of sympathetic magic: like attracts like. For typically the curse is a magical act (Aleister Crowley defined magic as: 'the science and art of causing change to occur in conformity with the Will'). Its essence lies in the imaginative projection of ill-will. Long part of the psychic arsenal of priest or magician, some say the curse works only if the victim knows of or believes in it. As a cancer-sufferer expecting to die is more likely to die than one who fights the illness, so a cursed person is said to die simply due to lost hope. The terrified unconscious undermines consciousness; especially if a guilty conscience is involved.

A curse may still work even if the victim either does not know of it or does not believe in curses, as with the death-prayers of the Kahunas of Hawaii (see chapter 13). Yet the Kahunas also held that, where no sense of guilt is involved, the unconscious mind will reject the attack.

In other cases, the curse seems to be non-specific to any particular individual, but strikes anyone in contact with a hexed object or place, or born to a hexed family. There are also numerous accounts of jinxed cars and ships that bring bad luck and disaster to all associated with them (see chapter 19). Such accounts are undeniable – unless, of course, you prefer to deny them simply because you do not want to face unpleasant reality.

And that is another kind of curse.

For those who do not doubt (and that includes most people in almost every society throughout known history), there are many traditional defences against cursing and the evil eye. These include charms, spells, amulets and the power to make the curse rebound on the curser.

All pure hokum?

It is anciently and widely believed that Mind controls Matter, and that there are hidden laws by which this control may be manifested, for good or ill. From time immemorial, folk have inhabited a magical universe. Only lately has this world view been challenged by scientific rationalism, which accepts only observed material cause and effect in defining what is 'real'.

Is science so rational? Even while believing itself entirely free of magical taint, orthodox scientific dogma (the curse of Faust lingering over it) curses various areas of inquiry as unscientific, damning those who enter taboo areas as mystics. A researcher deciding that astrology is not all nonsense is wise to keep quiet . . . even if he never walks under ladders. An anthropologist reporting on 'primitive' magical belief systems does so in a distanced, objective, scientific manner, not as a believer . . . even if privately he retells as fact a case of the Kahuna death-prayer working, or how in Australia he saw a man 'boned', or how in New York City today people are still literally hexed and scared to death.

Many such taboos and curses seem absurd. The priests of the Hos in West Africa could never cut their hair, on pain of death: their god lived in their hair. When the chief of Namosi in Fiji needed a hair-cut, he had first to eat a man to protect himself against the danger of (as with Samson) losing his virility by being shorn. The Mikado of Japan was shamefully degraded if his foot even so much as touched the ground. The sun and moon were not even allowed to shine on his head. Absurd? So it was that the Mikado's power was limited. He could not go anywhere or do anything private. High priests and kings were too important and too dangerous to society to be allowed free rein, so they were hedged about with taboos, a curse on them if they broke any of them. And there was the magical element. If they failed in their ritual duty, the land was cursed. Crops would wither, babies die, enemies invade. For, as in Arthurian myth, Land and King were said to be one.

Are we free of such 'superstition'? Might not the endless ritual media degradation of the British royal family reflect a widely held sense that the past they represent is dead, and that the land itself is under a curse – of unemployment, crime, uncertainty about the future? And how many of us during the 1960s wondered if the Kennedys were cursed, if only by their own gargantuan ambition? It is all in the mind, after all . . .

Or is it? How does author Salman Rushdie feel about the *fatwa* put on him by Iran's ayatollahs, so that any Muslim may 'lawfully' murder him?

Old taboos are only gradually broken. Many have to do with the social boundaries of what is acceptable behaviour and what is not. Those breaking social boundaries (by committing incest or murder, by betraying country or kin, or simply by refusing to toe the line) are traditionally cast out, to become invisible, without shelter, anathema. They are *cursed*. The fear of such a fate keeps most of us in line most of the time. Only in times of radical change, with society disordered (thus the old Chinese curse: *May you live in interesting times*) do the traditional moral prohibitions fail.

Then, with the old citadel fallen, and old beliefs burned triumphantly at the stake, the new conquerors soon proceed to establish *new* anathemas, *new* curses . . . as scientific rationalism has cursed all magical thinking.

This process is part of the most basic Western curse of all. Called Original Sin or the Fall, it lies at the very heart of Judaeo–Christian psychology. According to this potent theology, we have all been fatally cursed ever since Yahweh threw Adam and Eve out of Eden for eating the fruit of the Tree of Knowledge of Good and Evil. Their sin was to become self-conscious. As promoted by St Paul and others, we are cursed simply because we exist, because we think, because of the war in us between Reason and Instinct and Emotion, and most of all because we are sexual beings.

This curse, claims the Church, which since early times has never been averse to enjoining God's Wrath on those opposed to it, is immutable and cannot be undone save via the redemption of Christ.

Thus was created the mind-set that led to the triumph of patriarchy and to witch-hunts against women amid the scientific revolution, and today to the spread of cheeseburger imperialism.

For curses consist not just in individual malediction, but in states of paranoia and fear which can endure collectively for centuries. The witch-hysteria that gripped Europe in the sixteenth and seventeenth centuries was just such a curse, a madness from which collectively we have barely emerged; if we have emerged from it at all. This, after all, has been *par excellence* a century of pogroms and persecutions, of mass slaughter and the atom bomb, of cursed activity on a scale unmatched even by Genghis Khan or the Inquisition.

Since we inhabit the curse of our own contradictory nature, midway between angel and beast, it is no wonder we do not like to talk about curses.

In the east, folk talk less of *curse* than *karma*, meaning that whatever you do, or even think, has an effect, and that no way can you escape the consequences of your actions – especially if you were unaware of them.

Lack of awareness is the curse.

Even if you cannot or will not believe these tales of curse and malediction, they shed light on human nature, on what people always believed before becoming too embarrassed to admit to believing in anything at all. As Theodore Sturgeon, an American science fiction writer who died a few years ago, put it succinctly and to the point in what has become known as Sturgeon's Law: *Ninety-five per cent of everything is bullshit.* Which leaves five per cent that is not. Worth remembering, as we start trampling through the mires of human hearsay.

We will start with some modern examples of malediction. So maybe you should toss some salt over your shoulder before you turn the page . . .

2   Contemporary Curses

Even in the seemingly sceptical, materialist Western societies, priding themselves on having banished all superstition and magical thinking, the ancient practices of curse and blessing are alive and kicking. Not only in the Australian Outback, Dahomey or Haiti, but in London, New Orleans and San Francisco, men and women are killed by fear of curse. Stalls in Harlem, New York City, offer bat's blood and graveyard dust for sale. Studying voodoo death (see chapter 15) in the USA, Professor Kenneth M. Golden of Little Rock, Arkansas, reports many instances of effective hexing without medical explanation, including the case of a woman suffering uncontrollable spasms after rejecting lesbian advances from a voodoo woman, and of a black man, probably hexed by his own wife, who died of cardiac arrest after two weeks in the University Hospital. The autopsy showed there was nothing physically wrong with him at all. The woman's two previous husbands had also died for no apparent medical reason.

A leader of the Satanic Church in America, asked on TV if satanists practise human sacrifice, said: 'We perform human sacrifices by proxy, you might say – the destruction of human beings who would, let's say, create an antagonistic situation towards us in the form of curses and hexes.'[1]

DOCTORS BECOMING VERSED IN CURSES is the headline of an article in the *San Francisco Examiner* of Sunday, 2 May 1993. In it science writer Keay Davidson tells how some US doctors, treating Latino and Asian patients, no longer laugh at people claiming that their illness is caused by curse. To scorn such beliefs only drives the patient away to a 'traditional' healer.

'We physicians can tell them to take their clothes off, but we can't tell them to take their culture off,' says psychiatrist Dr Freda Lewis-Hall of Howard University in Washington DC.

David Waters, a University of Virginia psychologist, describes how some health personnel now hand the patient pills and say: 'This medicine will undo the curse and you'll have the last laugh.'

George Gafner, a social worker in Tucson, Arizona, reassures some of his Mexican–American patients by displaying in his office 'curse-busting' items like JINX REMOVING BRAND INCENSE, and the

POWERFUL INDIAN HOUSE BLESSING, a bottled concoction said to STOP EVIL.

'It's called "paradoxical psychology",' says Gafner, speaking of a seventy-six-year-old patient who claims he was first cursed in rural Arizona when just ten years old. 'He said a witch made some Anglo boys put sleeping potion in his soda pop. Then they hit him over the head with a bat.

'Instead of saying, "Quit talking about witchcraft," I said, "Let's talk about witchcraft." So I started reading him stories about Mexican witchcraft in Spanish and he started laughing. It allowed him to open up; his depression disappeared.'

Gafner tells how he accompanied this man to a *curandera*, a woman healer (see chapter 16). 'Within a few seconds, [she] established a warm personal relationship with this sick, stoic man, and brought him to tears.

'She had candles, a rosary, a little altar, incense, a prayer she said in Spanish. She spoke real positively about how he was going to get better. She massaged his leg – which was hurting him – and gave him some "bee-cream" ointment from a bumblebee.'

Family practitioner Dr Carlos Inocencio, of Los Altos south of San Francisco, reassures parents convinced that their child's illness has been caused by the evil eye, *mal de ojo* (see Appendix I), by stroking the child's head. Traditionally, it is said to alleviate the ill-effects of the evil eye. After doing this, he recommends standard remedies.

Yet not only 'Third World' immigrants believe in hex and curse. 'There are people in the Appalachians whose stories about what causes illness are almost equally bizarre,' says Dr Ralph Ocampo of San Diego, President-elect of the California Medical Association. 'And I really don't believe there's a generic difference between white, Anglo-Saxon, Protestant Christian Scientists . . . and the beliefs of someone from a remote Mexican village.'[2]

Curses can work even if unconsciously imposed by the victim's own fatalism, or by a mother's rage at filial disobedience.

Finis P. Ernest of Oklahoma City, a fifty-three-year-old nightclub owner, was admitted semi-conscious to the Veterans Administration Hospital in Oklahoma City, USA in January 1960. He was suffering from asthma, but was soon discharged, apparently cured. Six months later, having been in and out of private hospitals six times, he returned to the Veterans Hospital, by now suffering fits and convulsions. The doctors found nothing organically wrong. Having once again recovered, he went straight to his mother's home, but within forty-eight hours an ambulance returned him to hospital wheezing and in a near-terminal condition. Though he survived the attack, Finis P. Ernest was by now utterly depressed. He was allowed to go and visit his mother, but another relapse followed. At last realising what was going on, the doctors would let him out only on condition he avoided his mother. But around 6 p.m. on 23 August he phoned his mother. At 6.35 p.m. he was found gasping for breath. By 6.55 p.m. he was dead.

Perplexed and determined to investigate further, one of his doctors, Dr James P. Mathis, found out that Ernest's father had died while the boy was still in his teens, leaving him 'man of the house'. Before he was thirty Ernest had twice married against his mother's will, and in each case was soon divorced. Aged thirty-one, with his mother as partner, he opened a successful nightclub. Seven years later he met a woman, a schoolteacher, of whom his mother approved, and married her. For fifteen years all went well until, supported by his wife, Josephine, he accepted an offer to sell his business.

'Do this,' his furious mother warned, 'and something dire will happen to you.' Within two days asthma struck him down, but he went ahead with the sale. 'Something will strike you!' his mother shouted.

The visits to hospital began. The attacks and convulsions, and the doctors' inability to help him, convinced him that Mother was right. Aware of a connection between the asthmatic attacks and his mother's warning, on the afternoon of his death, Ernest reminded Dr Mathis that so far his mother had proved to be infallible in her malevolent predictions. As for the last phone call, Josephine told Dr Mathis that Ernest had found the nerve to tell his mother he meant to re-invest the money from the nightclub sale in a new venture, excluding her. His mother ended their conversation by reminding him of her warning of 'dire results'. He was dead within the hour. Dr Mathis had no option but to label the case a 'sophisticated version of voodoo death'.[3]

Or, as Hugh Rhodes wrote in sixteenth-century England: 'Dread the curse of parents thine/It is a heavy thing.'

The Hawaiian Kahunas (chapter 13) taught that the death-prayer works only if the victim (whether aware of the curse or not) has a guilty conscience. Is this what led American gangster Al Capone to be haunted to his dying day by James Clark, one of the victims of the St Valentine's Day Massacre? Some say it was only syphilitic hallucination; but other people also claimed to have seen the ghoul.

Thinking ill of others is a serious business, especially if the ill-thinking is deep-buried and unconsciously projected, and if the thinker is inherently imaginative. Take the cases of prominent English authors Robert Graves (1895–1985), and John Cowper Powys (1872–1963) . . .

While many an author, for one reason or another, has sometimes felt like cursing publishers, it is fortunately rare for two publishers who reject an author's manuscript both to die suddenly, while the third, who accepts it, promptly receives the Order of Merit. This is what happened in Graves's case.

Poet, novelist and mythologist of Irish–German parentage, Graves served in the First World War with the Royal Welsh Fusiliers. He was badly wounded and, nervously troubled thereafter, wrote poetry as therapy. He divorced his first wife Nancy, and in 1929 moved to Majorca with the American poet Laura Riding. The affair was stormy. One argument in London drove Riding to drink Lysol then jump out of a fourth-floor window. Graves jumped after her, though from a window on a lower floor. Both lived, but Laura Riding broke her spine.

Graves's autobiographical account of the war, *Goodbye to All That* (1929), made his name, and was followed by historical novels such as *I, Claudius* (1934), and *The Golden Fleece* (1944). These led him to view myths as a repository of (coded) factual revelation about the structures of pagan religion. In what he saw as his most important prose work, *The White Goddess* (1946), he argued for the existence of an ancient global religion rooted in the worship of a goddess of many names and triple aspect.

The circumstances surrounding publication of the book are as odd as the book itself. In 1944 Graves's work on *The Golden Fleece* was interrupted by a sudden desire to write about a mysterious 'Battle of the Trees', fought in ancient Britain. In just three weeks he completed *The Roebuck in the Thicket* – the first draft of *The White Goddess*. What had prompted this obsession? On his desk at the time was a brass box with an intricate lid, and on it he kept the brass figure of a hump-backed man playing a flute. Later he learned that the lid design represented Ngame, an African moon-goddess; and that the hump-backed flute-player was the herald of an African Queen-mother who claimed descent from Ngame. When references connected with the goddess kept coming his way, he felt driven to complete the book.

The first publisher to reject the manuscript died of heart failure. The second, who rejected it rudely, hanged himself from a tree in his garden while wearing female underwear. The third publisher who read it was the poet T. S. Eliot, and he accepted it. That same year he was awarded the Order of Merit.

Graves implied that all these events were meaningful. 'Chains of more than coincidence happen so often in my life that if I am forbidden to call them supernatural hauntings, I must call them a habit,' he remarked (perhaps disingenuously) of the entire *White Goddess* saga: 'Very well, put it down to coincidence.'[4,5]

Were these 'coincidences' worked by the goddess, or by Graves's own unconscious will? Perhaps, just perhaps, the two were the same . . .

John Cowper Powys was maternally descended from the poets Donne and Cowper and, though his name and concerns were more Celtic than Saxon, he was in fact English. He lived for years in the USA and it was there he wrote his great novels *A Glastonbury Romance* and *Weymouth Sands*. His possession of shamanic qualities is hard to deny. His biographer Wilson Knight wrote: 'Those who have incurred his anger have so invariably suffered misfortune that he has, as it were, been *forced* into a life of almost neurotic benevolence . . . Powys's early ambition to become a magician was no idle dream.'[6]

In his *Autobiography* Powys confirmed this, writing: 'The evidence of this – of my being able, I mean, and quite unconsciously too, to exercise some kind of "evil eye" on people who have injured me – has so piled up all my life that it has become a habit with me to pray to my gods anxiously and hurriedly for each new enemy.' He also referred to '. . . that formidable daimon which, as I have hinted to you before, *can* be reached somewhere in my nature, and which when it *is* reached has the Devil's own force . . .'

That this 'daimon' was not purely imaginary or imperceptible to others is suggested by two anecdotes about Powys.

The American novelist Theodore Dreiser told the story of how after a social call to Dreiser's New York home one evening, Powys promised to return later 'as a spirit or in some other astral form'. About two hours later, Dreiser looked up from his book to see the apparition of Powys by the door, a pale white glow coming from it. The ghost vanished when Dreiser strode close to it, and Dreiser phoned Powys's country home. 'I told you I'd be there, and you oughtn't to be surprised,' was all Powys had to say, then or later. It may be that he had no idea how he had done it, or that the apparition was in Dreiser's own mind. 'I used to be aware,' Powys wrote, 'of surging waves of magnetic attraction between Dreiser and myself.'

Powys's prediction '. . . that when I die it is the complete and absolute end of me . . .', was perhaps less accurate. A month after he died on 17 June 1963, a medium, Miss Frances Horsfield, was standing by Wilson Knight in Exeter Cathedral when she sensed the presence of a man and proceeded to describe Powys (whom she had never met): 'He has rather gaunt features, with high cheekbones and unruly hair. He *is* a personality. He is nearly controlling me, but I do not want that. He was himself an occultist . . . He wrote, didn't he?' Knight confirmed this. 'He is so close to you,' she went on. 'His power is so strong that you may well see him yourself some time.' She added that he had a 'wide, gleaming mouth' and a 'beaklike nose'. When Knight said Powys had latterly become a sceptic about 'survival', she said: 'Anyway, he knows all about it now.'[7]

It is often said that curses work best, if they work at all, if the victim is aware of the hex having been laid. Not only rabbits and birds mesmerised by hungry snakes seemingly acquiesce willingly in their fate. Often enough the human victims of curse, hex or death-prediction do likewise. The very expectation of death works to bring it about. Food or drink may be refused, while acute anxiety may influence the sympathetic nervous system. The victim's blood pressure falls while the heart beats ever faster; the lungs, paralysed by fear, cannot produce enough oxygen. Collapse and catalepsy precede death. The foretelling of death appears to be enough, in some cases, to bring it about.

Some fortune-tellers – a profession traditionally identified with the travelling Romany or gypsy people – will not predict a date of death for their clients. Yet, though they know the risks, others are not so sensitive.

In 1965 three Canadian doctors from Labrador described in the *British Medical Journal* how a mother of five children, a week short of her forty-third birthday, underwent a minor operation for incontinence. At first all seemed well. She regained consciousness. Then, an hour later, she collapsed with all the symptoms of shock. No treatment had any effect, and she died early next day. It emerged that when she was five years old, a fortune-teller had predicted she would die before the age of forty-three. For years she had told her daughter that she would be dead before this age; before going into the hospital she had confessed to her sister that she did not expect to survive the anaesthetic, while on the morning of the operation she had told a nurse she was sure she was going to die. And so she did.[8]

An even odder case concerns John Snell of Poole in England. He was told by an Indian palm-reader that he would die on his forty-fifth birthday, but for years the heavy-drinking long-distance lorry-driver chose to ignore the warning. However, in the year before his forty-fifth birthday he began to worry and gave up drinking. On his birthday he would not leave his house. Two days later the death was reported, in the local paper, of John Snell of Poole, on his forty-fifth birthday.

Somehow the palm-reader had got it both right and wrong. There had been two John Snells in Poole. They had lived only a hundred yards apart . . . and the John Snell whose palm had been read was still alive.[9]

Dr William Nixon of University College Hospital, London, had a patient aged thirty-five, who was terrified at the impending birth of her first child. It transpired that, walking on the South Downs as a child of ten, she had met a gypsy woman who had predicted that either she or her child would die in childbirth. In the event, mother and child both survived, but Dr Nixon had already encountered such a hex-death while working in Hong Kong's Tsan Yuk maternity hospital. A young woman, giving birth normally, refused to suckle her child or speak until the sixth day, when she said she had to die due to a fortune-teller's prediction. She had died, as predicted, though an autopsy showed nothing to explain her death.

The gypsies, of course, have always been associated with palm-reading, curse and fortune-telling. An old rhyme runs:

> And for every gypsy woman old
> A maiden's fortune will be told.

As mysterious in their origin (possibly from India, reaching Europe perhaps in the early fifteenth century) as in their occult power, real or imagined, the Romany fortune-tellers still read palms inside their booths and exotic trailers at fairs and amusement parks throughout the land. And even if for the most part their skill is not so much occult as a matter of reading character, typically from the mouth and eyes of the client, and of telling clients the *hobikens* (lies) they want to hear, deceit and imposture alone could not have built up and sustained a practice which has endured for centuries.

A certain Dr John Barker, curious after having treated two women terrified by the threats of gypsy palm-readers, went to a dozen contemporary English fortune-tellers to find out what they actually told their clients. He was impressed by some. Of a gypsy clairvoyant working on a south coast pier, he wrote: 'She was remarkably and uncannily accurate. I gave her no information whatsoever. After practising psychiatry for eleven years I could not possibly have told her a fraction about myself to compare with her quite amazing knowledge about myself and my past life.'

Another gypsy, 'a brusque elderly woman', began by telling him he would die suddenly of a stroke when just over seventy. He was impressed, as she also told him that he had nearly died three, also thirteen, years earlier – 'substantially correct since I had severe illnesses at both these times.'[10]

Brian Vesey-Fitzgerald, author of *Gypsies of Britain*, tells how Darklis Lee, a fortune-teller, admitted: 'I only tells them a lot of *hobikens*. Now my sister can *dukker* properly. My sister was my mother's seventh daughter. She can make or unmake luck. Seventh daughters can see more nor we can.'[11]

Suggesting that thought-reading is not so uncanny, the range of thought and desire in most people being so narrow and predictable, Vesey-Fitzgerald lists 'fourteen basic rules of fortune-telling' stipulated by Leland, the first president of the Gypsy Lore Society. These include telling middle-aged men they have had a lawsuit or property dispute; telling clients that fortune approaches but they must seize their chance; that in their lives they have three chances of fortune; that love is coming their way; that they have had trouble with relations or friends; that 'You have been three times in great danger of death'; that 'You have had enemies, but they are all destined to come to grief'; that 'You once got into trouble by doing a good act' – and so on. In other words: tell gullible folk what they want to hear.

Yet belief, if potent, may prove self-fulfilling. Of course, it helps if the curse or prediction is delivered with compelling eye and hypnotic look. Vesey-Fitzgerald, though viewing most gypsy fortune-telling as hokum, wrote in 1944 how one Urania Boswell told his fortune in 1928, foretelling things so amazing that '. . . I remember laughing and her reply, "You will see, young man." ' Commenting that '. . . I can say, in all honesty, that so far at least it has all come true', he adds: 'I have since, by the way, had my fortune told, spontaneously and without payment, by a young gypsy woman. The two fortunes agree in almost every particular.'[12]

Though forgotten today, Urania Boswell was responsible for many remarkable prophecies, most of them well-testified. In 1897 she foretold that 'Queen Victoria would see the leaves fall four times before she went to her long rest'; and that 'Men will fly like birds, and swim under the water in boats shaped like fishes. They'll sit by their own firesides and listen to voices and music a thousand miles away, same as if it was in the room.' She warned the American millionaire Cornelius Vanderbilt not to sail in the *Titanic* (see chapter 19) which was then being built; and in 1924 she said: 'I shall die in nine years, and it will be cold.' She did, and it was.

One (probably apocryphal) example of a gypsy curse concerns the Epsom Derby, England's premier horse-race. One year, it is said, a lady by name of Gypsy Lee predicted that a horse named Blew Gown would win the Derby and wrote down her forecast on a piece of paper. When it was haughtily pointed out to her that the spelling was *Blue*, not *Blew*, she became so angry that she issued a curse: no horse with a 'w' in its name would win the race so long as she lived. And so it went. But when she died in 1934 her family bet all they could on Windsor Lad, which came in first at seven-to-one.[13]

One of the oddest cases of a death-wish or prediction fulfilled led in Norway to the murder trial of Mrs Ingeborg Köbler, an Oslo woman accused of drowning her father, the wealthy and eminent Judge Dahl, as he swam in the Oslo fjord at Hanko on 8 August 1934. After he died it emerged that four months earlier Mrs Köbler, while supposedly in a sleeping trance, had predicted the time, place and fashion of his death.

The family was no stranger to tragedy: Ingeborg's powers of mediumship had developed after her brother Ludvig had drowned. Five years later her brother Ragnar had also died. Her father, convinced she had a message to bring humanity, had by now spent so much time and money supporting her work that the bereaved family was deep in debt. Her despairing mother, a local community treasurer in Fredrikstad, had gone so far as to purloin funds from her work.

At her séances, Ingeborg would enter a sleeping trance, then emerge from that into a waking trance. Messages would come from 'Ludvig' via a suspended pencil and planchette; 'he' would read lines from books selected by guests at the séances. She also wrote letters from the dead in their own handwriting – sometimes two letters simultaneously, one with each hand.

Communications from the 'other side' were also transmitted by code, each letter of the alphabet being given a number. In her sleeping trance Ingeborg (who consciously knew nothing about the code) produced a string of numbers that converted into messages. One fateful day the judge and his family received a message telling him how, when, and where he would die. From the evidence that emerged in the subsequent judicial inquiry it seems certain that he accepted this message calmly and with total belief, and that neither he nor anyone else ever mentioned it to Ingeborg.

On a warm August day, as he and Ingeborg walked on the beach at Hanko, Judge Dahl decided on a swim. Ingeborg stayed on the empty beach. There was no one else about. After swimming for a long time, cramp suddenly seized the judge. Ingeborg claimed that she had swum out, reached him, and got him back to shore. Failing to revive him, she went for help, but by the time they reached Judge Dahl he was dead.

Judge Dahl, it seemed, and for whatever reasons, had deliberately swum out to meet his death as predicted. And there it would have rested, with Ingeborg none the wiser, save that the press got hold of the story when Professor Thorstein Wereide, president of the Norwegian Society for Psychic Research, recounted it at what he thought was a closed meeting. Amid the subsequent furore Ingeborg was arrested and held in prison for five months while the investigation went ahead. Though in debt, Judge Dahl had, after all, been worth 60,000 kroner in accident insurance. She was released on the grounds that in her sleeping trance she could not have known about the message, nor had anyone told her later. Even then the family tragedies were not over. Ingeborg's mother later committed suicide.[14]

An even weirder (though much more circumstantial) tale involves one of Britain's most experienced exorcists and researchers into the nature of evil. Over many years and in many lands the Rev. Donald Omand, a Highland Scot and Anglican minister, combated black magic, sea-madness (sirenism), African and European witchcraft, and especially the spirit-possession of circus animals such as lions, bears and tigers. As General Secretary and International Chaplain for the Council for the Church in the Circus, he was routinely consulted by circus folk on matters relating to the paranormal.

Once he was handed a letter by an old lady, 'a true fairground queen', who asked him to keep it unopened until she died. Seven years later she died, and after he had conducted the funeral service, Rev. Omand opened the envelope before the family. In it was not a will, but a piece of papèr folded seven times, on it scrawled the day, month and year of her death.

Another time he visited the distressed family of a circus owner who had died of a heart attack a week after telling his sons he had just seven days to live. A doctor had told him he was in perfect health, but still he had died as predicted. The family showed Omand a bundle of thirteen envelopes they had found, all addressed to the dead man and in the same handwriting. Posted from different European cities, they had arrived once a year on the same date. Each contained a birthday card with the word 'birthday' crossed out and 'deathday' substituted, followed by a date and a signature. The date, always the same, was the date on which he had died. Later it emerged that the man who had sent the cards was a performer he had fired for drinking the same year the first card had arrived.[15]

Donald Omand's oddest case, however, was in 1973, when he attempted to exorcise the Loch Ness Monster.

In this he was accompanied by F. W. ('Ted') Holiday, an author and long-time researcher into fringe phenomena who had first sighted the weird beast in 1962. Noting Britain's many legends of 'loathly worms', and the disgust and dread with which such creatures have been regarded since ancient times, Holiday's studies had led him to an old Babylonian text, in which a 'Worm' of the marshes asks permission of the goddess Ea to 'drink among the teeth, and . . . devour the blood of the teeth and the gums . . .'

Holiday and other Loch Ness devotees he knew had sometimes suffered odd toothache and bleeding from the gums when monster-hunting. Aware that, up until the eighteenth century, exorcisms had been used against such water-monsters both in Ireland and Scotland, Holiday had come to believe that the elusive beasts associated with Loch Ness, and with many other lakes from Canada to Ireland, Russia to Australia, were not solid entities but malignant phantom projections from a prehistoric past, evil and hateful, leaving witnesses 'paralysed by fear' or speaking of 'an abomination'.

Omand, who had first seen what he assumed was an unknown mammal in 1967 while walking by Loch Long in Ross-shire, had reached a similar conclusion. In 1968, with a Norwegian sailor, Captain Jan Andersen, he had inspected 'the eeriest waterway in Norway', the Fjord of the Trolls. As their small boat entered the fjord his sense of apprehension grew. Suddenly the water boiled. Two humps rose above the surface, heading for the boat. 'It will not hurt us – they never do,' Andersen reassured him as the monster veered and dived. 'They don't do physical harm. The evil they do is to men's characters.' Omand suggested that they follow it, but Andersen, who thought such beasts connected with the biblical Serpent (see chapter 4), refused. 'Sufficient unto the day is the evil thereof,' he said. 'And I *mean* evil.'

Attending a psychiatric conference in Sweden in 1972 Omand was further intrigued to hear a paper read on the monster of Lake Storsjon. It claimed that the influence of such cursed creatures promotes domestic tragedy and moral degeneration in those hunting them or sighting them frequently.[16]

Subsequently involved in a newspaper controversy with another minister over the nature of the Loch Ness Monster, in *Experiences of a Present-Day Exorcist*, Omand wrote that 'What has been seen and is still visible to some on occasion, is not a concrete present-day monster but a projection into our day and age of something which had its habitat in Loch Ness and its surroundings millions of years ago.'[17]

In 1973 Ted Holiday contacted Omand, who had already agreed with the Bishop of Crediton that an exorcism at Loch Ness was desirable. Aware that exorcism is a dangerous profession demanding considerable self-discipline, Holiday agreed to meet Omand at Loch Ness on 2 June 1973.

Prayer has been used at Loch Ness before. The first mention of the monster, in Adamnan's seventh-century *Life of St Columba*, tells how this redoubtable soldier of Christ, en route to Inverness to convert the Pictish king Brude, confronted it as it rose from the loch 'with a great roar and open mouth'. Columba's prayers dismissed it back to the depths.

Donald Omand's exorcism was not so spectacular. Enacting the rite at points round the loch, after a protective ceremony in which he applied holy water in the form of a cross to the foreheads of all involved, he asked that: '. . . this highland loch and the land adjoining it may be delivered from all evil spirits; all vain imaginations; projections and fantasms, and all deceits of the evil one.'

Apprehensively, Holiday accompanied Omand in a small boat to the middle of the loch for the final exorcism. No monster appeared. Yet three days later at Strone, the lochside house where they were staying, there was an inexplicable manifestation. Though warned against it by Dr Omand, Holiday was thinking of visiting an alleged UFO landing site at the far side of the loch near Foyers, not far from the notorious Boleskine House, tenanted in 1899 by Aleister Crowley, the self-styled 'Great Beast 666'.

In 1969 in a cemetery near the house some American students had found, hidden under a grave-slab, a tapestry embroidered with humped, worm-like creatures, wrapped round a conch shell that made a braying sound when blown. The dryness of the tapestry suggested it had only just been hidden.

His hostess, Mrs Cary, was also warning Holiday against visiting the UFO site when all of a sudden there was a 'tremendous rushing sound like a tornado' outside the window. The garden was filled with 'indefinable frantic movement'. He heard thuds, as of heavy objects striking the wall. Through the window he saw 'what looked like a pyramid-shaped column of blackish smoke revolving in a frenzy'. Mrs Cary screamed, but her husband saw and heard nothing. After the disturbance ceased, Mrs Cary described seeing a 'white circle of light on Ted Holiday's forehead . . . I thought the house had been struck by lightning with this light shooting across the room.' When Omand was told about it, he described it as a 'reactionary manifestation'. Holiday notes that the beam, of which he was unaware, struck exactly the spot on his forehead which Omand had crossed with holy water . . .

Next morning, over the road atop the slope leading down to Loch Ness, Holiday saw a man dressed entirely in black, his back to the loch, glaring malevolently at him. Dressed in black leather or plastic, the figure also wore gloves, helmet, a mask and goggles. Warily approaching, Holiday saw no eyes behind the lenses and heard no breathing. Walking past the silent figure, Holiday eyed the loch, then began to turn. As he did, he heard an odd whistling sound – and swung round to find that the figure had vanished.

Now, 'Men in Black' (MIB) are prominent in UFO lore. There are a great many reports of UFO contactees being visited by these bizarre entities and being warned off further investigations. Typically, the victim is alone at the time, making it impossible to tell what, if any, objective reality they have. Their nature, if they exist at all outside the strained imagination of the contactee, is as ambiguous as that of the lake monsters. Yet visits by such beings (usually seen as demonic) have been reported for centuries. Their modern appearance (they may masquerade as journalists, salesmen or military personnel) may just be an adaptation by the modern imagination of some protean phenomenon as ancient as the shining disc – or lake monster.

Understandably, Holiday told nobody about this experience for months, not even Dr Omand. Omand said there would be no more manifestations round the house, but that the monster would doubtless continue to be seen, long-standing astral forms being hard to dissolve. The original exorcism would need to be reinforced by further rites. A year later, Holiday returned to Loch Ness, only to be struck down by a heart attack on the very spot where he had met the man in black. Five years later, a second heart attack killed him, aged fifty-eight.[18]

If by now, and against your desire or better judgement, these few cases already begin to persuade you that there may after all be something to this deeply unsettling subject, you may be glad to learn that there's no lack of contemporary advice available on how to guard against curses or the evil eye. What use most of it may be is another matter.

For example, in a curious little text called *A Witch's Book of Spells, Rituals and Sex Magick* (1983) 'Diana Dagon', who styles herself 'Coven High Priestess', devotes a chapter to *How to Back-Fire Curses and Defeat Evil Witchcraft*. Describing witchcraft as 'a practical Art', she says it is easy to tell if you've been cursed.

'You begin sleeping erratically, nightmares plague you. You become irritable and listless. You become ill; all sorts of things begin going wrong suddenly and without any apparent or reasonable cause.'[19]

In his book *Blessing or Curse: You Can Choose*, Christian evangelist Derek Prince lists seven problem areas indicating that a curse is at work:

1. Mental and/or emotional breakdown;
2. Repeated or chronic sicknesses;
3. Barrenness, or related female problems;
4. Marital breakdown or family alienation;
5. Persistent financial insufficiency;
6. Being 'accident-prone'; and
7. A history of suicides or unnatural or untimely deaths.

He notes that this corresponds closely with a list ascribed to the biblical prophet Moses in Deuteronomy 28.[20]

Among the antidotes described by Diana Dagon (of whom Prince would surely not approve) is the use of curse to counteract curse. Obtaining a black candle, the victim considers his or her misfortune, so working up a state of fury. The candle is lit, and the following counter-curse is delivered 'in an angry, commanding and hateful tone':

> 'O Dark Candle
> I Imbue Thee With
> The Curse of My
> Enemy.
> Take the Curse That
> Has Afflicted Me
> And Burn It;
> And Burn With It
> My Enemy.
> Visit Upon Him in
> Double Measure The
> Evil He Visited Upon Me.
> Let Him Understand
> That He Who Lives
> By the Sword
> Dies By the Sword.'

This method of projecting emotion in a state of willed concentration is hardly different to the way William Tufts Brigham counteracted a

Kahuna death-prayer in Hawaii (see chapter 13). Yet how to be sure you really were cursed to begin with? What if it was just paranoia, and you counter-cursed an innocent party? Diana Dagon claims that we have the right to fight fire with fire, and evil-doers cannot expect mercy from those they wrong, but agrees that some may 'prefer to fight darkness with light'. There is a protective ritual, to be performed with a white candle and a head of garlic on a Wednesday midnight after the full moon. You visualise a vivid white light surrounding and penetrating you, then recite a cleansing prayer, then take a bath and imagine the water washing the curse away.

This may well be the preferable approach. Prince, however, and other Christians to whom any magical working is cursed in itself, insists that curses, whether externally or self-imposed, may be revoked only by willing surrender to Christ.

Such spells and rites have been around for thousands of years, but it is in the distant past, at the very dawn of the art (if so it may be called) of malediction, that lies the most famous curse of all – one which, supposedly cast over three thousand years ago, never came into operation until early in the third decade of the twentieth century . . .

3   The Curse of King Tut

Of all early civilisations, that of Egypt exercises the strongest spell. Once called Khem ('black earth') Egypt's lost origins evoke a mystique still exploited by occultists, romancers and B-movie producers. Land of the Sphinx and the Great Pyramid; of Isis, Osiris and exotic animal-headed gods, ancient even to the ancient Greeks, it was here, claims Plato, that Solon first heard the tale of Atlantis from a priest of Saïs; and from Egypt that the Israelites fled; and in Egypt that concern with the afterlife became so potent that the dead were mummified to await rebirth. Laid to rest with their treasures, pharaohs and other great men and women were buried in tombs so magnificent that, over the centuries, most were robbed of their wealth. Few such tombs survived unlooted into modern times, but at least one did . . . and its opening led not only to the discovery of magnificent treasure, but to so many apparently inexplicable deaths that, some claim, it was a curse cast by the ancient priests who laid the dead pharaoh to rest that struck down many of those involved in opening and desecrating the tomb, and in dispersing its treasures.

This tomb, of the mysterious boy-king Tutankhamen (1358–49 BC), lay under the Valley of the Kings near Thebes. Opened on 26 November 1922 for the first time in over three thousand years, its discovery was due to the obsession of one man, Howard Carter, a self-taught English archaeologist who had spent three decades seeking unlooted pharaonic tombs in the baking hot, arid valley. For years he had been sure that at least one such tomb remained undiscovered, and that it was Tutankhamen's.

Inscriptions about Tutankhamen had been found in the nearby Temple of Luxor. During the 1907–8 season, while working for a wealthy American, Theodore Davis, Carter found a cache of large baked clay jars containing bundles of linen and funerary items. There, on seal impressions in the closures of the jars, and marked on one of the linen rolls, he found the name of the boy-king. Nearby was a pit grave; in it a crumbled wooden chest with gold plates bearing Tutankhamen's name. Davis thought this must be the boy-king's grave, but Carter doubted that a Middle Kingdom pharaoh would end up like a pauper. Somewhere in the valley there had to be a tomb not only undiscovered but unlooted; for no relics had ever been reported.

Carter's obsession attracted a new patron, George E. S. M. Herbert, fifth Earl of Carnarvon. Born in 1866, this rich English lord had survived a bad car crash, but thereafter had trouble breathing, especially in the damp English winters, and so from 1903 wintered annually in Egypt. There he met Carter through Sir Gaston Maspero, director of Cairo Museum. The meeting was a godsend to Carter who, despite his official appointment as administrator for antiquities, was not rich and needed patronage to continue his quest.

Carnarvon proved generous. For fifteen years he funded the search for Tutankhamen's tomb. Yet by 1922 Carter had combed almost the entire valley floor without success. All his colleagues thought he was on a wild goose chase – and eventually even Carnarvon wanted to give up looking. 'It has cost me a fortune,' he told Carter, 'I can't afford it.'

Only one small area was left unexplored, on the approach to the tomb of Rameses VI. Carter begged for one last chance.

'All right, Howard,' Carnarvon agreed. 'I'm a gambler. I'll back you for one more toss. If it is a loss then I am through.'

Early in November 1922 Carter began to dig again. After three days he and his workmen had found only the rubble of huts used by the builders of Rameses' tomb. But then on the fourth day a step was found, cut into the ground. It was the start of a staircase that led down to a sealed door.

On 6 November Carter cabled Carnarvon:

AT LAST HAVE MADE WONDERFUL DISCOVERY IN VALLEY STOP A MAGNIFICENT TOMB WITH SEALS INTACT STOP RECOVERED SAME FOR YOUR ARRIVAL CONGRATULATIONS

Carnarvon hurried to Egypt. When he got there work began again. It took several days to bypass the door and clear a rock-filled passage. Reaching a second sealed door, Carter made a hole in it big enough to take a candle.

Looking inside, at first he could make out nothing. Then, as his eyesight adjusted, he saw what lay in the chamber beyond: strange animals, life-sized black statues with gold kilts and sandals, a cup of translucent alabaster, a gold inlaid throne, three great gilded couches, strange black shrines, a pile of overturned chariots that glistened with gold.

Everywhere, the gleam of gold. Dumbstruck, he stared at the wealth within.

'Can you see anything?' Carnarvon demanded anxiously.

'Yes,' said Carter, finding it hard to speak, 'wonderful things.'

The date was 26 November 1922. There was no talk of a curse. So far, there was no reason for such talk.

Yet who was Tutankhamen? What did the Egyptians of his time

believe? What occult powers, if any, did they command?

About all that is known of this eighteenth-dynasty pharaoh is that he died violently, from a blow to the left side of his skull; that he was about eighteen when he died; and that his blood-group was A2, sub-group MN, making him 'rare-blooded'. No more is known now than in February 1923, when his tomb was entered and his sarcophagus found. The identity of his father, the circumstances of his birth, life and death remain entirely obscure. Not even a shred of papyrus describing his fate was found in his tomb.

All that is sure is that his reign saw a return to the worship of Amen and other, older gods, from worship of the sun-god Aten, as inaugurated by his royal predecessor, the equally mysterious pharaoh Akhenaten.

Did he die accidentally, or was he killed by those overseeing the re-establishment of traditional belief? If the latter, the crime was successful: his death marked the end of the turbulent eighteenth dynasty. Yet why should he have been killed? He, or those ruling through him, had already abandoned Akhenaten's sun-worship. Deserting Akhenaten's new city of Tell el-Amarna (*City of the Horizon*) for the ancient holy city of Thebes, he had also changed his name from *Tutankhaten* to *Tutankhamen* (or had had it changed for him).

Long before Tutankhamen's tomb was found, occult mystery had attached itself not only to all matters Egyptian, but especially to the eighteenth dynasty.

Myths like mushrooms thrive in darkness, while the craftsmanship of the wonderful artefacts laid to rest with Tutankhamen also encouraged the idea of a society or priesthood with powers beyond modern understanding.

Whatever the ancient Egyptians really believed or practised, by the time Carter and Carnarvon entered Tutankhamen's long-lost tomb, it was already firmly held by many that their powers included that of laying death-curses on those violating royal tombs.

If so, were such curses magically potent, or no more than functional prohibitions designed to deter the superstitious? Speaking in *Egyptian Magic* (1901) of what the Egyptians believed about the afterlife, Sir Alfred Wallis Budge notes that: 'The cemeteries were regarded with awe by the ancient Egyptians because of the spirits of the dead who dwelt in them.' He adds that Greek, Hebrew and Roman writers all confirm that Egyptians were 'experts in the occult sciences', being 'a nation of magicians and sorcerers'.

That collectively they were obsessed with the puzzle of death and what lies beyond it is plain. So are we all. As with almost all other known cultures, they had rites and ceremonies, not only to mark a person's death, but to assert their belief in the immortality (and subsequent rebirth) of the soul or 'subtle body' of each person.

The Egyptians, it seems, believed in the ghostly power of the *ka* (double), an image of the *khat* (perishable physical body), living with the mummified body in the tomb. But how does this connect with 'The Curse of the Mummy's Tomb'? Egyptians did not usually curse those violating their laws, nor, unlike some neighbouring, later cultures (the Bible is full of curses) did they often use the curse as weapon. Only pharaohs (and gods) could use the curse. As for curses laid on tombs, it may be that their deadly effect (if effective at all) was due to mechanical ingenuity, not occult science.

A curse tablet found in the antechamber of a tomb close by the Medum pyramid reads: *The spirit of the dead will wring the neck of a grave robber as if it were that of a goose.* Two corpses were found in the chamber: one mummified, the other not. The second corpse was a victim of the curse – a grave robber, killed by a stone that fell from the ceiling and struck him even as he reached out for the mummy's jewellery.[1]

A culture capable of building the Great Pyramid could also build traps to deter grave robbers. The curse keeps out the faint-hearted, the traps kill or maim the bold or desperate.

Even so, few pharaonic tombs had remained unrobbed by 17 February 1923, the day that Carter and Carnarvon, with some twenty others, first entered the marvellous main chamber of Tutankhamen's tomb.

Carter left nothing to chance. Closing the opening again, he posted armed men to guard the tomb night and day, and had the entrance reburied. Carnarvon and his daughter, Lady Evelyn, returned to England, where he gave the London *Times* world rights to the story. Meanwhile, Carter collected every expert he could find, then re-entered the antechamber. The treasures in it were photographed, sketched and prepared for conservation; the enormity of the find preyed on everyone. Later Carter noted that: 'by the time the antechamber was finished our nerves, not to say our tempers, were in an extremely ragged state.' And that was only the antechamber!

On Friday, 17 February 1923 the sealed door from the antechamber into the main burial shrine was opened. Chairs had been set up; electric lights strung. Standing on a newly built platform with hammer and chisel, Carter hacked a hole through the door. Beyond it was a huge gilt shrine. Protecting this with a mattress, he enlarged the gap, then crawled through it, followed by Carnarvon and the American archaeologist, Arthur Mace.

The shrine filled the entire chamber. At its eastern end were folding doors, closed and bolted. Drawn back, they revealed a second shrine, also with bolted doors, the seal upon them intact.

'I think at the moment we did not even want to break the seal,' Carter later wrote, 'for a feeling of intrusion had descended heavily upon us with the opening of the doors, heightened, probably, by the almost painful impressiveness of a linen pall, decorated with gold rosettes . . . We felt that we were in the presence of the dead king and must do him reverence, and in imagination could see the doors of the successive shrine open one after the other till the innermost disclosed the king himself. Carefully, and as silently as possible, we reclosed the great swing doors.[2]

So, step by step, they came to the inner sarcophagus, which contained a nest of three coffins, the innermost of which held the mummified body of Tutankhamen, wrapped in a bejewelled shroud. Over his face was a gold mask inlaid with quartz and lapis lazuli. A faded garland of lilies, lotuses, and cornflowers lay across his neck and breast. After three millennia in utter darkness, they still held a hint of colour.

Two months later, there was no colour left in Carnarvon's face. He was dead. His death was the first of many.

Were the deaths due to a curse activated by the sacrilegious act of opening the tomb? Or were they but a set of coincidences given apparent meaning by public hunger for the supernatural?

Carnarvon's death was certainly strange. Bitten by a mosquito on the left cheek, he contracted blood-poisoning, then pneumonia. For twelve days, in Cairo's Hotel Continental, he lingered. As he died at 1.55 a.m., all the lights in Cairo went out, then came on again – and at the same time back at his home at Highclere in Hampshire, England, his fox terrier bitch began to howl, sat up on her hind legs, then fell dead. This was confirmed by his son, who became the sixth earl. Stranger still, doctors who later examined Tutankhamen's mummy (not even unwrapped when Carnarvon died) found, on the boy-king's left cheek, a scab-like depression exactly corresponding to the position of Carnarvon's mosquito bite.

Next to die was the archaeologist Arthur C. Mace of New York's Metropolitan Museum, co-author with Carter of the first volume of *The Tomb of Tut-ankh-amun*. After Carnarvon's death, Mace complained of growing exhaustion and, for no apparent reason, fell into a deep coma. He died in the same Cairo hotel as Carnarvon. The following morning, George Jay Gould, an American railway tycoon, who visited the tomb as Carter's guest, was seized by a fever: by evening he was dead. Evelyn Greely, an American, killed herself on her return to Chicago after visiting the tomb. Professor M. Laffleur of McGill University in Canada, a house guest of Carter, died the day after he inspected the tomb. Sir Archibald Douglas Reid, a radiologist who cut the cords round the mummy of the dead pharaoh to X-ray the body, became debilitated, returned to England, and died there in 1924. Woolf Joel, a friend of Carnarvon, sailing on his yacht on the Nile en route to Luxor, fell overboard and drowned.[3] In another account, however, he is called Joel Wool, and his death, by fever, is supposed to have occurred after his return to England.[4]

The many discrepancies in the tales of Tutankhamen's Curse seem to confirm 'Sturgeon's Law' that ninety-five per cent of any body of information is rubbish. That leaves five per cent that is not. The question is, *which* five per cent? In dealing with a subject as weird and ephemeral as this, it can be hard to tell, though suggestions like Erich Von Daniken's that extraterrestrials put the curse on Tutankhamen's tomb may reasonably be assumed to belong to the ninety-five per cent.[5]

Carter (whose death in 1939 at the age of sixty-six was oddly natural) and many other sceptics dismissed the curse as superstition. Even so, the sudden deaths of people directly or indirectly involved with tomb or treasure continued. By 1929, according to one count, twenty-two had died prematurely, thirteen of whom had been involved in opening the tomb. These included Professors Winlock and Foucrat, the archaeologists Davies and Harkness, the assistants Astor and Callender, and Professor Douglas Derry, who on 11 November 1925 performed the autopsy on Tutankhamen's mummified body. Though reluctant to do so, either through scruple or fear, he went ahead with the examination, and soon after died of circulatory collapse.[6]

Carnarvon's half-brother, Aubrey Herbert, present at the opening of the sarcophagus, died during a bout of 'temporary insanity' (one version) or peritonitis (another). Carnarvon's wife Almina died, oddly enough, of an 'insect bite' in 1929. The Hon. Richard Bethell, who had helped Carter to catalogue the treasures, died in the same year, aged forty-nine. One version of his death says he was found dead in bed of circulatory collapse, another that he died in a chair at the Mayfair Club in London, cause unknown, while a third hints at suicide. Oddest of all was the fate of his father, Lord Westbury (seventy-eight years old in one account, eighty-seven in another), who leapt to his death from the seventh floor of his London home.

'I really cannot stand any more horrors and I hardly see what good I am going to do here,' his suicide note asserted. 'So I am going to make my exit.' An alabaster vase from the tomb was in his bedroom. En route to the crematorium, his hearse knocked down and killed an eight-year-old boy, while fifty-seven-year-old Edgar Steele, a custodian in Sir Alfred Wallis Budge's department of Egyptological antiquities at the British Museum, died on the operating table in a London hospital.

Several Egyptians connected with the tomb also died mysteriously, among them Prince Ali Fahmy Bey, shot dead in a London hotel soon after viewing the tomb, though whether by his French-born wife or by an unknown intruder never clearly emerged. His brother committed suicide soon after.

The deaths continued. When in 1966 the Egyptian government agreed to exhibit the treasures in Paris, Mohammed Ibraham, governmental

Director of Antiquities, dreamed he faced great danger if the treasures left Egypt. He fought but failed to get the decision reversed. As he left a final meeting with the Cairo authorities he was hit by a car, and died two days later.

Six years later his successor, Dr Gamal Mehrez, died of circulatory collapse, aged fifty-two, on the very day that Tutankhamen's golden mask was once again disturbed, being flown to London as part of an exhibit commemorating the fiftieth anniversary of Carter and Carnarvon's discovery of the tomb.[7]

The story attained such power that, when San Francisco policeman George LaBrash had a stroke while guarding a museum display of the treasure during its 1979 world tour, he sued the city for disability payments, claiming his stroke to be a job-related injury caused by the curse. He alleged that, as he guarded the boy-king's gold funerary mask in San Francisco's Museum of Fine Arts, King Tut's spirit had 'lashed out at him', causing the heart attack. The case was dismissed. Even in California, the claim was thought too far-fetched, though some lawyer had obviously thought it worth a try.[8]

Carter himself always scoffed at belief in a curse. After all, if anyone should have been struck down, it was him. Instead, he lived another sixteen years, continually irritated by the belief. At first he refused to discuss it but, with the legend not only not dying but gaining ground as the years passed, finally he broke silence, insisting that: 'Rumours of a Tutankhamen curse are a libelous [sic] invention.'

The evidence that it existed in a formal, written fashion is equivocal, to say the least. It is said to have been found in two forms. The first was written in hieroglyphics on an ordinary clay tablet allegedly found by Carter in the underground tomb's antechamber. Decoded, it read:

> Death will slay with his wings
> Whoever disturbs the peace of the pharaoh

That this (unphotographed) tablet was not mentioned in the written record, and never appeared in the artefact collection, is explained by believers as due to the fact that Carter and his associates, worried that it would scare off their local Egyptian work-force, kept quiet about it. A contradictory claim made in 1980 by Richard Adamson, expeditionary security officer, is that the curse story was invented to scare off would-be robbers.[9]

The second form of the curse is said to have been found on the back of a statue in the main burial chamber. It read:

> It is I who drive back the robbers of the tomb with the flames of the desert. I am the protector of Tutankhamen's grave.[10]

Unconfirmed reports of fearful events on the day the antechamber was first penetrated in November 1922 claim that, as the last man returned to daylight, a sandstorm blew up to hide the mouth of the tomb. As it died away a hawk, the royal emblem of ancient Egypt, was seen to soar over the tomb to the west – in Egyptian belief, the direction of the Land of the Dead.

Whatever the truth, public fascination with the curse grew. In 1924, with Carnarvon and others already dead, French Egyptologist J. S. Mardrus asserted that the deaths were due to it. Pointing out that the tomb was the *first* intact pharaonic tomb to be found and opened in modern times, he contended that, given the known occult interests of the ancient Egyptians, Carter and Carnarvon should have realised the need to 'be suspicious of the unknown and to take certain precautions, both against the visible and invisible'. Though mocked by his colleagues, his case was apparently made stronger not only by the growing number of sudden deaths associated with Tutankhamen's tomb, but by the unexpected deaths of other Egyptologists, including the odd case of professor H. G. Evelyn White of Leeds University. Shown a secret room in an Egyptian Coptic monastery, he had removed from it a trove of apocryphal books. Back in England late in 1924 he killed himself. In his suicide note he wrote: 'I knew there was a curse on me, though I had leave to take those manuscripts to Cairo. The monks told me the curse would work all the same. Now it has done so.'[11]

Commenting on such cases, Mardrus said: 'I am absolutely convinced that [the Egyptians] knew how to concentrate upon and around a mummy certain dynamic powers of which we possess very incomplete notions.' Now he found his beliefs taken more seriously. 'It is a deep mystery,' said the *New York Times*, 'which it is all too easy to dismiss by skepticism.'

Scientists counter-attacked. Alan Rowe, a University of Pennsylvania archaeologist, pointed out in 1930 that the air in an Egyptian tomb opened five years earlier had been so bad that anyone breathing it got a violent headache after just a few minutes. If someone is found dead in a garage, he went on, carbon monoxide poisoning is blamed. But if the same fate befell a worker in a tomb, then 'a guilty conscience and a lively imagination combined to attribute the deaths to a curse'.[12]

In 1933 Professor Georg Steinberg, director of the Egyptian Institute of the University of Leipzig, published a monograph tracing the deaths of the alleged victims of the curse. Discovering that most of them had nothing to do with the tomb, and concluding that a 'curse of the pharaohs' did not exist, he also scorned the tale of the inscription allegedly found in the antechamber by Carter. His analysis was supported by Professor Jean Capart of the Royal Museum in Brussels. When nobody met Capart's challenge to provide particulars of the inscription, he dismissed the claim as 'the product of the fancy of a storyteller in search of thrilling sensations'.

Yet within the year Dr Albert M. Lythgoe, curator emeritus of the Metropolitan Museum of Art's Egyptian collection, was struck by a mystery illness. Described in the press as one of the few survivors of the group at the opening of the tomb, Lythgoe soon died – a victim of the 'curse'. To dampen the publicity his successor, Herbert E. Winlock, pointed out that of fifty-four people variously present at the opening of the tomb (1923), the sarcophagus (1924), and the mummy's unwrapping (1925), only eight had since died. 'The "curse" is a superstition so wholly devoid of foundation,' he concluded, 'that only the most credulous and ill-informed persons can give a moment's credence to it.'[13]

A similar analysis led James Randi, stage-magician and well-known debunker of the paranormal, to conclude in 1978 that the death rate was just what one would expect, given that many expedition members were elderly and in a country lacking modern health and sanitary measures.[14]

Sceptics also noted that others besides Carter who might have been expected to die remained unafflicted. Lady Evelyn Beauchamp (*née* Herbert), at her father's side when Carnarvon first entered the tomb, lived to a ripe old age, as did her brother, the sixth earl. Neither believed in the curse.

Moreover, if pharaonic curses were so effective, then no Egyptian tombs would ever have been robbed. Why bother even trying if a rapid and hideous death is the sure result? Yet from the start the guardians of Egypt's royal tombs fought a losing battle against robber-gangs, many probably organised by court officials. Over a century before Tutankhamen's time the desperate guardians had exhumed the mummies of thirty-six pharaohs from their sacked tombs and, with such gold as remained, hid them in a sealed, camouflaged cave outside the Valley of the Kings. This cave was found only because, in the 1880s, ancient relics began turning up in Cairo's antique markets. On investigation the Director of the Cairo Museum, Sir Gaston Maspero, learned that a family had found the cave in 1871 and had been selling the plunder ever since. Led by an informant, Sir Gaston's assistant Emil Brugsch entered the tomb and there he saw row upon row of the mummified remains of over thirty ancient pharaohs, along with such treasure as remained unstolen.

No tale of a death-curse ever arose in connection with this particular theft, one of greater magnitude than the rifling in 1923 of the tomb of just one pharaoh, Tutankhamen.

The Curse of Tutankhamen is like the Smile of the Cheshire Cat: now you see it, now you do not. The desire to believe or disbelieve is everything, and depends largely on one's cultural or religious attitudes.

How could such a curse work over time and at a distance? Anyone who asserts that such weapons or mental devices created by the imaginative will of long-dead priests do really exist risks being denounced as credulous, yet it is the common opinion of humanity through the ages that curses *can* be cast and *do* kill. The victim does not even have to be aware of it.

Unsurprisingly, a tendency to depression is common among Egyptologists and people who dig up graves. Howard Carter suffered from such deep depression that he gave up archaeology several times. His friend Dr Evelyn White, who had also been present at the opening of the tomb, though seriously ill with nervous depression, told every doctor who tried to treat him: 'Don't bother. I know what the matter is.' Lord Westbury, unable to 'stand any more horrors' after the death of his son, Richard Bethell, committed suicide while depressed by jumping from a window; his widow killed herself five years later. Dr Zakariaj Ghoneim, chief inspector for the antiquities department of Upper Egypt, killed himself in 1959 after suffering from deep depressions for years.[15] In themselves these few examples prove nothing, but suggest that those involved in the morbid activity of unearthing old tombs are likely candidates for effective cursing, or self-cursing.

Maybe there is more to it than that . . .

In 1968 a team of British radiologists led by Professor R. G. Harrison of Liverpool University visited Egypt to X-ray Tutankhamen's mummy, hoping to learn what had killed him. During their stay, says Harrison, they were beset by 'strange happenings'. As they worked in the valley, the lights went out in Cairo, just as they did the night Carnarvon died; and one of the team died suddenly, of no obvious cause.

A suitably mysterious postscript is the fact that under the headmask of the mummy inside the third gold coffin, Carter and his helpers found an iron headrest. This, along with a dagger blade and an amuletic bracelet, proved that eighteenth-dynasty Egypt had entered the Iron Age. The author Arnold C. Brackman, a sceptic about the curse who none the less has noticed what seems to have evaded everyone else, points out that there is a possible relationship between the headrest and a curse. For in the Egyptian *Book of the Dead*, composed during the eighteenth dynasty, the symbolic meaning of the mummy's headrest is described as follows:

Rise from non-existence, O prostrate one! . . . overthrow your enemies, triumph over what they do against you.[16]

4 Ancestral Voices and Original Sin

Back to the start of things, to the dawn of history, to much that is more about myth than fact, more about superstition and folklore than about history. The next few chapters tell of that dark time in Europe when thousands of people were burned to death for imaginary crimes, and there is no way to understand that accursed era without insight into the religious beliefs and demonic myths that underlay the medieval terror.

Few 'true' tales of curses from ancient times survive, because not many people two or three millennia ago could write, and because their idea of 'truth' was not ours. Before the ascent of science and reason, the common world-view was magical – the boundary between myth and 'reality' was vague. It was believed that sorcerers took animal form; that gods walked among men in disguise; that an unpredicted eclipse or comet's appearance meant disaster; that omens lay in bird-flight or a stabbed man's writhings; that menstruating women must never go near growing crops, food or anything else their touch might harm; that spirits lived in trees, rivers and stones; or that you might die if an enemy wrote your name on a piece of lead, wax or pottery, spoke a curse over it, and then buried it. This led, the world over, to the concept of the 'real' or 'secret' name, whispered into a man's ear at birth and never spoken aloud lest it be used against him.

In Bath, England, in 1980, archaeologists uncovered the remains of a temple dedicated to the Roman goddess Minerva. In it were found 'curse tablets' written out and directed at people by priests paid by enemies of those people. Likewise Ezekiel, the biblical prophet, condemns 'women who sew magic charms on their sleeves and make veils for the heads of people of every height to hunt souls!' (Ezekiel 13:18).

The worst curses of all were cast by gods. In Greek myth, Bellerophon tries to ride the winged horse Pegasus up to Olympus but is hurled down to spend the rest of his life as a lame, despised outcast. Prometheus steals fire from the gods and is chained to a rock: his liver, pecked out daily by an eagle, grows back in the night, to be pecked out again next day. Icarus flies too close to the sun: his wax wings melt and he falls to his death. Actaeon, the original Peeping Tom, spies on the goddess Artemis bathing naked and, turned into a stag, is torn into pieces by his own hounds. The gods were jealous and vengeful.

Crimes like parricide and incest were especially cursed. Oedipus, though warned by the Delphic Oracle, unwittingly kills his father Laius and marries his mother Jocasta. When he realises what he has done he blinds himself, and is hounded to death by the Furies, though not before cursing his twin sons Polyneices and Eteocles. Born of his incest, they fulfil the curse by killing each other when fighting for the Theban throne. Just as bleak is the Greek drama of Orestes, son of King Agamemnon of Argos, the Greek leader at Troy, whose mother Clytemnestra beheaded Agamemnon after her lover Aegisthus cut him down in his bath. Agamemnon had murdered her former husband Tantalus, as well as a new-born baby suckling at her breast. Clytemnestra had no reason to love him; Orestes none to love her. Reared in exile, Orestes asks the Delphic Oracle if he should kill his father's killers. Apollo speaking through his priestess warns Orestes that he will become an outcast if he does not: the oracle warns that the Furies will punish matricide. Either way Orestes is doomed. Returning disguised to Mycenae he enters the palace, kills Aegisthus, then beheads his mother.

For this act of retributive matricide he is chased by the Furies and goes mad, but is absolved by Athene, goddess of wisdom. So the madness ends; the Furies retire: good sense and 'holy Persuasion' win the day.

These tales say a lot about how our ancestors viewed human nature and fate. Oedipus unwittingly commits the crimes he was warned to avoid; Orestes is damned if he avenges his father and damned if he does not. People saw human life itself as the curse, and attempts to improve it ('rebel against the góds'; 'eat of the Tree') were regarded with deep suspicion.

In Eastern belief the curse is in our failure to see through illusion, (our self-delusion, rather than a supernatural imposition); but the idea that we are all innately damned still runs deep in the West, via the Bible story that Adam and Eve got expelled from Eden, and the dogma of Original Sin. It is the first curse in a book full of curses: by one count, the word 'curse' is found in the Bible about 230 times ('blessing' occurs about 410 times).[1] The main vehicle of both blessings and curses is words. Proverbs 18:21 states that: *Death and life are in the power of the tongue*; while Proverbs 26:2 says that: *Like a sparrow in its flitting, like a swallow in its flying, a curse that is causeless does not alight.*

Numbers 5:11–31 describes a curse used to decide a wife's faithfulness. The woman has to drink a cup of water mixed with dust from the Tabernacle floor and with ink scraped from a written curse. If she is guilty, then . . . *the water that brings the curse shall enter into her, and cause bitter pain, and her body shall swell, and her thigh shall fall away* . . .

The primary cause of all curses, and their justification, is said by

Moses in Deuteronomy 28:15 to lie in disobedience to God's laws.

Which brings us to the strange history of the first and greatest curse of all, cast by God on all humanity – the curse of Original Sin.

Millions of fundamentalist Christians still hold as literally true the tale that the Lord God, having made the heavens and the earth, put Adam in the Garden of Eden, telling him he could eat of any tree but that of the knowledge of good and evil, 'for in the day that you eat of it you shall die'. Then from Adam's rib He made Eve, the first woman. So Adam and Eve walked naked and unashamed, until Eve meets the Serpent, who asks her if the fruit of any tree in the garden is forbidden.

Eve explains, but the Serpent says: 'You will not die. For God knows that when you eat of it your eyes will be opened, and you will be like God, knowing good and evil.'

So Eve eats the forbidden fruit and gives it to Adam, who also disobeys God. Suddenly conscious of being naked, like beasts, they make fig-leaf aprons, then hide in fear from God. Adam blames Eve, who blames the Serpent, but Yahweh curses all three and expels Adam and Eve from Eden.

Why do so many Christians still believe so literally in this curse as to insist that all non-Christians are damned, and Woman more so than Man? Certainly the early Church 'fathers' adopted the dogma of Original Sin to strengthen their own position against pagan competition. St Paul said Adam's act brought sin and death into the world, but that grace and eternal life came in greater wealth via Christ (Romans 5:12–19). St Augustine regarded spontaneous sexual desire as proof of Original Sin.[2]

Some say the allegory of the Fall refers to the emergence of a new type of consciousness, one that now dominates the world: ego-based, rational 'head'-consciousness. This made people feel shut up in themselves, separated from nature, lost in a world flooded by sin. The Serpent split in two: one half now the wrathful sky-god, the other the satanic worm; both hostile to Man who, thrown out of Eden, was at first bewildered, then, as in the case of Cain, became murderously angry.

Evidence includes a stone altar carved about 1230 BC (before Genesis) for the Assyrian king Tukulti-Ninurti. It shows him kneeling before a god's empty throne. No king before had ever been shown kneeling. A cuneiform tablet of the time says: 'One who has no god, as he walks along the street, Headache envelops him like a garment.' Soon afterwards the Assyrian race went berserk, falling on their neighbours like wolves on the sheepfold. Bas-reliefs celebrating their conquests record a new sadism, mass slaughter, the decapitation and flaying alive of captured civilians. Even minor crimes were violently punished. Trapped in egotism, human feelings had become unreal to them. Cast from Eden, they were cursed by continual nervous tension (thus 'Headache envelops him like a garment').[3]

The curse spread. A new,. heartless, rational violence invaded the world. Communion with the old gods, with nature and the intuitive mind, was lost. Greek philosophers began to master the new way, but most folk clung to the older, broader, more ecstatic mind-set. Drunken, orgiastic cults like that of Dionysus revolted against this curse of reason; a revolt persisting since via millennarianism, magical or occult beliefs, psychedelic cults and espousal of feminism. Some tried to create new Edens ('New Age', or 'New Jerusalem'), or revolutionary new social orders like Communism.

Adam and Eve ate the apple and lost 'Eden', their state of communion with the intuitive mind. Cursed and expelled, we were now alone with ourselves. Many believe the curse of lost Eden still prevails, redeemable only by Christ.

Another condition anciently regarded as accursed is still widely called 'the curse'. The mysterious female connection with the moon has been long acknowledged due to women's monthly bleeding in obedience to the lunar cycle. Menstruation, associated with both female fertility and female temperament, led early man to see the waning moon, like menstrual women, as 'sick' or 'cursed'. In Germany, the menstrual period was called 'the moon'; in French, le moment de la lune. The Maori call menstruation mata marama, 'moon sickness', saying a girl's first menstruation comes only when the moon sleeps with her. From India to North America the words for 'moon' and 'menstrual blood' were similar or identical. Throughout the ancient world, menstruating women were taboo – unclean, holy, set apart from normal life, secluded in the menstrual lodge. Their bleeding was supernatural, not an earthly wound. They were dangerous. Their touch might cause illness. Their presence in the house might put out the hearth-fire. Food brought to them was left at a distance. No menstruating woman walked round ripening crops for fear of blighting them. An Australian aborigine, learning that his wife had lain on his blanket while menstruating, might kill her, then himself die of fright within the fortnight.

Adolescent youths were initiated into manhood by fearful rites to test their courage and separate them from mother, but the initiation rite for pubescent girls was the natural rite of their first menstrual seclusion.

The word Sabbath, since applied to the Christian day of rest, Sunday (also to the sabbat of witches), may come from the Babylonian sabattu, or sabat, meaning 'Heart-Rest'. On this Day of Rest, or Evil Day, when the moon was full, it was said Ishtar the moon-goddess was menstruating. On this day it was unlucky to work, eat cooked food, or go on a journey.

This monthly day later became a weekly day on which everyone observed the ancient taboo of menstrual inaction. Jungian psychologist Esther Harding argues that the taboo arose as an attempt by men '. . . to protect themselves by segregating the dangerous female, and in this way protect themselves from the devastating effect of their own sexuality.'[4]

That belief in the cursed female condition can still of itself blight the lives of women today is suggested by a letter from a woman in her thirties, received in 1987 by the Christian evangelist Derek Prince. The woman reveals that her periods had always been irregular, a condition doctors attributed to hormonal imbalance. In August 1985 she heard a set of tapes by Prince on 'Blessings and Curses'. At the end of these was a prayer. She spoke it aloud. Hearing the tape again some time later she was struck by Prince's assertion that 'almost if not all, menstrual disorders, are a result of a curse'. Checking her diary, she realised that since August, when she had first recited the prayer, her periods had been regular. She concluded that, since her school years she and her peers had called menstruation 'the curse', this identification alone had been enough to trigger irregularity.

As to the ancient curse of barrenness (Deuteronomy 28: 'Cursed shall be the fruit of thy body'), Prince tells the story of a couple, who had been childless for twelve years, though medical tests could detect nothing wrong. In July 1985 the couple attended one of Prince's prayer meetings, at which he spoke on curses that hang over families. Feeling that this was their problem, they asked him to pray over them. Prince pronounced the curse broken; his wife Ruth told the woman that she would be 'neither barren nor unfruitful'. Some two years later, says Prince, at another meeting in England the couple came forward with their new-born baby boy.[5]

The practice of sorcery was always seen as accursed, especially as it annexed divine power to impious mortal ends. The Bible (Deuteronomy 18:10–11) denounces all forms of necromancy, divination, soothsaying, sorcery or wizardry as being an 'abomination to the Lord'. Yet I Samuel 28 tells how Saul, King of Israel, disheartened by the defection of his people, the conquests of the Philistines, and God's refusal to answer his questions, went illegally to a diviner, the Witch of Endor, to ask about the future.

In disguise he came to her by night and ordered her to conjure up the spirit of the prophet Samuel, recently deceased. At first the woman refused, aware that Saul had executed many witches like herself and suspecting he was trying to trick her to death. But when he swore by the Lord that no harm would come to her, she conjured up Samuel, whom she alone could see as 'a god coming out of the earth', and as 'an old man . . . wrapped in a robe'.

The apparition of Samuel asked Saul why he had been disturbed.

Saul told him it was because God had turned away, answering him no more, either by prophets or by dreams. He needed Samuel's advice.

Samuel then cursed him with the knowledge that he and his sons were about to die, Israel was about to fall to the Philistines, and David would become king. Saul, who had not eaten all day or night, collapsed in terror. The witch kindly killed an unfatted calf, baked unleavened bread, and fed Saul and his two servants, who then rose and went away . . . to die the following day.

Of the witch and her fate, no more is said. The biblical scribe seems unhappy at having to admit even the existence of such ungodly activity.

Classical Roman authors are less prudish. Thus we may thank Lucan for the surviving tale of Erichtho, the Crone of Thessaly. In his *Pharsalia*, Lucan tells us how from that dread and barren land came the most potent sorcerers of all. Thessalian witches could influence the weather, make love enter the hardest hearts, and encourage 'even the severity of age . . . to burn with youthful fires'. Even Babylon and Memphis in Egypt, famous ancient centres of black magic, were said to have been overcome by such power. 'The chant of the Thessalian witch penetrates the furthest seat of the gods and contains words so powerful that not even the care of the skies, or of the revolving spheres, can avail as an excuse to the deities to decline its force,' Lucan claims by way of prologue to his tale of how Sextus Pompey, son of Pompey the Great, attempted to learn the future by consulting the dead via Erichtho, who 'kept on good terms with the infernal powers by squatting in tombs'.

Lucan describes Erichtho, the most potent and hideous of all Thessalian witches, as pale and thin, her hair matted, her breath foul. Defying the midnight lightning, her very footsteps poison the fruits of the earth. Living in a grave from which the ghost of the corpse has been expelled, her habits are as unwholesome as her powers are immense: 'She tears the limbs of the dead and digs out their eyes. She separates with her teeth the rope on the gibbet and tears away the murderer from the cross. She applies to her purposes the entrails withered by the wind and the marrow that had been dried by the sun. She bears away the nails which had pierced the hands and feet of the criminal, the clotted blood which had distilled from his wounds and the sinews that held him suspended.'

Waiting until a wolf has begun tearing at a body from a battlefield, this pleasant ancestress of the three witches of *Macbeth* (see chapter 20) will 'wrench the morsels from his hungry jaws' to collect ingredients for her potions. Watching over a dying man, she will 'bite his lips, compress his windpipe, and whisper in his expiring organ some message to the infernal shades.'

Lucan describes how Sextus, nervously seeking Erichtho out at midnight in a rocky place by deserted graves, asks her to force the dead to confess what they know of the future. Answering that she can change individual fate and even restore an old man to youth but cannot break the chain of fate, the hag tells him that she will try to show him the future. For this, she says, she will need a newly slain corpse with sound lungs, as older corpses 'only squeak incoherently'. Making the night still darker by her arts, winding a 'pitchy cloud' round her head, she takes Sextus to a nearby battlefield to search among the bodies of the unburied dead. Even the wolves and birds of prey flee at her approach. Selecting a body, she passes a hook under its jaw, and drags it over rocks and stones to a cave under a projecting ridge where the yew-tree grows thick. Covering her face with her hair and with a wreath of vipers round her brow, she scolds Sextus and his men for their fear. She goes to work on the corpse, applying to it froth from the jaws of a dead dog, the entrails of a lynx, the marrow of a stag which has fed on serpents, and other odious items. At last she chants a long, terrible, impious incantation to the Furies of Hell. Her voice resembles the barking of a dog and the howl of a wolf, the hooting of a screech-owl, the yelling of a wild beast and the fearful hiss of a serpent. Finally the spirit of the dead man appears, standing before her, pale and soundless, speaking only when commanded. Having given the required information, it asks to be laid to rest forever. She builds a funeral pyre on which the corpse places itself: she applies the torch, and that's the end of it.[6]

Another ancient sorcerer was Simon Magus who, according to the New Testament, set himself up as Christ's rival. Legend tells how, in a magical battle with St Peter in Nero's palace in Rome, this Gnostic magician flew in the air, but was felled by the saint's well-aimed prayer, and died.

Necromancy and divination prospered. Just as Napoleon and Hitler later believed that certain quatrains of Nostradamus were about them, so Julius Caesar thought a famous Sibylline prophecy referred to him. It spoke of a great king ascending to power in the east, destined to conquer and unite all the peoples of the world, his reign ushering in an age of splendour.

As it turned out, the only prophecy still associated with Julius Caesar was shouted at him from the crowds by one Vestricius Spurinna:

'Beware the Ides of March!'

Few people in ancient times failed to see an omen, usually unlucky, in any unexpected event, particularly unexpected celestial events.

Comets, fiery-tailed visitors moving even more independently in the night sky than the planets, were always feared. Some still regard them as accursed. Noah's Flood was blamed on a comet; the English astronomer Sir Fred Hoyle has speculated that comets seed the earthly atmosphere with organisms that bring new strains of influenza. Others claim that these heavenly snowballs, irregularly orbiting the sun, do not affect us, and that the only damage comes from 'self-fulfilling superstition'.[7]

The Roman historian Tacitus, writing in the reign of Nero, tells of a comet which appeared around AD 60 and caused the emperor's subjects to act 'as if Nero were already dethroned' and 'to ask who might be his successor'. Nero's astrologer, Balbillus, advised the emperor to deflect this celestial wrath by 'using his most prominent subjects as omen-conductors and letting the message in the sky be fulfilled in their deaths rather than his'. So, as Suetonius writes, Nero: '. . . resolved on a wholesale massacre of the nobility . . . all children of the condemned men were banished from Rome, and then starved to death or poisoned'. And so the expectation of the people was gratified: powerful and hated folk *had* perished according to the comet's prophecy. Nero survived, and even a visit in AD 66 by Halley's Comet failed to shake his imperial power: he died in AD 68, aged thirty-two.

As for Halley's Comet, it returned in 1066, when the Normans conquered England. Following another of its visits, in 1910, Oklahoma sheriffs in the USA only just managed to prevent the sacrifice of a virgin by lunatic cultists called the Sacred Followers, many of whom committed suicide to escape the celestial wrath. That same year King Edward VII of England perished 'from the comet complicated by bronchitis'.

When in 814 no comet appeared to herald the death of Charlemagne, the chroniclers recorded a comet anyway. The Incas viewed comets as death-threats from their sun god, *Inti*: one appeared in 1531 before the Spanish *conquistador* Pizarro arrived. More recently it is claimed that President Kennedy's assassination in Dallas, Texas, in 1963 (see chapter 17), was prefigured by the comet *Pereyra*. Those foretelling this event were not decapitated, but that was the fate which, according to legend, befell the Chinese imperial astronomers Hi and Ho, too drunk to notice and warn of a coming solar eclipse. The Emperor Yao charged them with 'having done violence to the five fundamental forces and having idly abandoned the three fundamental regulations'.[8]

Fear of judgement in the hereafter led to many customs designed to dispel guilt and fear, and to ensure a welcome in heaven, no matter how raucous earthly life had been.

Scapegoats have been resorted to throughout the ages. In Ireland the sins of the newly dead were passed on to a hereditary family of 'sin-eaters'. Food left for the dead to aid their journey beyond the grave was eaten by the 'sin-eater', who thus accumulated a vast weight of sin. When his own time came, all the accursed sins he had eaten were eaten in turn by his son or successor. On the Jewish Day of

Atonement, the High Priest laid his hands on a goat, confessed over it the sins of the Jews, then drove it into the wilderness. At least it was left alive. In the Himalayas folk made a dog drunk then, chasing it out of the village, stoned it to death so that no disease or ill-luck would visit them for another year. In one part of Nigeria two human victims were killed each year to remove the sins of those paying for the sacrifice. Once a year in Thai cities an adulteress was driven out, thrown on a dunghill to attract evil spirits, and forbidden ever to return. In many ancient cultures the annual torture, murder and ritual cannibalising of the divine king or elected corn-god, took place to placate the gods and ensure fertility.

Such scapegoat rites persist: Christians still claim that Christ died for their sins; while recent history has revived one of the most pernicious scapegoat superstitions: anti-Semitism, the cursing of the Jews as Christ-killers, condemned to wander homelessly forever.

A Jew (Hebrew *Yehudi*) is a member of Judah, meaning either of the tribe of Judah, one of the twelve that claimed the Promised Land, or of the later Kingdom of Judah (as opposed to the northern Kingdom of Israel). Initially called Hebrews (*Ivrim*), the Jews were called Israelites (*Isre'elim*) until the end of their exile in Babylon in 538 BC. Thereafter, the term *Yehudi* was used of all adherents of Judaism.

Anti-Semitism may have arisen from envy of the Jewish claim that there is but one god – Yahweh, who in the myth of Eden cursed all humanity. Yahweh also blessed those obeying him, and the Jews in particular as his Chosen People, as given in Numbers 24:9:

> Blessed be everyone who blesses you,
> And cursed be everyone who curses you.

Thus, whoever opposed Israel opposed God himself – an attitude calculated to enrage other races. In 333 BC, Alexander the Great overran Judaea. After his death, Hellenic influence led to Roman rule and to continual Jewish revolt, from that of the Maccabees (*c.* 167 BC) to the mass Zealot suicide at Masada (AD 74) after the emperor Titus took Jerusalem. A century after Christ, a final revolt led by Simeon bar Kochba failed. Enslaved and dispersed, the Jews' plight worsened when Constantine (AD 279–337) embraced Christianity as Rome's state religion. With usury banned to Christians, the Jews were found useful – as usurers.

The Crusades brought renewed anti-Semitism. Many Jews had settled in England and Germany, but they rejected assimilation and their laws forbade them from marrying non-Jews. Amid crusading hysteria, fantastic myths abounded: that the Antichrist, when born, would be a Jew of the tribe of Dan; that he would love the Jews most of all; and that the Jews ritually murdered Christian children for blood to use in Passover rites. This, the infamous 'blood libel' (attributed to Hugh of Lincoln: England 1255), was used to justify atrocities. In vain, tortured Jews insisted that Judaism forbids the consumption of blood; on this aversion neurotic Christians built the reverse fantasy, so as to justify the slaughter of the 'demonic' Jew.

In 1290 the Jews were expelled from England, in 1395 from France, in 1492 from Spain. Forced into ghettoes throughout northern Europe, they were blamed for the Plague that killed a third of Europe's population from 1348 to 1350. It was claimed they had poisoned the wells. In 1349 the people of Brussels, Frankfurt, Mainz and Cologne burned or drowned every Jew they could find, 'because they thought to please God in that way'.[9]

The legend of the Jew condemned to wander the earth until Judgement Day for insulting Christ on the way to Calvary is ascribed to Matthew of Paris, who said he heard the tale from an Armenian bishop in 1228; that the man's name was Ahasuerus, and that he had been a doorkeeper in Pilate's palace. This Wandering Jew had struck Jesus, who had said: 'I will stand here and rest, but thou shalt go on until the last day.'

The demonic myth did not die. Late in the nineteenth century, as occultists like MacGregor Mathers ascribed old magical texts to Jewish Qabalists, anti-Semites like Richard Wagner and Houston Stewart Chamberlain fanned the ancient flames of hate.

In Russia, in 1903, *The Protocols of the Elders of Zion* appeared, masquerading as proof of an 'international Jewish conspiracy' for world conquest. It was a fraud that many believed eagerly. In 1919 the White Russian army murdered some 60,000 Jews, blaming them for the 1917 Revolution. Even in 1921 the London *Times* thought the *Protocols* genuine. When in 1933 the Nazi leader Adolf Hitler came to power in Germany, he used the myth of the demonic Jew to begin a persecution leading to the 'Final Solution': the attempt to exterminate all Jewry. Some six million Jews died, many in the gas chambers of Auschwitz and Belsen. Fourteenth-century horror was echoed, more horribly, in the twentieth.

Today the Jews have regained their homeland, Israel. But the *Protocols* remain in circulation; and apocalyptic Christian sects still claim that Armageddon, the final battle between Christ and the Antichrist, will take place in the 'Holy Land'.

Anti-Semitism may arise out of a common dislike of any who hold themselves to be exclusive or 'chosen by God' – the gypsies, also exclusive and itinerant folk, have likewise been persecuted by Nazis and others. But it may also be the result of a curious religious confusion typical of monotheists, who see all things as opposites, black and white, absolute good and absolute evil, with no intermediate shades of moral judgement (or doubt) permitted.

Which is another kind of curse.

5 Papal Magicians and the Templar Head

Curses are not just *individual* maledictions; some are the fruit of a dark, hostile, paranoid mind-set as found in institutions using fear and torture to control human beliefs. Long before the birth of the Soviet NKVD or Nazi SS, the Dominican Inquisition knew how to screw false confessions out of terrified victims – in the name of Jesus Christ, God of Love.

From its earliest days the Church resorted to malediction and the use of terror, but it took over a millennium for it to embrace the murderous fanaticism of the Middle Ages, when Cathars, Templars, and unknown thousands of women (and some men) were tortured and burned alive as heretics or witches.

St Paul had denounced false teachers and 'those who do not love Christ' as cursed, cast out of God's grace; but only when Christianity became the Roman state religion could the Church begin to assert itself. Before a crucial battle in the year AD 312 the emperor Constantine and 'all his troops' saw a 'sign of a cross' in the noonday sky, inscribed with the words 'By this, conquer'. That night Christ visited his dreams; the following day Constantine had his men paint the sign of the cross on their shields. Or so he told the Christian bishop Eusebius.[1] With Christianity now official, bishops assumed the power to curse all and sundry for many different sins. They cursed emperors, they cursed rich and poor alike. The poor, with no other outlet, cursed everyone, or adopted new beliefs which the Church or emperor promptly anathematised and cursed as heresy.

Church power grew slowly. In AD 545 the Byzantine emperor Justinian demanded agreement that the Monophysite party was heretical. In Rome Pope Vigilius, who had paid two hundred pounds in gold to be elected, refused to sign the edict. Hiding under the altar of St Peter, the Pope clung so fiercely to its legs that it began to collapse on him when the emperor's soldiers tried to pull him out by his beard. Promised safe conduct, he went to Constantinople, only to find himself a prisoner. In AD 553 Justinian summoned a church council which the Pope refused to attend. The heresy was condemned, and all those upholding it were cursed. At last caving in, Vigilius confessed his errors. Justinian released the Pope, and he started the journey back to Rome, but died before he got there.[2]

The Roman Church did not gain its present authority or form for many centuries. It was not until 1074 that Pope Gregory VII ordained priestly celibacy: married priests must abandon their wives, or be cursed forever. There was uproar, but Gregory got his way, and the prohibition remains in force today. Not surprisingly, Pope Gregory was not popular among the clergy, but the citizens of the Holy Roman Empire, in revolt against Emperor Henry, made a direct appeal to the Pope. When Gregory was attacked, wounded and kidnapped in Rome, the citizens attacked those who threatened his life, and they in turn fled to Henry for refuge. In a dangerous game of tit-for-tat Pope Gregory, as head of the Roman Church, officially summoned Henry to Rome; while Henry officially summoned a church synod at Worms for the purpose of cursing and deposing the Pope. The result was that Gregory got in first and cursed and deposed Henry. Henry presented himself at the papal castle in January 1077, humbled and contrite, and had to stand outside barefoot and in rags for three days and nights before the Pope would let him in. Later he regained his power, but the die was cast – popes and emperors would fight for centuries thereafter. At the Synod of Brixen, at which Clement VII was elected as anti-Pope, Gregory was denounced as a magician and necromancer. In 1085 he died a fugitive, in exile.

It is said that, one day during his papacy, Gregory arrived at the Church of the Lateran only to realise he had forgotten his *grimoire*, or magical book. He sent two servants back to his villa to get it, threatening them with terrible curses if they opened it. Curiosity got the better of the servants who not only opened it but began reading the invocations aloud. Several demons appeared.

'We'll obey your commands,' they said, 'but if you trifle with us, we'll fall on you and destroy you.' Terrified, the servants told the devils to hurl down the wall before them, which they did. It isn't known whether Gregory heard of it but, if he did, perhaps he shook lightning out of his sleeve – a feat believed to be among his powers – and slew the servants.

Gregory was not the only papal magician. John XX and Gregory VI before him were equally enthusiastic dabblers in just those arts for which so many folk were later to be sent to the stake. The best known papal magus of all was Gerbert, alias Silvester II. Gerbert, who learned Arabic and imported Arabic numerals into Europe, is said to have sold the devil his soul in exchange for the Papacy and, like Albertus Magnus and Roger Bacon in the thirteenth century, to have made a brazen head which would answer all questions and solve the most obscure problems. Oddly, one of the charges against the Templars when they were arrested in 1307 was that they too worshipped a mysterious head.

One of Silvester II's successors, Benedict IX, elected Pope at the age of twelve, reportedly used demonic magic for more down-to-earth purposes. 'Among other things he caused the matrons of Rome by his incantations to follow him in troops among the woods and mountains, being bewitched and their souls subdued by the irresistible charms of his magic.'[3]

In 1095 the First Crusade to recapture the Holy Land was invoked by one of the two Popes struggling for supremacy: Urban II. He thought if he took up the cause of Holy War it would seal his authority, and so set in motion a conflict that lasted two centuries. It was during the First Crusade that the Knights Templar were founded. Two centuries later, a Pope and a King conspired to destroy them, thus invoking a curse which destroyed both King and Pope.

We all know Friday the thirteenth is supposed to be unlucky. Thirteen's bad image is explicable, given its old association with pagan lunar/female Mysteries. The early Church fathers crushed these, yet awkward *thirteen* refused to go away. Christ and twelve apostles or the judge and twelve jurors make thirteen; our twelve-month year is false: there are not twelve but thirteen ($13 \times 28 = 364$) moons in a year. Thirteen is bad news – like walking under ladders or breaking mirrors – and today many high-rise towers have no thirteenth floor. Yet why *Friday*, when Monday (alias Moonday) surely shares thirteen's sinister features more exactly?

One reason may be that the date commemorates a horrible crime. At daybreak on Friday, 13 October 1307, soldiers of the French King Philip the Fair raided Templar houses throughout France. The plot had been months in the planning. The order for the arrests, drawn up on 14 September, had gone out to royal officials throughout France, and with it a list of charges, on the basis of which the Knights were to be tortured into confession.

Why? Because Philip was broke. Having banished the Jews in 1306 and seized their wealth, now he wanted the Templar gold.

But the surprise had to be total. The Templars, though driven from the Holy Land in 1291 after the fall of Acre and the end of the Crusades, were still a formidable force. Owning their own fleet, banking for kings, farming their own tithes and answering only to the Pope, they were envied, feared and hated for their riches, ferocity and arrogance. While the Crusades lasted they had been invulnerable, but now their enemies – Dominicans, the rival Knights Hospitaller and pragmatists like Philip – saw an opening. To justify seizing the Temple's wealth, Philip realised, he had to act as moral champion of the Church, uncovering a conspiracy so foul that even brave men would blench. The Temple had to be degraded, demonised, then destroyed. With the agreement of the French Pope Clement V, he invented the office of General Inquisitor, ordering Guillaume Imbert, his Dominican confessor, to legitimise the destruction of the order.

Imbert knew what was wanted. The Templars would be accused of denying Christ, defiling the Cross, perverting the Mass, and adoring an idol (a head); also of ritual murder, obscene kissing, sodomy and (like Cathars and witches) wearing a cord. The bigger the lie, in fact, the better.

The origins and real purposes of this order of warrior-mystics remain as mysterious as its fate after 1307, its history cloaked in extravagant myths of high-level intrigues, buried treasure, the Ark of the Covenant and the Holy Grail.

To this darkly glamorous mystique may be added the terrible tortures endured by French Templars in 1307, and the curse hurled at King Philip and Pope Clement by the last Templar Grand Master, Jacques de Molay, as he died over a slow fire on an isle in the Seine in March 1314.

The Order of the Poor Knights of Christ and the Temple of Solomon was founded, it seems, in Jerusalem in 1118 by a knight of Champagne, Hugues de Payens, and eight companions. Arriving at the palace of Baldwin I, King of Jerusalem, they demanded recognition as an order to keep the roads and highways safe, and to protect pilgrims. Baldwin quartered them in his palace, said to be built on the foundations of the Temple of Solomon. Thus, Knights Templar.

Sworn to chastity, poverty and obedience, they were supposedly so poor they had to share horses when out protecting pilgrims. Yet in 1128 Bernard of Clairvaux, head of the dynamic new Cistercian order, drew up their Rule and championed them, urging the wealthy to support the order and sinners to join it. Murderers, thieves, adulterers and even heretics were welcomed, so long as they embraced harsh vows and accepted the constant threat of bloody death. Bernard was so persuasive that in 1130 Hugues de Payens returned to Europe with 300 knights. The money poured in – and power with it. In 1139 Pope Innocent II made them answerable to himself alone; even as Abbot Suger of St Denis in Paris had his church rebuilt in a new style, later called 'Gothic', using pointed arch and flying buttress to draw eye and spirit up. Some claim the Templars brought this new architecture back with them from Palestine; and that their role as 'protector of pilgrims' was a front for occult work and (it was alleged at their trial) heretical perversions.

However unorthodox their doctrines, their harsh Rule was unlikely to encourage perversion. They owned no money, property or books. Instant obedience to superiors was required, whatever the consequences. They could never surrender, or retreat before odds of less than three-to-one. Taking their castle at Safed in 1270, the Kipchak sultan Baibars gave them a night to convert to Islam, or die. Their commander ordered them to choose death. Baibars had the man skinned alive before them all, but to a man they chose death.[4]

Chief of the three ranks within the order (knights, sergeants and clerics), the knights wore a red eight-pointed cross on a white mantle, signifying their purity. They also wore a sheepskin girdle at all times, as a symbol of chastity.[5] In 1307, their torturers pointed to this girdle as 'evidence' of satanic heresy.

Certainly they dabbled in old pagan lore thinly Christianised as Grail myth. The German knight Wolfram von Eschenbach in *Parzival* (1216) describes the Grail knights as 'Templeisen'. In the *Perlesvaus* (1206–12), Sir Gawain enters a castle housing two masters and thirty-three other men 'clad in white garments' with red crosses on the breast: Templar garb. This was dangerous stuff. A bloody crusade against the dualist Cathars ('Pure Ones') of Provence had begun, and the Templars too were suspect.

Believing in reincarnation, the co-equality of good and evil and that Yahweh was a false god, the Cathars promoted doctrines that the Church had persecuted for a millennium. Yet by 1208 Catharism was so popular that the corrupt Roman Church was in danger of being driven out of Provence. Stern steps were needed. Pope Innocent III, preaching crusade, let the northern French invade. The French responded eagerly. 'Kill them all,' the Abbé de Citeaux reportedly said when at the Siege of Béziers his men could not tell Catholics from Cathars among the defenders, 'God will know his own.'

So the Pays d'Oc was devastated in a thirty-year war, and the Inquisition, originating in the dark pieties of a Spaniard, Dominic Guzman (founder of the Dominican Order) was formed to root out heresy. By 1244 it was all over. Many lapsed Cathars, rather than perish on mass pyres of up to two hundred victims at a time, took refuge among the Templars.

Sixty-three years later, on Friday, 13 October 1307, Philip of France struck.

Under their new Grand Master Jacques de Molay, the Templars felt secure up to the end. After all, who would dare attack the Temple?

How many were seized is unclear. There were about two thousand Templar knights in France, maybe four thousand in the whole of Europe – but the knights were only the tip of the organisation. Maybe up to twenty thousand others were directly affected by Philip's dawn raid and by the later papal anathemas.

Most escaped, many to Portugal and Scotland. Yet even as their fleet vanished from La Rochelle, never to be seen again, the Franciscans and Dominicans launched a huge propaganda campaign. The Templars, people were told, had practised 'all the supremely abominable crimes which even the sensuality of unreasoning beasts abhors and avoids . . . they defile the earth with their filth, they undo the benefits of the dew, they corrupt the purity of the air and bring about the confusion of our faith.'[6]

The General Inquisitor Guillaume Imbert now began breaking his captives. Terrified men chained naked in stinking solitary cells were told their brothers had confessed, and that if they did too they would be spared. If not, they would be executed – if they survived torture that included oiling then roasting their feet over a slow fire until the bones fell from their sockets. One survivor of this ordeal was helped to a council of inquiry carrying his blackened foot-bones. His torturers had let him keep them as souvenirs.

Devices used to extort confession included the hot iron, applied to any part of the body including the genitals; red-hot pincers that nipped away the flesh; cold pincers to pull fingernails and teeth, the tooth sockets being probed to add to the pain; and clever contraptions to crush and break the bones of foot, ankle and knee. Recalcitrants were, between ordeals, shut in the *oubliette* – a pit or cell, too small to stand in, too narrow to lie in, situated right under the main sewer-drain in the dungeon floor.[7]

Under torture many went mad; few could resist. At the first Paris interrogations, only four men out of 138 (thirty-six died under torture) denied every charge. A fortnight after the arrests thirty-two Templars confirmed their confessions publicly. Only six of the 138 denied spitting on the cross on entering the order, thus rejecting the Crucifixion as the Cathars had done. Most confessed to the *osculum infame*, the 'kiss of shame' on mouth, navel, penis and buttocks. Seventy admitted being ordered to commit sodomy, all but two or three denied having done so. Only officers knew of the mysterious idol or head, Baphomet, maybe because Philip's initial order was that *only* officers should be asked about it. When he broadened the order to include all captives it emerged that they all knew of it. Yet their accounts of it under torture were wholly various, as in agony they agreed with whatever was suggested.

For at least five centuries the 'confessions' wrung out of broken, terrified men were taken by historians as proven.

As for the idol or head called Baphomet, did Imbert invent it further to damn the Templars? Pagans had worshipped heads; Pope Silvester, Bacon and Albertus were said to have made brazen heads; and in early Grail texts the Grail is a plate bearing a severed, bleeding head. Accused of believing it could save them and fertilise the land, some Templars described it as long-haired, bearded, and existing as carvings shown at the order's general chapters. It has been argued to be the image on the Shroud of Turin, which the Templars kept in a casket: the Grail.[8] Or the Grail was the Ark of the Covenant, kept at Axum in Ethiopia, and Templar knowledge of it led Wolfram to write *Parzival*.[9] Or Baphomet was a cipher for Sophia, in Gnostic lore the female epitome of wisdom. Nothing is known for sure, save that Brother Imbert got the results Philip wanted.

Collapsing under the threat of torture, the order's treasurer said he would freely admit to killing God to avoid such pain.

Jacques de Molay was at first no braver, denying Christ and

publicly claiming that the Temple had long been seduced by Satan. Only when about to die after seven years in jail did he redeem himself. Publicly paraded to affirm the guilt of the Temple before being burned alive in Paris on 14 March 1314, he recanted all confessions, affirming the order's innocence.

'I admit that I am guilty of the grossest iniquity,' he told prelates and princes assembled by Notre Dame. 'But the iniquity is that I have lied in admitting the disgusting charges laid against the Order . . . to save myself from terrible tortures by saying what my enemies wished me to say.'[10]

With Brother Geoffroi de Charney, once Templar preceptor of Normandy, he was hustled away to die amid a slow fire on an isle in the Seine. Long agony would precede death as no mercy was permitted; no smoke to asphyxiate the dying; no strangulation prior to the torch. With boatloads of curious spectators watching from the river, the two men shouted out the innocence of the Temple until they fainted. At the very last de Molay cursed King Philip and his family for thirteen generations, and called Philip and Pope Clement V to join him for judgement at God's throne within the year.

Clement died a month later; Philip's sudden and wholly inexplicable death followed in November. Thus, the Templar Curse.

The Inquisition soon found a new enemy: witches, meaning Woman.

6   Bothwell and the Witches

With the Cathars and Templars suitably treated, the Dominican Inquisition needed a new enemy to justify its continued existence, preferably one of vaguer description and thus with a longer shelf-life. So, who or what to demonise next?

Being an order of men of secluded disposition, world-rejecting, and denied contact with women, it soon came up with an answer. In 1321 Pope John XXII, a nervous individual convinced his enemies were trying to kill him by magic, was persuaded by black-robed Dominican advisers to agree to a crusade against *maleficium* – evil sorcery, black magic. And their terms of reference were broad. *Maleficium* to them meant what were widely known as the 'cunning arts' – the ancient folk traditions and lore in every Christian land of medicine, power and fertility, often practised by women, and commonly known as 'witchcraft', and its practitioners as 'witches' (Anglo-Saxon *wicca*).

This was an uphill task. In effect it was the next stage in the uprooting of the old pagan nature religions, clearing the way for science and the Industrial Revolution. Few folk then thought of cunning men and women with their knowledge of herbs and obscure ways as wicked, i.e. inherently evil and to be feared. Everyone already knew such arts were as capable of promoting evil as good, according to the will of the practitioner, but so what? That was like everything else.

Yet there were straws in the wind. In 1320, just six years after Jacques de Molay burned in Paris, Petronilla de Meath suffered the same fate. The first witch to be burned in Ireland, she was a scapegoat, confidante of the powerful Norman lady Alice Kyteler who, accused of getting rich via commerce with a 'demon', had fled to protectors in England. The 'demon' was named as 'Robin Artisson', but no such individual was ever identified or apprehended.[1] He was a man, after all. And though too many men too were to die in the years to come, accused of the most fantastic crimes their inquisitioners could imagine, by and large the civil war that arrived with Renaissance and Reformation was a war against Woman. It was a war waged by the emergent and paranoid intellectual mind, all thought and up in the air with the sky-god ('risen Christ', etc.), against the old, dark earth-ways; against the flesh; ultimately against nature itself.

It was slow to take root. One of the first burnings for *maleficium* in Europe was of Jehane de Brigue in Paris in 1390. Her crime? She was accused by a man she'd cured of possessing a demonic familiar. Yet fifty years later Swiss records speak of potent witches able to curse marriages, kill infants by concentrated death-prayer over a charmed lizard then placed under the doorstep of a house, or (by those denied Christian baptism) cause violent storms and dissension between friends.[2] And almost another fifty years passed before the slow fire smouldering since 1321 was at last fanned into full, murderous blaze.

This was accomplished by two German Dominicans, Kramer and Sprenger, who in 1486 published the witch-burning manual *Malleus Maleficarum* ('The Hammer of Witches'). This grim, retributive volume caught the uneasy new mood in Europe. With the Black Death and the pogroms against the Jews a century past, Gutenberg had just invented the printing press and Columbus was about to sail. The old certainties were gone. Increasingly folk abandoned the countryside for towns. Losing touch with the old ways, they were ready to believe anything. It was time for the torch, and Kramer and Sprenger (not forgetting Gutenberg) lit it. The *Malleus* was an instant bestseller, with twelve editions in fifty years. The ecclesiastical version of Machiavelli's *The Prince*, it was pragmatically brutal, justifying the insane hysteria it promoted and unleashed under a cloak of Christian piety – justifying any amount of cruelty to detect, convict and cure those accused of *maleficium*, witchcraft. It condoned torture to gain 'voluntary' confessions. Of course such torture was to be conducted piously, the torture chamber being 'constantly sprinkled with holy water and a smoke made with blessed herbs'. Four activities were 'necessary to damnation'. They were: renunciation of the Faith, devotion and homage to the Devil, the dedication to him of unbaptised children, and indulgence of carnal lust with incubi and succubi, the erotic demons of the night.

The sadistic panic now unleashed was most marked in Protestant lands like Germany, Switzerland and Scotland. Protestant belief is marked by denial of any female principle at all. Catholics at least have the Virgin Mary, but Protestants only have God the Father, God the Son, and God the Holy Ghost – two men and a don't-know. Psychologically speaking, that's bad news.

Popular texts, such as Jean Bodin's *Démonologie*, John Knox's *First Blast of the Trumpet Against the Monstrous Regiment of Women* and Guazzo's *Compendium Maleficarum*, kept the hysteria well fired. Bodin consoled those appalled by the cruelty now unleashed by explaining: '. . . the witches are so bent on [Satan's] devilish service that there is no torture or punishment that can frighten them; and they say that they go to a true martyrdom and to death, for love of him, as gaily as they go to a festival of pleasure and public rejoicing.'[3]

White or black, witchcraft of any sort was declared satanic. The witches' horned god was the Devil. In effect, femininity itself was suspect. Any woman thought 'odd' was at risk. So the epidemic spread, a collective insanity nobody could stop.

Some now claim there never were any witches, and that the madness arose from mass sexual frustration caused by the impossible moral standards demanded by the Church. Perhaps, but in the seventeenth century the plague was everywhere. The mother of Johannes Kepler, who discovered the Laws of Planetary Motion, was charged with witchcraft. At Bamberg in Germany between 1609 and 1633, over nine hundred women were tortured in the 'witches' chair', a contraption made of iron, and heated over a fire. Confessions thus obtained led to the stake. In parts of Germany the female population was almost exterminated.

Yet the idea of witchcraft was so fascinating that some 'witches' *voluntarily* confessed. In 1662 Isobel Gowdie of Auldearn, Scotland, claimed carnal relations with Satan. She identified this individual as 'Black Johnnie', describing him as a 'a meikle, blak, roch man', as 'cold within me as spring-well water' and thus condemned herself out of her own mouth.

For six weeks, without need of torture (though she was stripped and examined for signs of the devil's mark), this local lass eagerly told appalled elders from nearby Nairn just how riddled with evil the stolid, boring little community was. Along with Janet Braidhead, another self-proclaimed witch, she said she could turn herself into a hare, and had once in this form been chased by dogs, only in the nick of time transforming herself back into human shape.

Isobel described how her coven had buried the body of an unchristened child in a farmer's dung-heap to destroy his crops; stuck pins in a clay image, which was then burned to kill the male children of the local Laird of Parkis (all of whom *had* died, one after another); and yoked toads to a tiny model plough drawn twice round a field to make it sterile. She and her companions believed they could make thistles sprout instead of corn, and that their own land became richer as a result.[4]

She took great delight in shocking her sober inquisitors by describing exactly how 'Black Johnnie' had his wicked way with her and the other female witches, and how much he had enjoyed whipping them. It sounds like a gossipy spanking party that had got a bit dull. She had to tell someone else. The bored young wife of an impotent older man, she clearly had psychological problems. After all, as a girl in 1647 – the year 'Black Johnnie' had recruited her – she must have been shocked by the terrible Battle of Auldearn. This had left two thousand men of the Covenanting army slaughtered or bleeding to death in local ditches.

In the seventeenth century there was no television and few books; thus no entertainment for Isobel on long nights other than her fevered imagination, the excitement of coven meetings and the pleasure of cursing others who were better off.

Isobel Gowdie's fate is unrecorded, but it is probable that she and her confederates were burned.

It is the second best-known Scottish witchcraft trial.

Seventy years earlier, in Edinburgh in 1593, Scotland's 'Witches of Berwick' were persuaded to admit to trying to kill King James VI and his Danish bride by raising a magic storm to sink the king's ship and by burning a wax image of him. (They were also accused of sailing to sea in a sieve, of robbing graves for the bones needed in their rites, and of employing sundry curses, charms and spells.)

The king's cousin Francis Stewart, fifth Earl of Bothwell, was accused of setting up this and other plots to kill James by black magic. Godson of James's mother, Mary Queen of Scots, who had been beheaded in England six years earlier, Bothwell was a violent man even by the standards of one of Scotland's more desperate eras. He was formally denounced as the 'Devil' who had driven the Berwick Witches to try to destroy James, 'the wisest fool in Christendom'.

As for James, soon to be King of England too, he showed great interest in the trial and the accused, whom he questioned himself. He was unhappy when Bothwell was acquitted on the grounds that the trial was political, but may have derived some consolation from the torture the accused endured and the death of five of the 'witches' at the stake. Scots torture techniques lacked continental refinement, but they were usually enough to persuade victims that confession, implication of others, and a more-or-less rapid death by fire was, all things considered, preferable. Why suffer crushed limbs to be crushed further? Why not just say what you're told to say and get it all over with?

Bothwell's trial opened in the Edinburgh Tolbooth on 10 August 1593. If he was found guilty . . . It was not long since Lyon, King of Arms, had been burnt alive for sorcery alone. He seemed unperturbed, but then he had taken the precaution of packing Edinburgh with his Borderers. Many were in court, and his friends on the jury would not, in such angry times, establish a precedent by executing him simply for conspiring against a despised king. He knew half of them were deep in conspiracies of their own.

He was pleased to note that, when three times the crier called out for anyone with evidence against Francis, Earl Bothwell, to step forward and speak, nobody in the courtroom moved a muscle. Not even a hair. They knew what would happen if they did.

He was equally pleased to note that the chief witness against him, the warlock Richard Graham, was unable to testify in person. He had already been strangled and burned. His deposition, as assembled from his confessions, was read, and as it and those of Agnes Sampson, Effie M'Calyean, Barbara Napier, Margaret Thompson and others were recited, the court grew ever more agog at the alleged satanic plot.

It had all begun when David Seton, the alert Bailiff Depute in Tranent, had started wondering why his servant Gillie Duncan 'slept out every other night'. She was known to be a healer – was she in league with Satan? It was his duty to find out. But even tightening a twisted rope round her head had not made her confess. It was only when he had found the witch's mark on her throat that she had broken down. Soon he had a list of names – many, surprisingly, of respectable men and women. They included Agnes Sampson, the 'Wise Wife of Keith', a famous midwife and healer; but most important of all, Gillie accused young Dr Fian, or Cunningham, Master of Saltpans School.

This satanic individual, a veritable Scottish Dr Faustus, had sold his soul to Satan, who had given him a mole's foot 'so that he should never want silver'. He had used magic for all sorts of devilry and mischief. The court rocked with laughter, however, at the story of how Fian failed to get the love of a lady who loved another man. Fian had put a spell on his competitor, so driving him mad for an hour and discouraging him, but even so the lady had not turned to Fian. So he had asked the girl's brother to get three hairs of her head so he could make a love charm, but she woke up when her brother was removing the hairs and complained to her mother, who guessed what was happening. So the old mother cut three hairs from the udder of a virgin heifer, wrapped them in the enchanted paper Fian had provided, and told her son to take the parcel back to Fian. Over the hairs Fian had muttered the spell to bring their owner in love to his arms. Next time he was at the kirk, the lovestruck heifer came leaping at him, and chased him wherever he ran!

But there was serious evidence to come.

One night, with Agnes Sampson and others, Fian had set sail in a boat like a chimney (the jurors found this hard to imagine) and came to another ship, *The Grace of God*. Here they met another witch and drank wine, then left it, and the Devil raised a wind and sank it, with everyone on board.

That was a terrible thing – and it was alleged that it was not the first ship they sank! The court buzzed with rumour and hearsay.

Next they heard how the king was bringing his bride back to Scotland when Fian and his hell-mates decided to stop them sailing. They had raised a northeasterly so strong James had had to stay in port. This they had done probably by untying three knotted threads, just like Finnish wizards. The first, everyone knew, brought moderate wind, the second a half-gale, and the third a hurricane. In any case, it had not worked. Soon the Devil told them that James and his bride had put out to sea. They would have to try again.

So they gathered together one night, baptised a cat in Satan's name, tied to each of its feet a finger or toe joint from a human skeleton, then took it to the pier-head at Leith just before midnight, and threw it out as far as they could while chanting spells. The cat, though, swam back to shore. Still, they were ready for that too. They had a second cat, to which they tied 'the chiefest part of a dead man and several of his joints', and with it they had set sail in their waterproof sieves. When they were quite far enough out so that the cat could not swim back, the warlock Robert Grierson dropped it in the sea. Presumably then they got back to shore as fast as they could, because a great storm blew up. A ship loaded with gifts for the queen sank between Kinghorn and Leith. But the royal party, though their ship sprang a leak, was only slightly delayed. Fian's last attempt, to divert James back to the English shore by making the captain of the royal ship lose his bearings in a magic fog, worked no better.

Sterner measures were required. Three covens of witches attended the Lammas Sabbat, held at Achison's Haven near Musselburgh. The Devil was also there, as a 'black man', but known to all. When Agnes Sampson said they needed his help, he said it might be difficult, but that they should make a potion. They must roast a toad, mix its fluid with strong urine, add the skin of an adder, and the pituitary gland of a new-born foal. This devilish brew, the court now heard, was to be 'laid in his majesty's way' to destroy him. Agnes Sampson was told to make a wax image of the king, then burn it so the king would die. Margaret Thomson was to get hold of linen the king had worn, in which to wrap the image.

These instructions were carried out. Then it was Hallowe'en. The three local covens, and as many others as cared to come, met in the awesome kirk of Old Berwick, overhanging the stormy sea. Agnes Sampson came first, to make the preparations, then Fian, flying through the air, then a hundred or so others, all flying, or in sieves, or mounted on devils. There were only about six men. All masked, they reeled widdershins (anti-clockwise) in the kirkyard, facing out so they could not see each other's faces.

Fian then burst into the kirk, where Satan waited, 'a muckle black man' with a tail, his beard like a goat's, his nose the beak of a hawk. The court was enthralled.

Next the jurors heard how Fian now directed the robbing of graves, 'two within and one without the kirk', to get the bones they needed for the next part of their magic against the king. Then they had argued about what to do.

Jocky Grey-Meill, 'ane auld silly pure plowman', said the king hadn't been hurt by their efforts so far, and for this he had 'got a great blow' from the Devil . . . who, it was insinuated, had been Bothwell himself.

And maybe it had been. Bothwell smiled . . . at his friends.

Gillie Duncan's confession had led to many arrests, all leading to the torture chamber, where Calvinist fantasies as brutal as those of the Dominican Catholics the Calvinists despised were similarly proven: by mutilation of living human bodies. The best any of them could hope for was to be strangled before being burned. Barbara Napier was reprieved when found to be pregnant as she was being taken for execution. This upset King James so much that he lectured the jury on the perils of kindness to witches.

As for John Fian, under torture he admitted everything, then escaped. After he was recaptured his legs were crushed so 'that the blood and marrow spurted forth in great abundance', but this time he denied everything. Taken on a cart to Edinburgh's Castle Hill, he was strangled and thrown on to the fire.

There was also the mysterious Richard Graham, his name often volunteered by those under torture. Arrested, examined by James, then 'encouraged', this Borders lord admitted to raising the Devil often, once so fearfully that his co-conspirator, the late Justice Clerk Sir Lewis Bellenden, had taken fright and died. Graham said he had given Bothwell 'some drug or herb', so that with it the earl could touch the king's face, and thus englamour him.

He said Bothwell had told him how an Italian necromancer had foretold that Bothwell would return to Scotland, gain great wealth and power, but would kill two men. The earl would be pardoned for the first offence, but not the second. Bothwell, having killed Sir William Stewart and Davie the Devil, had already been pardoned once. Having plotted treason against the king, Graham said, Bothwell had asked him to hasten the king's end, so as to prevent his own premature fate. So Graham had prepared a wax image of the king, hung between a fox and the head of a newly killed calf.

Fortunately for Bothwell, by now Graham was already dead. All that stood against him was the evidence of five witches already burned, and four who had, against the odds, been acquitted. And since all evidence so far had been produced by torture, what jury could possibly convict? Not even Graham had spoken against him until he had been promised his life if he did – a promise since broken in the most brutal way possible.

Bothwell walked free. Yet it seems likely that he was indeed the 'Devil' who, half-believing in such powers, had whipped up the happenings that led to the trials, tortures and execution of the Witches of Berwick. They died. He got away with it, just like Black Johnnie and Robin Artisson.

7 Sister Jeanne and the Devils

August 1634 at a jail in the French town of Loudun in Anjou, and the priest Urbain Grandier, his head shaved, both legs shattered by the torture-machine called the Gehenna, had only hours left to live before he was burned at the stake. His crime? He had, his enemies claimed, caused the nuns of Loudun's Ursuline convent to be possessed by devils.

It was all nonsense – almost everyone knew it. He was going to die not because he was a sorcerer but because he had made too many enemies. He had been less than discreet, especially for a Roman Catholic priest. He had broken his vow of celibacy – not once, but many times.

But what was a man to do? Continence was known to be impossible for young men, so how could any vow demanding it be binding! So he had argued fourteen years ago when he had come to Loudun, fresh from the Jesuit College at Bordeaux, fresh and sharp with his roving eye. From the start he had excited the envy of the small-minded by moving straight into the highest social circles, hob-nobbing with d'Armagnac, Loudun's Governor, and Sainte-Marthe, the famed historian and poet. How could he have known, as he captivated the devouter sex with his large dark eyes, his gravitas, his Vandyke beard, his pomaded moustache and mocking wit, that in August 1634 his enemies – all men! – would convict him for sorcery on the evidence of Astaroth, chief of the devils said to possess those miserable nuns?

But not just his love affairs had ruined him. His financial dealings had made him more enemies than he needed, his sharp tongue had made him still more, and as for what he had done to poor Philippe . . . The shame of it still hurt even through the agony of his crushed legs and his terror at what lay ahead. So stupid too! To have made her pregnant after he had been entrusted as her tutor and confessor. Entrusted by her grandfather, once his best friend – Louis Trincant, Loudun's Public Prosecutor.

It was his eloquence at Sainte-Marthe's funeral in 1623 which had begun it. He had so impressed poor Trincant – Trincant, with his love of the Muses who did not love him. With Sainte-Marthe gone, the gatherings at Trincant's town house had been better than no social life at all, though the company in the Prosecutor's drawing-room had been so boring! What else to do but poke fun at long-nosed Adam the apothecary, and pot-bellied Mannoury the sober surgeon? So he had made two new enemies, and then of course . . .

Philippe, with her gawky yet beautiful grace. Why had he not stuck with his vintner's widow? Was plump Ninon every Tuesday night not enough? But virginal, pretty Philippe! It was Trincant's fault for making him her confessor! At last she had surrendered, but frankly it had been disappointing. After she told him about the baby he had avoided her, knowing it could ruin him. He had denied it all. When the bastard was born, Philippe's friend Marthe claimed it was hers. But everyone knew. Some Protestant had pinned an 'Ode to the Public Prosecutor's Bastard Granddaughter' to the law-court doors. Trincant, who overnight had become Grandier's most dangerous enemy, made Marthe sign a deed recognising the child as hers. But everyone knew. That, it was clear now, had been the beginning of the end.

But still he had felt untouchable, now pursuing Loudun's most celebrated *dévote*, Madeleine de Brou, at thirty an unwed prude. A real challenge! The problem was that he had fallen in love with her, and this new scandal had led the apothecary Adam to defame her in public. Sued for slander, Adam had been found guilty – and ruined.

Grandier's enemies had begun recruiting powerful friends, like the King's Advocate Pierre Menau, who had been pestering Madeleine for years, and who hated the priest for winning her love. There was also Jacques de Thibault, one of Richelieu's unpaid agents. One day outside the church of Sainte-Croix they had argued, and Thibault had struck Grandier with his malacca cane.

Grandier had gone to Paris to appeal to the *parlement* and to the King. Louis XIII had promised him justice, but Grandier's enemies had got a warrant for his arrest from the Bishop of Poitiers. In November 1629, after days shut up in the Bishop's palace dungeon, he had been stripped of his priesthood on the charge of scandalous immorality. Set free to appeal, however, he had won on a technicality, because Trincant, to save his own good name and protect Philippe, had refused to confirm Grandier's guilt. He had been reinstated. Even his friend the Archbishop of Bordeaux had told Grandier to get out of Loudun while he could, but he had stayed on. A big mistake. For he had got involved with the Ursulines, with Sister Jeanne – which was why he was about to die.

And there lay the irony. He had never had anything to do with them.

They were a small poor convent in a rented house, paying their way by educating young ladies. Their prioress, Sister Jeanne, only twenty-five, was given to mystical transports. Less mystically, she was also fascinated by the notorious M. Grandier; and the parlour chatter said she was not alone. The other sisters and all Loudun's most virtuous ladies felt the same.

Grandier knew nothing of them until the death of Canon Moussat, their senile old confessor. Heart in mouth, Sister Jeanne wrote to Grandier. His refusal to become their confessor, claiming he had too much other work, enraged her, so that her imaginary love turned to hate. When Grandier's lover Madeleine de Brou came to visit her niece at the convent, Sister Jeanne sent her packing with a torrent of abuse, then invited lame, ugly old Canon Mignon to be their confessor. Everyone knew he hated Grandier. Yet in her dreams Grandier still visited her, doing unspeakable things. She told her sister nuns about it and soon two of them, both named Claire, also began dreaming that Grandier visited them carnally by night.

Of course they had to confess their dreams to Canon Mignon. For a time he just listened. But when one Hallowe'en some of the younger nuns dressed up as ghosts to scare the children, playing on the fact that the house was said to be haunted, Canon Mignon suddenly saw how to destroy Grandier. Reprimanding the jokers, he told them to keep quiet and, rather than console the victims, he terrified them further. 'Those weren't ghosts,' he told them. 'More probably devils.'

To Sister Jeanne and others now reporting nightly visitations he said: 'These aren't dreams. These are devils, agents of Satan!'

Did Sister Jeanne realise her role? Either way, she played it.

Visiting Grandier's enemies to explain his plan, Mignon asked the prior of the local Carmelites to lend him an exorcist. The prior lent him three. With Mignon they set to work, telling the now near-hysterical nuns that they were possessed by devils, and in particular by Grandier. Soon all but the oldest nuns were nightly visited by the ghostly Grandier. They began to writhe and grimace by day, to speak obscenities and demonic names like Ecos, Celsus, Acos, Cedon, and the arch-fiend, Astaroth!

How could they know these names, how could they blaspheme as they did, how could they writhe and contort and expose themselves as they did?

'It's Grandier!' the devils told the exorcists. 'He sent us!'

Soon all Loudun knew that the sisters were possessed by devils sent by Grandier. 'They're demented,' Grandier shrugged. 'Melancholy plus *furor uterinus* leads them to imagine that incubi visit them by night.' Hearing this, Mignon just smiled. 'He laughs longest who laughs last,' he said as reinforcements arrived to fight Satan, including the *curé* of neighbouring Chinon, Pierre Barré. This bigot, who saw the Devil everywhere, let the mob in. From now on, the public could see for itself just how obscene and disgusting was Grandier's work, expressed through the Devil.

On 6 October 1632, Barré and Sister Jeanne put on their first public performance. It was wholly convincing. She was seized by 'dreadful spasms', and by 'many violences, vexations, howlings, and grindings of teeth, two of which at the back of the mouth were broken'. Rolling about, she showed her legs. Astaroth, speaking Latin in her voice, answered Mignon's questions, confirming that Grandier was responsible. His Latin was poor. 'The Loudun devils had only studied up to the third grade,' said a contemporary wit.

Two days later, Barré and Sister Jeanne gave an even better show. This time, the main demon was Asmodeus – one of seven, it emerged, possessing the Prioress. Barré at last defeated Asmodeus with the aid of M. Adam the apothecary, who poured a quart of holy water into a huge brass syringe. Writhing, Sister Jeanne was held down as the exorcising enema was administered. Not surprisingly, Asmodeus quit. Sister Jeanne, who had thought it impossible to be possessed against her will, was now convinced by Mignon and Barré that, though Asmodeus had gone, six other demons still inhabited her body. As for Mignon and Barré, they left no record of their own state of mind.

A week later, Loudun's officials demanded entry, among them the town's mayor, de Cerisay, an open-minded man, but they were told that the devils would not perform today. The exorcists would submit an official report later.

Increasingly nervous, Grandier went to the Bishop of Poitiers, who told him that if he wanted to complain of victimisation he should do so through the civil authorities. Grandier formally charged Mignon with conspiracy. On 28 October the sceptical de Cerisay issued a court order against the slander. When dissenting priests produced medical men to sign an oath that possession by demons was indeed involved, the mayor outlawed further exorcisms. But not only did they continue, they became more public, more violent. More nuns were possessed. The civic and church authorities locked horns. Only with the Archbishop of Bordeaux about to visit did the nuns calm down. For days and nights there were neither fits nor seizures. Maybe this was because Mignon was prohibited from conducting further exorcisms, while Barré could only do so in the presence of outside Jesuit witnesses.

'There are no devils,' said the archbishop, flatly.

The *furor uterinus* died down. With guilt and shame replacing fame and ecstasy, the nuns were disgraced, and their pupils were withdrawn. Faced with ruin, Sister Jeanne wrote for help to her relative M. de Laubordemont, a royal counsellor and servant of Cardinal Richelieu, France's true ruler.

Laubordemont was cautious. He had to sound out his master. Richelieu suffered such foul diseases and smelled so bad that few could bear to remain in the same room with him, but when he said 'Do it!', everyone jumped. Sometimes he derided the supernatural, sometimes not. It would not do for Laubordemont to act rashly.

One night Laubordemont visited the convent with Prince Henri de

Condé, the notorious sodomite. The excited nuns greeted the royal personage with an especially salacious display. Impressed by their writhings, Condé urged Laubordemont to act. Seeing their chance, Grandier's enemies persuaded Laubordemont that the sorcerer Grandier was also a subversive who six years earlier had published a pamphlet satirising Richelieu. Whether this was true or not, Laubordemont, who had seen to the burning of witches before, decided to act, and was soon back from Paris with full royal powers to arrest and investigate Grandier who, though warned, refused to flee. The poor fool thought himself innocent. Arrested, he was jailed in Angers Castle, though nothing more incriminating than a polemic against clerical celibacy was found in his house.

He was already doomed. The exorcists stripped, shaved, blindfolded and pricked him all over to find the devil's mark, the one spot where he felt no pain. They failed. He was taken to the attic of a house Mignon owned, which was bricked and blocked up so he had neither light nor air.

The public exorcisms began again. The better to condemn the pastor, the nuns were paraded from church to church and kept in hysterics. Their convulsive blasphemy and thrashing white legs convinced sightseers from all over France that Grandier was indeed a master of demons. Politically, it worked. The Jesuits sent an envoy to Loudun to protect Grandier – then quietly withdrew him. It was too late. Grandier had already been taken before the sisters. They had gone berserk, offering details of his sexual tastes that might have surprised even Condé. By now it seemed everyone wanted him dead, not just the Carmelites and Franciscans. Doubters kept quiet. The hysteria had become dangerous. The numbers of possessed women had grown and two groups of public exorcists were now daily at work – sweating, lamenting, clearly deeply affected by the presence of evil. Among these were the Holy Reverend Fathers Lactance and Tranquille, Franciscans by no means so sane and bland as their names suggested.

It was spring now, with Sister Jeanne claiming that demons in the form of cats, dogs, goats and stags daily entered her body. When she asserted that Grandier had indeed got the Devil's Mark, a freelance surgeon, given *carte blanche*, entered Grandier's airless cell, and, 'treating him with extreme inhumanity', proceeded to find not only one but five insensible spots.

Two of the nuns suddenly came to their senses. Realising that Grandier would die because they had let the exorcists manipulate them, Sisters Clara and Agnes stood up in open church and declared publicly that they had lied: there were no devils, Grandier was innocent. They were denounced as being maddened by Satan. The strain was growing.

'M. de Laubordemont is crazy,' one demon had a sister declare.

Her remark was taken down in an unread report which Lauborde-mont automatically signed. This later caused great amusement at the French court.

With Grandier committed to trial as a sorcerer who had sent devils to possess the nuns, their evidence was taken. The lies were too much for Sister Jeanne. After making her deposition she stood for hours in pouring rain, a rope round her neck, then told Laubordemont she had accused Grandier falsely. She was going to hang herself, but was stopped. Laubordemont chose to see her contrition as a trick by the devil Balaam or Leviathan. There was no backing out now, even though many in Loudun knew it was a charade. Against these sceptics Lactance and Tranquille railed from the pulpit for weeks.

Yet public protest grew, despite threats of huge fines and worse for critics of the lunacy. Public meetings were banned as thousands of tourists poured into town for the execution. Everyone knew Grandier was going to die. Only Grandier believed that justice would prevail – until at last he appeared in the dock. He defended himself passion-ately, but then saw the judges laughing, whispering, shifting about, and knew he had no chance.

Even when they ordered him to be tortured then burned alive, his ashes scattered to the four winds, he was so calm that, the friars noted, some judges were impressed. Father Tranquille quickly told them that it was not true dignity, just unrepentant pride, the brazen insolence of hell.

Then they took him, stripped him and shaved him completely, even the eyebrows. Laubordemont, telling the surgeon to pull out his fingernails, was astonished when the man refused. Taken back to court, Grandier denied his guilt yet again, begged hopelessly for mercy, then spoke of the martyrs so touchingly that many were moved to pity. Many women wept.

'Clear the court!' Laubordemont shouted.

Then they started trying to make him confess.

They tied Grandier up, stretched him on the floor, then locked his legs between four oak boards, the outer two fixed, the inner two movable. To stop Satan easing the pain of the torture, Fathers Lactance and Tranquille carefully exorcised the ropes, boards, wedges and even the mallets.

In between the boards they drove first one, then two, then three wedges. Through his shrieks, Grandier still refused to confess. At the fourth wedge, bones in his feet and ankles broke; briefly he fainted. Taking over from the executioner, in turn the sweating friars ham-mered in a fifth, sixth, seventh, and then an eighth wedge, shattering his bones from feet to knees. He was screaming continually by now, but still they could not make him confess to lies. 'I have been a man,' he whispered, 'I have loved women.'

'You are a sorcerer,' they insisted, Laubordemont lurking behind them. 'You have had commerce with devils.'

Eight wedges was the usual limit of the Question Extraordinary, let alone the Ordinary. When the executioner, sent for more wedges, returned with two no thicker than the last of the first set, Laubordemont was so angry he threatened to whip the man. Teeth bared, Lactance drove home the ninth wedge, and his colleague, Tranquille, the tenth. Grandier fainted again. Worried that he might die before they could get him to the stake, they revived and laid him on a bench, a green rug covering his shattered legs. They even gave him a glass of wine. The Capuchin called Archangel came to poke at his broken limbs. By then he was incapable of complaining.

'Satan makes him feel no pain!' Father Archangel declared.

'God!' he whispered, almost inaudibly.

'You see?' The Capuchin swung on his accomplices. 'When he speaks of God, he means Satan! When he says he hates Satan, it means he hates God! He must feel the full heat of the fire, or his soul is lost forever!'

Laubordemont now sat by him, sighing and sobbing, a secretary nearby with written confession, ready pen. 'Why not sign?' Laubordemont sounded incredulous. 'Admit your guilt before God! Brother, in the Name of God and Sweet Jesus, help us to save you! Sign!'

Grandier refused. 'I cannot sign what God, and you, and I know to be false,' he whispered. 'There is no truth in any of it.'

After two long hours Laubordemont gave up. With a final sigh he turned with a shrug to an observer, M. de Gastyns. 'What more can I do?' he asked, but de Gastyns just looked disgusted. Laubordemont's mask of pity dropped.

'Get La Grange!' he snapped. 'Tell him to fetch the executioners.'

Awaiting the captain of the guard, Grandier closed his eyes.

Six thousand people crowded the Place Sainte-Croix. The roofs were packed, every window was rented. A grandstand had been built for Laubordemont and his friends, who were able to sit only after, in a pitched battle, the rabble was driven off it with pike and halberd. The crowd was so dense it took Grandier, bound to a bench on a cart drawn by six mules, half an hour to cover the last stretch. He wore a rope round his neck, and a sulphur-soaked shirt. Fifteen feet high, the stake stood by the north wall of the church. A small iron seat was fixed to it two feet above the pile of logs, faggots and straw. Lifted on to this, Grandier was lashed to the post, facing the crowd – and Trincant's house. Trincant was at the window with Mignon and Thibault. Mignon waved. Trincant raised his wine-glass ironically as the friars made their exorcisms.

La Grange told Grandier he could speak, and that he would be mercifully strangled before the fire was lit. He tried to address the crowd, but the friars threw holy water in his face and hit him on the mouth with an iron crucifix. *'Dicas!'* Lactance kept screaming. 'Confess!'

'I have nothing to confess,' Grandier whispered. 'Now give me the kiss of peace and let me die.'

Lactance refused, but the crowd became so vociferous that in a fury he climbed the pyre and kissed Grandier on the cheek. 'Judas!' howled the crowd, so angering the friar that he jumped down, seized a twist of straw, lit it in the brazier, then waved it in Grandier's face.

'Confess that you are the devil's servant!'

'I am about to meet God, who is my witness . . .'

'Confess!' Lactance screamed. 'You have only a moment to live!'

'Only a moment,' Grandier said mildly, 'and then I go to that just and fearful judgement to which, Reverend Father, you too must soon be called.'

Enraged, Lactance threw the burning straw on the pyre. Archangel fired the other side. 'Is this what you promised me?' Grandier cried. Too late the captain of the guard tried to stamp out the fire even as Tranquille lit the pyre at another point, with Lactance at the brazier again.

'Strangle him!' La Grange roared.

The crowd responded: 'Strangle, strangle!'

But then the executioner found that a friar had knotted his noose so it could not be used. By the time the knots were undone a wall of flame hid Grandier. Screams were heard as the friars energetically tossed holy water on to the fire. A huge black fly flew into Lactance's face and dropped on to the open pages of his book of exorcism. Beelzebub! Lactance shuddered.

Buzzing, it took off and disappeared into the smoke.

The screaming stopped. There was coughing. 'Forgive them,' the friars heard, 'Forgive my enemies.' Then the cords binding the blackened carcass to the stake burned through and the body tumbled into the flames.

Grandier was dead. Soon Lactance, Tranquille, Mannoury the surgeon, and others cursed by believing too much in devils, would follow him.

For the devils survived Grandier's death. That night Sister Jeanne went into convulsions. 'The black fly,' Lactance demanded anxiously, 'which devil was it? Why did he throw himself on my holy book?'

'Baruch, the parson's familiar,' cried the prioress. She bent backwards and did the splits. 'He was trying to throw the book into the fire!'

Next day at Sainte-Croix the sisters played before a huge crowd. Sister Jeanne identified the demon in her as Isacaaron. He was alone in her. The other five had gone down to hell to warm up Grandier's reception party.

'Is he suffering down there?' Lactance demanded.

'The privation of God is the worst!' screamed Sister Jeanne.

'Yes, but how is he being tortured? And how did he *suffer* when he was being burned, or did the devil stop that?'

'There's a special torture for each of his sins, especially those of the flesh! And Satan couldn't stop him suffering, for you good friars didn't let him get close!'

That night Lactance looked pale. The following morning he had a raging fever. He kept saying God was punishing him; he kept seeing Grandier at the stake, Grandier asking God to forgive his enemies. Then armies of demons came, invading his body, making him rave blasphemies. Bleeding and purging did no good. For a month he lingered. On 18 September he knocked the crucifix from the hand of the priest administering extreme unction, and died.

Mannoury the surgeon went next. Returning by night from bleeding a sick man, suddenly he stopped, staring into the darkness. His servant with the lantern saw him shudder then fall to the ground, screaming for pardon from Grandier's ghost which he saw before him, naked as he had been when Mannoury had pricked him to find the devil's mark. Within a week he too was dead.

Then Louis Chauvet, a judge who had refused to take part in the trial, was accused by Sister Jeanne and other nuns of being a magician. Fear that Richelieu might take their raving seriously and send him Grandier's way so unhinged him that he went mad. He declined and died that winter.

Tranquille's fate was more long drawn out and dreadful. Little by little the devils, particularly Dog's Tail and Leviathan, possessed him. By 1638 he was raving like the nuns, rolling on the floor, literally barking mad. He neighed, hissed and cursed, and threw up whatever he tried to eat. After Whitsunday he took to his bed. When on Monday after Whitsun extreme unction was administered, the devils fled him and promptly entered another friar kneeling by the deathbed. Their new victim went so wild the other friars had to stop him kicking Tranquille's barely dead body.

As for the nuns, the possession and the exorcisms continued.

But Sister Jeanne received special attention.

In December of the year Grandier died, the Jesuit Jean-Joseph Surin arrived in Loudun to join the team. A melancholic pained by excruciating headaches, he never doubted the reality of the possession. By now Sister Jeanne, sure that the demon Isacaaron had made her pregnant, no longer menstruated. Her belly was growing. In despair she decided to cut the baby out of her body, baptise it, then recover or die. But a miraculously invisible force seized the knife from her hand. The image of Christ on her crucifix held out his hand to her. She decided to change her ways. Yet the phantom pregnancy persisted until a particularly strenuous public exorcism ended it.

Even so, her possession endured – and Surin became its victim even as he tried to conquer it. One night he prayed that he should be allowed to suffer in her place. He was willing to let the devils in and be regarded as a lunatic. He became obsessed, like all the other exorcists, still alive or newly dead. Driven mad by overmuch concentration on evil, if he tried to make the sign of the cross on his mouth, his mouth would bite the finger. After a long struggle he wrote to a fellow Jesuit, Father d'Attichy, telling him that he was fighting 'four of hell's most malignant devils . . . I find it almost impossible to explain what happens to me during this time, how this alien spirit is united to mine, without depriving me of consciousness or inner freedom, and yet constituting a second "me", as though I had two souls . . . [which] do battle within the limits of a field, which is the body.'

Surin was different from the others, though. His over-identification with evil was matched by a powerful sense of good, so that even during his obsession he sought Sister Jeanne's salvation; praying for her, following her when she fled, ignoring her tantrums, whispering prayers in her ear when she went into convulsions – only to find himself possessed and speechless while she screamed with demonic laughter. This war lasted for years.

During one exorcism, as she writhed on the floor with her tongue hanging out, stigmatic marks spelling saints' names began to appear on her body. The stigmata lasted from 1635 until 1662, then ceased as mysteriously as they had begun. Confronted by them, Isacaaron fled early in 1636, but Behemoth was tougher. After ten months of wrestling with him Surin broke down, and another Jesuit, Father Ressès, took over. Early in 1637 Sister Jeanne, at the point of death after weeks of violent nausea, was miraculously visited by a vision of Saint Joseph, who laid hands on her, 'After which I came to my senses and was completely cured,' she wrote later in her *Autobiography*.

She went on a pilgrimage, and moved in a blaze of glory. Famous now, she was greeted warmly wherever she went. In Paris she was received by Richelieu, and stayed with Laubordemont. Marvels and wonders were noted of her; there were crowds everywhere. Eventually she returned to Loudun. The doors of the now quiet convent shut behind her. The madness was over.

But Surin went all the way down. Between 1639 and 1657 he was incapable of reading or writing, often even of speech, while the smallest act, such as changing a shirt, was such agony that it took him all night. He knew he had lost and that the devils were heating up his seat in hell. Christ glared at him, the Blessed Virgin raised her hand to discharge avenging lightning at him, the shock of it jolting his entire body. He wanted to set fire to the houses he stayed in. In May 1645 he threw himself from the cliff-top window of a Jesuit house, but when he hit the ground he suffered only a broken hip. After that he was always watched. He was mad, but lucidly so, and his terror so paralysed him that he could no longer even walk.

Finally his confessor induced him to feel some hope again. One day in 1657 he picked up a pen and was able to write down three pages of his thoughts. Three years later he began to walk again. A quarter of a century after Surin had first come to Loudun, he recovered his wits and his faith so that, when he died in 1665, he was at peace – the last, longest-lasting, but most lucid victim of the terrible curse which had overtaken not only Sister Jeanne and the Ursuline nuns of Loudun, but all who had convinced themselves that Grandier had indeed been the master of devils.[1,2]

The case of Urbain Grandier and the possessed nuns of Loudun is the best-known of hundreds of insane prosecutions which usually led to the stake. Galileo's telescope showed the moons of Jupiter; the apple fell on Newton's head, but the madness continued to rage, even crossing the Atlantic.

Almost sixty years after Grandier died, a similar terror swept the village of Salem, Massachusetts, in 1692. Swallowed by a stiff-necked Puritan community, the fantastic lies of a pack of hysterical girls sent many innocents to the gallows. It was the last and most celebrated of the witch-hunts. In the eighteenth century, the insanity began to fade away, though as late as the early nineteenth century in England helpless old women were still being ducked and tormented on suspicion of witchcraft.

When the twentieth century dawned, people could look back and say that, finally, that particular madness was over. At last, Reason was in the saddle and never again could such insanity prevail – or so many thought . . .

8 Celtic Curses

The Celtic world was always rich in tales of the evil eye, second sight and curse. Semi-mythic early Irish kings and heroes like Conchobar or Cuchulainn were bound by magical prohibitions (taboos: see chapter 12) called *geas* (singular), or *geasa* (plural); from *guidh*, 'to entreat'. To break any of the often mutually contradictory demands of one's *geasa* was to invite fatal retribution. These demands were typically fantastic. Cormac, son of Conchobar of Ulster, could not yoke his horses with ash-poles, hunt a stag with golden horns or listen to the harp music of the bard Craptine. Neglecting these *geasa*, he died. Cuchulainn could not speak his name to any other warrior and so he was prevented from identifying himself to a son who did not know him. Defending himself against the young warrior's challenge, Cuchulainn was forced to kill him. Nor was Cuchulainn permitted by his *geasa* to swerve from his path when joining combat, enter a meeting uninvited, eat dog meat or refuse a feast. When he met three hags by a ford who invited him to feast on roasted dog, then he knew he was cursed and that his end was near.

Such *geasa* and the fate attendant on breaking them were partly designed to rein in the mighty. Where kings were concerned, they involved the royal destiny. If a king broke his word, or failed to conduct the rites on which the health of land and folk relied, then he died, the people suffered and the land was cursed. Thus in Arthurian lore the Wasteland is caused by the sin of the king.

Other forms of curse or spell-casting were common. The evil eye (see Appendix I), by which a prolonged stare causes misfortune, was thought to arise from malice or envy. Its owner might not even know he or she had the power, and it could be cast at a distance. This form of curse was usually attributed to old women; suspected witches were often accused of it, especially if their eyes were differently coloured. If a child (the prettiest) or a beast (the finest) fell suddenly ill, the evil eye was blamed. Horses afflicted by it would sweat, tremble and grow weak. It turned ale or milk instantly sour. Charms against it included rowan, juniper and iron.

The Celts believed that successful cursing or spell-casting required highly concentrated will-power, aimed solely at the person or object involved, and was typically cast by means of incantations chanted in verse. To concentrate the force more potently, the wizard might cast the curse while standing on one leg with one eye closed, forefinger pointed at the victim – a routine to send shivers up the most sceptical spine.[1]

Tales of prophetic malediction abound all over Britain, but the most elaborate are found the further north and west one goes. Particularly in Highland Scotland, where mass poverty and frequent tyranny went hand in hand with the Gaels' fertile imagination, the curse was the usual means used by the weak to retaliate against the strong.

In fact, so many old Highland families carry a curse of one sort or another that the problem lies in which to select.

The curses on Mar, Moy, Glamis, Fyvie and Brahan are all well-known, those on Fyvie and Brahan especially so. The shadowy thirteenth-century True Thomas, alias Thomas the Rhymer, is associated with the curses on Mar and Fyvie. The curse on the Seaforths of Brahan is ascribed to the equally shadowy Coinneach Odhar Fiosaiche – Sallow Kenneth the Enchanter – to whom many of the best-known Highland prophecies are attributed.

Though attributed to True Thomas, the Curse of Mar – one of Scotland's oldest families – was probably cast in the sixteenth century by the Abbot of Cambuskenneth, furious at being evicted from his abbey during the chaos and anarchy of the time. So it belongs to that body of ecclesiastical curses (more common in England: see chapter 10) called down on those buying former church lands. In this case, the guilty party was John Earl of Mar, who promptly sold the abbey and began building a fine palace in Stirling.

As given in Sir Bernard Burke's *Romance of the Aristocracy*, the curse runs (and runs seemingly endlessly) as follows:

Proud Chief of Mar, thou shalt be raised still higher, until thou sittest in the place of the King. Thou shalt rule and destroy, and thy work shall be after thy name, but thy work shall be the emblem of thy house, and shall teach mankind that he who cruelly and haughtily raiseth himself upon the ruins of the holy cannot prosper. Thy work shall be cursed, and shall never be finished. But thou shalt have riches and greatness, and shalt be true to thy sovereign, and shalt raise his banner in the field of blood. Then, when thou seemest to be highest, when thy power is mightiest, then shall come thy fall: low shall be thy head among the nobles of the people. Deep shall be thy moan among the children of dool [French *dolour*: sorrow]. Thy lands shall be given to the stranger, and thy titles shall lie among the dead. The branch that springs from thee shall see his dwelling burnt, in which a King is nursed – his wife a sacrifice in that same flame; his children numerous, but of little honour; and three born and grown who shall never see the light. Yet shall thine ancient tower stand; for the brave and the true cannot wholly be forsaken. Thou, proud head and daggered hand, must dree thy weird, until horses shall be stabled in thy hall, and a weaver shall throw his shuttle in thy chamber of state. Thine ancient tower – a woman's dower – shall be a ruin and a beacon, until an ash sapling shall spring from its topmost stone. Then shall thy sorrows be ended, and the sunshine of royalty shall beam on thee once more. Thine honours shall be restored; the kiss of peace shall be given to thy Countess, though she seek it not, and the days of peace shall return to thee and thine. The line of Mar shall be broken; but not until its honours are doubled, and its doom is ended.[2]

Unusual not only in being so detailed but in being as much a forecast of blessing as of curse, this prediction would never have been cast in such language, if indeed it dates from the sixteenth century, as its detail seems to suggest. Nobody in Scotland then wrote like that, and it had certainly been rewritten in more modern language by the time Burke recorded it centuries later. There is no doubt it was known in this later form before fulfilment of its final terms.

Briefly holding the title of Regent of Scotland before he died – violently, like so many Scottish nobles of the time – in 1572, Earl John did indeed sit 'in the place of the king'. Cambuskenneth may be 'The ruins of the holy'; while as for the work which 'shall never be finished', Earl John's palace at Stirling, known as 'Mar's Folly', never got beyond a façade. Confiscated, the Mar estates were recovered by his son, John the seventh earl, and for nearly a century this Catholic family did well when Catholic Stuarts occupied the throne, but not so well in the 1640s and 1650s when Puritan Covenanters, allies of English Cromwell, ruled the kingdom.

With the last Stuart king – James II of England, James VII of Scotland – deposed in 1689 and Dutch William of Orange now on the Protestant throne, another John was Earl. Privately Jacobite and Catholic, he trimmed his sails to keep in with authority, thus earning the epithet of 'Bobbing John', but in 1715, at Queen Anne's death, he raised the Jacobite standard on behalf of James II's son, the Old Pretender. He would have done better to have kept on bobbing. He lost the battle of Sheriffmuir through sheer military incompetence, and fled to France. His estates were confiscated and sold to the Earl of Fife ('Thy lands shall be given to the stranger, and thy titles shall lie among the dead'). His son, Thomas Lord Erskine, died childless in 1766, twenty-one years after the '45 Rebellion led by Bonnie Prince Charlie, the last Stuart to try to regain the crown. Some forfeited Mar estates had been bought back by Thomas, and the land now came to John Francis Erskine, son of Bobbing John's daughter. He settled in Alloa Tower, which James VI of Scotland, I of England had visited as a child. In 1801 a lighted candle placed near a bed caused a fire in which Erskine's wife died. She left several children, three of whom had been born blind – again as forecast ('The branch that springs from thee shall see his dwelling burnt, in which a King is nursed – his wife a sacrifice in that same flame; his children numerous, but of little honour; and three born and grown who shall never see the light.')

The fulfilment continued. During the Napoleonic Wars a cavalry troop was quartered at Alloa, fifty horses being stabled in the old hall ('horses shall be stabled in thy hall'). In 1810, visitors found a weaver working in the State Chamber ('and a weaver shall throw his shuttle in thy chamber of state'). Years later, an ash sapling sprouted from the roof ('Thine ancient tower . . . shall be a ruin and a beacon, until an ash sapling shall spring from its topmost stone'). The curse was almost done.

Now came the blessing. Visiting Scotland in 1822, with the last Stuart safely dead, George IV restored the Earldom of Mar to John Francis, the old grandson of Bobbing John ('and the sunshine of royalty shall beam on thee once more. Thine honours shall be restored'). Years later in Stirling Castle, the young Queen Victoria met Lady Mar, at Court for the first time. Whether or not the queen knew of the curse, on saying goodbye she kissed Lady Mar ('the kiss of peace shall be given to thy Countess, though she seek it not, and the days of peace shall return to thee and thine').

In 1866, when the second Earl, grandson of John Francis and also Earl of Kellie, died childless, his cousin claimed both Kellie and Mar, causing dispute with a nephew of the late Earl. This was solved only in 1885, when Parliament recognised two Earldoms of Mar – an Earl of Mar and Kellie and an Earl of Mar. So the last line of the curse was fulfilled ('The line of Mar shall be broken; but not until its honours are doubled, and its doom is ended').

Quite as famous (though much more ambiguous) is the curse laid on Fyvie, the 'crowning glory of Scottish baronial architecture', a great house in Aberdeenshire by the River Ythan. It lies not far from Gight, where the young Lord Byron spent a miserable childhood.

Now in the National Trust, its elegant drive offers an impressive first view of the battlemented façade and five towers, each commemorating one of the five families to own the place since 1400.

A treasure trove of tapestries, antiques and paintings by Raeburn, Reynolds and others, Fyvie is also rich in the supernatural. The Green Lady – Lillias Drummond, murdered 400 years ago by her husband Alexander Seton (her bloodstains are still visible on the floor of the murder room) – haunts the corridors; while below the Meldrum Tower is a secret chamber with another curse on it that, should anyone ever enter it, 'The Laird of that day would surely dee, and his leddy would go blind of her e'e.'

In its earliest days Fyvie was a royal property, which during the late thirteenth century was tenanted by Richard le Cheyne, Baron of Inverugie. It may have been in his time that, according to tradition, the first and major curse was laid on Fyvie by Thomas the Rhymer.

Born about 1220, this legendary poet-magician got his title, Thomas of Ercildoune, from land he owned at Earlston in Berwickshire. He was known as a seer during his lifetime, and it is possible that he did compose some of the fifty or so prophecies ascribed to him. Yet there are so many myths about him that it is hard to separate fact from fantasy.

Legend has it that one day, lying down by 'Huntlie Bank', in the Border country, Thomas met the Queen of 'fair Elfland', kissed her, and was carried away from 'living land' through 'mirk mirk night' to the fairy realm. There he dallied with her for seven years, and from her supposedly gained his magical, prophetic powers – including the power to curse . . .

Even to this day a tale persists at Dumbuck by Dumbarton, Tom-na-hurich by Inverness, and at Eildon near Roxburgh that, like King Arthur or Charlemagne, he sleeps in a fairy knowe, awaiting recall. In each place it is said that from time to time he emerges from the knowe to buy horses for his host of sleeping warriors. When he has them all, the great king whose reign he prophesied (Robert the Bruce, who defeated the English at Bannockburn in 1314?) will emerge, the great battle will be fought, and 'The lands of the north sall a' be free'.[3]

Yet he did live and there is an interesting fictional reconstruction of his life by the novelist Nigel Tranter.

Although he was also supposed to have foretold the death of Alexander III, who rode his horse over a cliff one stormy night while going to meet his bride, Thomas did not always predict bad luck. At Inverugie in Aberdeenshire legend has it that he stood on a certain stone and composed a rhyme predicting that, so long as that stone was undisturbed, the Keiths, then Earls Marischal of Scotland and owners of Inverugie Castle, would flourish, but that its removal would see the family fall. The stone was removed in 1763; in 1766 the last Earl Marischal sold up.

The Haigs fared even better; Thomas's prediction being so beneficient that they had it carved above their front door, where it may still be read:

> Tyde what may betyde,
> Haig shall be Haig of Bemersyde.

After the First World War Field-Marshal Earl Haig, a distant relative of the Haigs of the direct line, was granted the estate by the nation.[4]

Fyvie fared less well. It seems Thomas was not averse to a spot of magical blackmail if displeased, threatening the high-and-mighty (whom he was fond of visiting) with curse and woe should their hospitality fail him.

Robert Chambers in *Popular Rhymes of Scotland* (1842) tells how Thomas had long been threatening a visit to Fyvie, so the castle gates had been left open for seven years. The precaution was in vain. When at last he came, it was during a storm so violent that the leaves whirled from the trees and the castle gates slammed shut in his face – and this though not so much as a breath of wind stirred the grass on which he stood. Finding himself locked out, even though through no fault of Fyvie's tenants, in a rage he proceeded to pronounce the following, somewhat obscure, curse:

> Fyvie, Fyvie, thou's never thrive,
> As lang as there's in thee stanes three;
> There's ane intill the oldest tower,
> There's ane intill the ladye's bower,
> There's ane intill the water-yett [gate],
> And thir three stanes ye's never get.[5]

Another version of the curse, as given by the Rev. Walter Gregor in *The Folklore of the North-East of Scotland* (1881) runs as follows:

> Fyvie's riggs and towers,
> Hapless shall your mesdames be,
> When ye shall hae within your methes [boundaries],
> Frae harryit kirk lands, stanes three –

And so on as before. This version seems to refer to how, when *c.* 1390 Henry de Preston became owner of Fyvie and extended the original peel-tower by adding the Preston Tower, he took stone from a nearby religious house he had demolished – 'harryit kirk lands' – a phrase that may also refer to the 'harrying of Buchan' by Robert the Bruce earlier that century. The 'methes' may have been the boundaries between Fyvie and neighbouring Church lands.

Either way, the curse is vague. Presumably it means that misfortune would attend Fyvie, and particularly its mistresses ('Hapless shall your mesdames be') until the three stones mentioned are found and discarded – or, less probably, discovered and incorporated into Fyvie's walls. Two have been found, but the third, under the water-gate leading to the River Ythan and perhaps built into the very foundations, remains undiscovered. As to the one in the 'oldest tower', long said to be Preston's Tower, it is said the battlements once contained an odd stone that stayed dry when its neighbours got wet, and vice versa. It became wet so often that it crumbled away and no longer exists.

As for the stone in 'the ladye's bower', this was long ago identified, and today rests on two bowls in the charter-room at Fyvie. On two bowls because, like its companion, it is a weeping stone.

The lines are usually interpreted as promising that no heir would ever be born at Fyvie, or that the house would never pass from father to eldest son. Certainly Fyvie has often changed hands in the last seven centuries. Time after time the male succession has failed – but not always. Reginald Le Cheyne, probably the tenant when the curse was uttered, had no son, nor did any later tenant, until after 1433, when Sir Henry Preston's younger daughter, given Fyvie as her portion, married Alexander Meldrum.

The Meldrums, with several sons succeeding, held Fyvie until 1596, when Andrew Meldrum sold the estate to the Setons. Two Seton sons inherited before, over a century later, the second Earl of Aberdeen bought Fyvie, settling it on his eldest son, General William Gordon.

In his old age the general, having married one of his servants, Isobel Black, ignored the second curse and tried to enter the secret room in the Meldrum Tower ('The Laird of that day would surely dee, and his leddy would go blind of her e'e'). Unsurprisingly (he was eighty) he soon died. What is more peculiar is that his wife Isobel did indeed go blind.

His son died childless in 1847, the estate passing to relatives only to be put up for sale in 1885 and bought in 1889 by Alexander Forbes-Leith, in whose family it stayed before recently being taken over by the National Trust, to become one of northern Scotland's chief tourist attractions.

The Curse of the M'Alisters is less dramatic or detailed than those cast upon Mar, Fyvie or Brahan (see next chapter). Some time before the reign of Queen Anne (1701–14), the M'Alisters, a bunch of rowdy Highland thugs, were at war with their neighbours. In a skirmish one of their chieftains, M'Alister More (More = Big), captured the two sons of a widow. Ignoring her pleas for mercy, he and his men hanged her sons on a gibbet in front of her door. Understandably enraged, she cried, 'Never shall there be a son to the house of M'Alister.' But they just laughed, telling her that if she made any more fuss they'd torch her house.

From one generation to the next the M'Alisters had many daughters, but never a son – until near the end of the seventeenth century a boy was born at last. His name is not known, but apparently he grew up a staunch Jacobite. When in 1715 Bobbing John Mar (see the Curse of Mar) raised the Stuart standard, he left his wife and went to join the rebel army at Perth. For months no news came through the hills to the remote M'Alister lands, though rumour had it that Mar had won a great victory and that the son of James VII of Scotland, II of England, had been crowned James VIII at Scone.

It was not so. One wild night M'Alister's young wife went to bed and fell asleep, only to be awakened by a horse's clattering hooves. It sounded like her husband's charger. Entering the courtyard, the riderless horse dropped dead of exhaustion. As she waited anxiously upstairs, the young woman heard her husband's footsteps approach. The door opened. Into her room came a headless man in uniform. She screamed and fainted. On the following day came the news that the battle at Sheriffmuir had been lost, and that her husband had been captured, tried for treason and executed.

This vaguely detailed account is almost certainly apocryphal.[6]

A similar tale, from Moy on Speyside in the Central Highlands, tells how the Mackintoshes of Clan Chattan warred with their neighbours, the Grants. Peace was eventually made, guaranteed by a solemn oath sworn by both sides. Yet the Mackintoshes broke their word by capturing Grant of Urquhart and a lesser Grant chieftain, Alva, betrothed to Urquhart's daughter. Deciding to hang both men, the Mackintoshes made the daughter choose whether her father or her lover should die. After an agony of indecision, she decided to save Alva and let her father die; but the Mackintoshes hanged both men before her eyes. Standing under the gallows, she cursed the Mackintosh of Moy, saying that never again would there be a direct heir.

Sir Walter Scott turned the tale into a ballad complete with an old hag who appears when at last a male heir is born. But the Curse of Moy does not seem to have worked very well. Scott has it that the witch reminds the assembled company of the existence of the curse, and then departs, before the death next day of the new-born child. This is romance. Though brothers or nephews frequently inherited Moy over the next few centuries, son succeeded father several times.

Lockhart also mentions the tale of Moy's cursed bed. Around the turn of this century, in the time of the twenty-seventh Chief of Clan Chattan, there was a house party at Moy. Among the guests were three elderly ladies of well-known Highland families. One night one of them remarked that it was now nineteen years since all three had last been at Moy together, when 'that dreadful thing happened'.

Begged to explain by another guest, she told how, at that earlier party, she had one morning come down late for breakfast. Apologising to her host, she explained that she had rung repeatedly for her maid, who had not appeared, so that in the end she had had to dress herself.

The maid's door had been found locked. No sound came from within. When the lock was forced, they came upon the maid dead in bed, the imprint of a large body in the sheets beside her. At this the old housekeeper reminded all present that the bed was the cursed bed, and should never have been used. Either she knew nothing or would not tell what she knew of the curse, but she would only say that there was something very wrong with the bed. Usually it was kept in a lumber-room but, on this occasion, the house being full of people so that an extra bed was needed, it had been brought out. Following this tragedy, the bed had been taken out that very day and burned.[7]

It is no surprise that the villain of Shakespeare's Scottish tragedy, its name rarely spoken by actors for fear of bringing down the curse associated with it (see chapter 20), was associated by Shakespeare with Glamis Castle on Tayside in eastern Scotland. Glamis, after all, is among the most famously haunted sites in Britain. Yet though the historic Macbeth, or Maelbeatha, King of Scotland *c.* 1040–57, may once have been Thane of Glamis, it wasn't until centuries after his lifetime that the eerie legends connected with the secret chamber at Glamis Castle originated.

Though dating from the seventeenth century in its present form, parts of Glamis are much older. 'The extreme antiquity of the building is vouchsafed by the immense thickness of the walls,' wrote Scott who, following his own visit in 1793, speculated about the secret chamber. Of this room, which was to seize the imagination of the Victorians, it was said that only Lord Strathmore of Glamis, his heir, and the factor of Glamis, knew where its door lay and what it hid, and that they could reveal the dire secret only to their successors.

One legend, as given by Robert Chambers in *Picture of Scotland* (1827), tells that the secret room is occupied by the ghost of Earl Beardie, alias Alexander Earl of Crawford, notorious for his rebellion against James II. The tradition is that, losing at cards and warned to desist, he swore in a fury that he would 'play until the day of judgment'. Immediately the Devil appeared and Earl Beardie, his cronies and the room itself vanished. Wherever the room is, in it, says this tradition, the wicked laird and his friends may be found, still gambling and cursing one another.

According to another tale, several Ogilvies came to Glamis seeking refuge, during a feud between themselves and the Lindsays. Pretending to help them, the owner locked them in the secret room, then left them there to starve. A later Lord Strathmore was so upset by the mouldering bones that he had the room walled up.

The most gruesome tradition is of a monstrous child born two or three centuries ago and shut in a secret room hollowed out of the walls. As each earl came of age he was told the awful secret and shown the rightful earl, who is supposed to have lived until the 1920s.[8]

Whatever lies hidden in the secret room, it seems sure that *something* at Glamis has preyed for centuries on the Strathmores. 'If you could guess the nature of this secret,' the old earl told an inquirer soon before his death in 1905, 'you would go down on your knees and thank God it were not yours.'[9]

Following a visit to Glamis in October 1879, the diarist Augustus Hare, commenting how 'Lord Strathmore himself has an ever sad look', goes on to tell how the Bishop of Brechin, feeling the profound sadness of the house, offered his ecclesiastical services to Strathmore who, though deeply moved, said 'that in his unfortunate position *no one* could ever help him'.

Hare adds that Strathmore had built a new wing for the servants and children to sleep in, as the servants would not sleep in the main house, and he would not let the children do so.[10]

In the summer of 1793 Sir Walter Scott spent a night at Glamis, and in his *Letters on Demonology and Witchcraft* (1830) he tells how he was conducted to a room in 'a distant corner of the building' and left on his own. As he heard door after door shut, he began to think himself 'too far from the living, and too near to the dead'. Reminding his readers that King Malcolm II had been murdered in Glamis, he 'experienced sensations, which, though not remarkable either for timidity or superstition, did not fail to affect me to the point of being disagreeable.'[11]

Which is one way of saying he was scared half to death.

Variations on the tale of the secret of Glamis, of its numerous ghosts, and of pounding or hammering sounds that presaged death in the Strathmore family, are legion, which is not surprising because Glamis has had a chequered history of the sort that lends itself to dark tales.

Local lore has it that Macbeth murdered Duncan here, though it is certain that Duncan died much further north, near Elgin, after his defeat by the Norseman Thorfinn, at Torfness (now Burghead) on the Moray Firth.

And it is by the western end of the Moray Firth, just north of Inverness and west of the so-called Black Isle, where the River Conon flows into the Cromarty Firth, that the site of Brahan Castle is found.

9   The Brahan Seer and the Seaforth Doom

Of Highland Scotland's many tales of prophetic curse, by far the best known concerns the cruel death of Coinneach Odhar Fiosaiche (Sallow Kenneth the Enchanter), later called the Brahan Seer. According to the legend, a vengeful red-haired woman, Lady Isabella Mackenzie, had him burned to death in 1663. He cursed her family, the Seaforth Mackenzies, predicting their doom in such detail that when, over a century later, it all came to pass many, including Sir Walter Scott and the scientist Sir Humphry Davy, swore they had known of it long before its eerie, prolonged fulfilment.

Coinneach was a wiry man with a cam left eye who came from the Isle of Lewis and worked as a field-labourer at Brahan in Easter Ross. This estate, north of Inverness by the wild River Conon, with all its legends of the kelpie or water-horse, was owned by the third Earl of Brahan, Lord Kenneth Mackenzie of Kintail, Coinneach's protector.

Coinneach needed protection. Famed for his doomy predictions ('Sheep shall eat men, men will eat sheep, the black rain will eat all things; in the end old men shall return from new lands', runs the short version of the best known, about which folk still argue), he was also feared for his sharp tongue. He respected nobody, and it was his open contempt for the gentry as much as his reputation as a sorcerer that got him thrust head-first into a barrel of burning tar, with Kirk blessing, by order of the Lady Isabella.

This happened at a time when no Highlander, even the educated, denied the reality of *an da shealladh*, the Two Sights. The fearful ability to enter sudden trance and predict a birth, or a death, or a stranger's arrival was as much part of daily life as cutting peats, or milking the cow. Nobody wanted to be a seer, it was involuntary, it set you apart. And of many cursed with the gift of vision, *taibhsearachd*, in none was it more potent than in Coinneach. Nor was any seer more dangerous, which is why he was styled *fiosaiche*, 'sorcerer'. He was a bad man to insult, cruelly honest with all, sure of his own invulnerability – until he overstepped the mark.

It was the gentry and clergy, not the poor, who hated the legendary Coinneach. The poor feared but did not blame him for the gifts that

e him so bad-tempered and sarcastic. He dug peat and dyked with
he rest; his hovel in Strathpeffer was as poor as the rest; and it was
there they went for prophecy, bringing a jug of *uisquebaugh* in
payment. They would duck into the dark, smoky hovel, and writhe on
the barbs of his wit as he drank, and drank, until suddenly he would
jerk, go rigid, and bring his sparkling white stone up to his blind left
eye, his right eyeball rolling so far up into his head that only the white
was visible. In a hoarse sing-song he would chant the vision, and they
would hear what they thought they needed to know.

As for this magic stone on which Coinneach's clairvoyance relied,
one tale says that his crofter mother was herding above the burial
ground one night when she saw the graves in it burst open. Out flew
the ghosts of the dead, to vanish into the night. Boldly she waited, and
near dawn back they came. Curiosity led her into the graveyard where
she saw every grave but one now shut again. She laid her rowan staff
over the last, still-open grave – for as everybody knows, no spirit can
cross rowan. The last spirit rushed back; a beautiful woman in white,
a golden band in her hair. Finding her way barred, she explained she
was the drowned daughter of an ancient King of Norway, and that on
one night every year the dead were allowed back to their homes, but
her journey to Norway was so long she was always late back. Please
could she return in peace to the Land of the Dead? So Coinneach's
mother lifted the staff, and in gratitude the princess gave her a hollow
stone, sparkling white, to give to Coinneach when he was seven,
saying that it bestowed the gift of prophecy. This was done, and when
the boy first looked into it, he 'saw' a whale stranded by a far-off cave.
The Uig men went out and found it, and that was the start of his
reputation.

Another version of the tale claims the princess told Coinneach's
mother to pick two white stones off her grave: these would bring him
luck if used to help others. But when the woman picked them up the
ghost became fearful, prophesying: 'He will help a red-haired woman,
and she will repay him with hell-fire.' So at his birth his mother threw
the stones into a deep well. Years later, however, the well went dry
and Coinneach found them. His mother warned him: never help a
red-haired woman. But in time this is what he did, the red-haired
woman being the Lady Isabella.

A third version has Coinneach finding the stone when, full-grown,
he was out cutting peat and fell asleep waiting for his wife to bring his
lunch. Waking up, under his head he felt a stone, small and round
with a hole through it, and through it saw his wife coming with curds
poisoned by an enemy, though she knew nothing about it. When he
looked through the stone with his left eye he went blind in that eye; at
least to the outer world. Like Tiresias in the Greek myth, in exchange
for his outer sight he got inner vision; the power to see not only the
future, but into every human heart and mind.

★ ★ ★

Today, Brahan is found on a wooded north slope above the River Conon, a popular salmon river spating east from the bleak Northwest Highlands into the Cromarty Firth. Many prophecies attributed to Coinneach endure here, most to do with floods erupting over this, North Britain's northernmost fertile stretch of land. It is a lovely but unpredictable land, bare mountain and cold sea all about, its precarious fertility abruptly arrested by the slopes of Ben Wyvis to the north and by the wilderness to west and southwest.

Loch Ussie just north of Brahan is overhung by the vitrified fort atop the knoll of Knockfarrel, from which myth says the giant Fingal strode with one step on to Ben Wyvis on the north side of Strathpeffer below. Into Loch Ussie with its wooded isles Coinneach hurled his stone as he was marched to his death. Indeed, one tale claims the loch was formed by Coinneach hurling his stone into the puddle shaped by a cow's hoof, the waters then welling up from it. It is also said the stone was eaten by a pike, and will one day be found by a man with two navels and six fingers on each hand, who will inherit Coinneach's prophetic gift.

As for Brahan Castle, it was razed at the end of the Second World War. Nothing remains but a grassy sward. Just after the entry to Brahan itself, on the left by the roadside is the Hood Memorial, a stone plinth erected by Lady Hood Mackenzie, marking where her sister Caroline was killed when hurled from the pony carriage that bolted down the road, in the year 1823, seven years after Lady Hood's inheritance.

This death fulfilled the final part of Coinneach's prediction, that the Seaforth line would end when the Brahan lands 'shall be inherited by a white-hooded lassie from the east, and she is to kill her sister'.

Some ten miles east, in the semi-derelict cathedral at Fortrose on the south shore of the 'Black Isle' – a peninsula, not an isle – is a memorial tablet detailing the sad fate of the last Lord Seaforth and his 'four fair sons', all of whom died according to the Brahan Seer's uncanny prediction.

Lord Kenneth Mackenzie, third Earl of Brahan and Kintail, was a Royalist, jailed for his beliefs by Cromwellian Covenanters during the Civil War. When in 1660 Charles II restored the monarchy, Mackenzie recovered Brahan and married Isabella, the shrewd, sharp-tongued, red-haired daughter of a local laird, but the match was not happy.

In 1662 Lord Kenneth went to France on a diplomatic mission, but even with the earl, his protector, absent, Coinneach still thought himself invulnerable, and refused to curb his tongue despite all his local enemies among clergy and gentry. At a party in Brahan's grounds that summer, he heard some sycophant remark that rarely was such a fine gathering of gentlemen's children to be seen. Unable to stop himself, Coinneach sneered that he saw more evidence about him of the children of footmen and grooms than of the gentry.

Realising his stupidity too late, he made himself scarce.

For Isabella this insult was the last straw. She knew her husband enjoyed Coinneach's disrespectful wit, which is why he protected the evil little man, but Kenneth was far away – too far away for her liking. Angry, abandoned, lonely, fearing that all about her secretly derided her, she decided to destroy this devil's chiel who so openly despised his social superiors.

One account says Isabella had him pursued, seized, tried and executed on the spot, and that before he died he delivered the curse. The better-known tale is that she pretended to forgive him, so that soon he came out of hiding on the moors and went home. Then on her birthday she summoned him to ask, before her family and servants, just what her husband was up to in Paris.

Though briefly he had been afraid, now Coinneach's confidence was back. So he came, and was ushered into a luxurious drawing-room at the castle.

The day was warm, yet Isabella lay on a cane day-bed by a blazing fire, all those round her sweating in the heat. She looked hectic and unwell, yet still he felt secure. His bow was a mockery. 'Lady, what do you want to know?' he demanded, arrogantly ignoring her long, calculating look. He saw only her distressed, angular white face, her sleepless red-rimmed eyes, the rapid rise and fall of her breast under her red satin dress.

'Use your stone,' she said harshly. 'Tell me if my lord is well.'

'First,' he said agreeably, 'tell me where he is.'

'Paris!' She spat the word. 'Look in the stone. Tell me!'

Lifting the stone to his cam left eye he saw what he saw and, unable to stop himself, laughed out loud. Only after lowering the stone and seeing the look on her face did he begin to sense the trap. Why else had she called in all these other narrow Kirk-obsessed fools if not to witness his witchcraft?

'Why do you laugh?' she snapped, now up on one elbow.

He breathed deep. 'Fear not for your lord,' he said as smoothly as he could. 'He is safe and sound, well and hearty, merry and happy.'

She glared. 'What do you mean, *happy*? Where is he? What is he doing?'

In a sweat now, he widened his lopsided grin and tried to charm her. 'Ask no more questions. Be content: he is well and happy.'

She sat up, hot eyes boring at him. He felt the heat of her hate. 'But where is he? Who is he with? When is he coming home?'

He was in a dilemma. Tell the truth and he was dead. There was no mercy in her eyes. She had witnesses. She had trapped him. If he lied to save his skin, it would be all round the Gaeltacht inside a week.

Coinneach crawled before her! He was frit!

In a monotone he said: 'I see your lord in a magnificent room. He is in fine company and far too agreeably occupied to think of leaving Paris.'

His words fell like stones. Somebody gasped. She stood, unsteadily. The fire roared behind her; there was fire in her eyes, but her smile was white marble, like the smile of the Sphinx.

'Tell me now, seer,' she said softly. 'Tell me what you saw.'

She had him. Her witnesses would say whatever she told them to say; the Kirk would gladly sentence him to death in the name of Jesus Christ the lord of love. They relied on her, not on him, and most of them feared him as much as the Kirk hated him.

Knowing he was lost, he burst out: 'Since you want to know what will only displease you, I will tell you the truth! Your lord has little thought of you, or of his children and his home. I saw him in a gay gilded room, grandly dressed in velvet, silk and cloth of gold. He was on his knees to a fair lady, his arm round her waist, his lips pressed to her hand.' He paused, then added: 'That is the truth.'

Amid the silence the fire roared, behind her, in her eyes. She seemed about to faint. She shrugged off support. Her gaze never left him as she licked her parched narrow lips and, hoarsely triumphant, declared: 'You have spoken evil of dignities. You have defamed a great chief in the eyes of his servants. You have abused my hospitality and outraged my feelings. You have sullied the good name of my lord in the hall of my ancestors.' She paused, and said sweetly: 'You shall suffer the death.'

Frozen, he stared at her. A dirk pricked his back. They'd kill him now if he so much as moved. How had it come to this? Then he knew he'd been ready for years. *Go with the old gods!* he commanded himself.

Scowling, he took the stone from the pouch at his waist and raised it to his cam left eye. The familiar swirling dizziness seized him, then the mists cleared, and he *saw*, he saw every detail, and he cried harshly: 'I see into the far future, and I read the doom of the race of my oppressor. The long-descended line of Seaforth will, ere many generations have passed, end in extinction and sorrow. I see a chief, the last of his house, both deaf and dumb. He will be the father of four fair sons, all of whom he will follow to the tomb. He will live careworn and die mourning, knowing that the honours of his line are to be extinguished forever, and that no future chief of the Mackenzies shall bear rule at Brahan or in Kintail. After lamenting over the last and most promising of his sons, he himself shall sink into the grave, and the remnant of his possessions shall be inherited by a white-hooded lassie from the east, and she is to kill her sister. And as a sign by which it may be known that these things are coming to pass, there shall be four great lairds in the days of the last deaf and dumb Seaforth –

Gairloch, Chisholm, Grant and Raasay – of whom one shall be buck-toothed, another hare-lipped, another half-witted, and the fourth a stammerer . . .'

He paused to look about that hot, shrouded room. He saw some crossing themselves. He saw Isabella bite her lip and make a sign, and knew he was about to be thrown into Brahan's cellars, there to rot with the rats until dawn, when he would be dragged out to die. And her look said it was not an easy death she was planning. Somehow he controlled his fear and his rage. Raising his left arm he pointed hard at her and completed the curse. 'The chiefs thus distinguished,' he whispered hoarsely, 'will be allies and neighbours of the last Seaforth; and when he looks around and sees them, he may know that his sons are doomed, that his broad lands shall pass to strangers and that his race shall come to an end. And of the great house of Brahan not a stone shall remain.'

The fire now burned not only in her eyes and behind her on the hearth but as twin blotches consuming her cheeks. With difficulty amid the silence she broke the spell and signalled. In the sudden uproar he felt an eerie sense of relief as rough hands seized him and sent him on the start of his last journey. 'You'll die at dawn,' they said, but none dared meet his eye.

There is no more agreement as to whether this version of the Doom – as given by Alexander Mackenzie in *The Prophecies of the Brahan Seer* (1877) – was delivered in the castle, or just before Coinneach's execution,[1] than there is about the actual circumstances of his death. One tale says Isabella handed him over to the Kirk to be tried as a witch, and that he escaped, but was soon recaptured in a small glen by a running burn. He was tried and convicted, and died by fire at Chanonry Point. Another legend tells that he did not die at Chanonry at all, nor by fire, but was hanged by a burn, into which, having uttered his curse, he hurled his stone, so that a spring immediately gushed out, to form Loch Ussie. But the most popular tale is that, with Kirk authority, Coinneach was quickly tried, convicted and taken bound the few short miles to Chanonry Point – a bare, windy spit of land on the south shore of the 'Black Isle'.

Here a tar-barrel awaited Coinneach, iron spikes thrust through its sides to increase his final torment. Into this he was plunged head-first, to be torn by the spikes and to choke on the tar before fire was set to send him on to eternity. Before he underwent this final torture, Lady Seaforth is said to have crowed at him that he would never go to heaven. But he replied: '*I* will go to heaven, but *you* never shall; and this will be a sign whereby you can determine whether my condition after death is one of everlasting happiness or of eternal misery; a raven and a dove, swiftly flying in opposite directions will meet, and for a second hover over my ashes, on which they will instantly alight. If the raven be foremost, you have spoken truly; but if the dove, then my hope is well founded.'

This final prophecy was apparently fulfilled in Coinneach's favour, the dove being first to alight.

Meanwhile, Lord Kenneth had left Paris and was near Brahan when he heard of the trial, whereupon he rode so hard his horse died under him. He arrived too late. Obviously, if Coinneach's execution followed his vision of Lord Kenneth's lovemaking in Paris as quickly as folklore says, then this final embellishment is romantic nonsense. In 1663 it took more than a day and a night to get from Paris to north Scotland. Nor is there any evidence that Coinneach Odhar lived and died as these popular tales claim.

But, whoever laid the curse, the curse was laid.

Lord Kenneth died in 1678. It seems that he was away in Paris for barely more than a year; that he too was second-sighted, and was a womaniser and drinker, and thought to have married below his station. And Isabella? She survived her husband by almost forty years, dying in 1715, a formidable matriarch, domineering and efficient, not at all well-liked. Did her local unpopularity lead to the libellous legend that she had seen to Coinneach's death, and brought the curse down on her family? It seems likely. The surviving portrait of her by David Scougal shows a pensive face, angular, all nose and mouth and remote large eyes; richly gowned, she clutches a spray of roses. The bloody Isabella of legend? Nothing proves it.

Yet the curse remained.

A century passed. Kenneth's son Kenny, the fourth earl, sided with King James VII during the 1688 'Glorious Revolution': a bad move politically. With Dutch William now king both of England and Scotland, James was exiled to France; Kenny followed him there and in 1701 died in Paris, aged forty. In 1707 came the union of Scotland and England. Many Scots, feeling betrayed by Edinburgh lawyers, stayed loyal to the Jacobite cause, among them Isabella's grandson, William Dubh, the fifth earl, who lost his lands and titles after the 1715 uprising. Allowed back to Scotland in 1726, he lived out his life on the Hebridean island of Lewis. When he died in 1740, his eldest son Kenneth inherited the clan, and began recovering the Seaforth estates, both at Brahan in the east and Kintail in the west. Lying low during the 1745 rebellion led by Bonnie Prince Charlie (James VII's grandson), the Seaforth Mackenzies survived the next catastrophe, when in April 1746 the bare moor of Culloden, a few miles east of Inverness, soaked up Jacobite blood. Prince Charlie fled this, the last pitched battle in Britain.

The Highlands suffered. Men carrying arms or wearing the plaid could be killed on sight. Children heard speaking Gaelic were whipped. Victory belonged to King George II's brother, William, Duke of Cumberland. In England, a flower was named after him: 'Sweet William'; in Scotland, a weed was named after him: 'Stinkin' Billy'. Soon, entire Highland clans were being forcibly cleared out of their ancestral glens to make way for the more profitable Cheviot sheep. Tens of thousands of folk were transported overseas, many dying en route, many more never returning. So the first part of the Black Rain prophecy was fulfilled. It was a hard time in the Highlands. There was a curse on the land as a whole, not just on any one particular family.

Then, nine years after Culloden, the last Seaforth was born. His name was Francis Humberston Mackenzie and he inherited the estates of Brahan and Kintail via the misfortunes of others. In 1771 the earldom had been restored to Kenneth, grandson of the fifth earl, exiled after the 1715 uprising, but he died childless and his title lapsed. Brahan went to a second cousin, Thomas Mackenzie, who also died childless, in a naval battle. He was succeeded by his brother: Francis Humberston Mackenzie.

And so the curse's fourfold prediction came true: (1) the last Seaforth would be deaf and dumb; (2) he would survive his four sons; (3) his estates would pass to a 'white-hooded lassie from the east', who would kill her own sister; and (4) when these things came to pass there would be four great Highland lairds, each with a recognisable deformity.

Born in London in 1755, Francis Humberston Mackenzie was schooled at Eton, where, when he was twelve, scarlet fever broke out. Among those struck down by it, he was put in the sick-house dormitory along with fifteen other boys, many, like him, dangerously ill. One night the nurse on duty heard him cry out and found him agitated in his fever. When she managed to calm him down, he told her how, when she had left the room for a moment, he had seen an ugly hag enter by a door opposite his bed, a wallet hanging from her neck in front of her. He had seen this old hag, like the Celtic banshee, move from bed to bed of his fellow sufferers, staring at each of them. The first she had passed but, reaching the second, she had paused, from the wallet removing a mallet and a peg. In his delirium Mackenzie had seen her use the mallet to drive the peg into the boy's forehead. He heard the crunch of splintered bone as the peg was driven in, though the victim never stirred. The old hag continued round the dormitory, staring at some boys longer than others, then driving pegs into their foreheads. When at last she reached him, he was paralysed with fear. He lay unable to cry out or resist. One cold hand felt at his ears, while the other seemed to reach for a peg. At last after a long cold stare but without pegging him, she had left, finally vanishing through the same door she had entered. At last released, he had cried out, so that the nurse came. She had derided his tale, but later told it to the doctor on his rounds who, seeing the boy still excited and obviously feverish, made him tell it again. The doctor wrote down what the boy told him, and later, to his horror, realised that those described by the boy as having had a peg driven into their foreheads were those who had died of the fever; while those whom the *cailleach* (Gaelic for hag) had passed, recovered.

Those at whose bedside she'd paused, like young Seaforth himself, were all damaged by their illness. Francis survived, but he was stone-deaf thereafter, and for a long time dumb, though later he recovered his speech. He married Mary Proby, daughter of the Dean of Lichfield, who bore him four sons and six daughters. Despite his deafness, he enjoyed a distinguished career. He sat in Parliament, raised a regiment of the Seaforth Highlanders, and became Governor of Barbados, where he ended slave-killing. In 1808 he gained the rank of lieutenant-general. All seemed well. Yet one by one his sons died.

William and George, the eldest, died in infancy – not unusual then. Francis, the youngest, died at Brahan in 1813. William, the third-born, was already MP for Ross-shire when he too fell ill, and went south to recover his health. When news came that he had rallied, the old piper at Brahan remarked sadly: 'It's decreed that Seaforth will outlive his sons.'

Soon it was known: William had died in Edinburgh.

How to imagine Francis' grief? He was aware of the curse, and knowledge of it must have tyrannised him ceaselessly. First made deaf and dumb, then 'the father of four fair sons' and all the time awaiting their destruction before his own, knowing that others about him were anticipating the prophesied disaster, well known as it was. 'After lamenting over the last and most promising of his sons,' Francis himself indeed sank rapidly and died barely two months later. There were no male descendants. So the major part of the prophecy was fulfilled.

Due to the mismanagement of the West Indian estates, Francis had had to sell his lands in Kintail. At his death, the surviving estates at Brahan were inherited by Mary Frederica, his eldest daughter.

In Barbados she had met then married Sir Samuel Hood who, later admiral of the British fleet in the Indian seas, had died in India barely a month before his father-in-law. So Mary returned to inherit Brahan, mourning not only her husband but her father and her two younger brothers.

That was in 1816. Seven years later occurred the accident in which her sister Caroline died, when the horses drawing their trap bolted down the long westward slope of the road towards Contin, so fulfilling the last part of the curse, that '. . . the white-hooded lassie . . . would kill her sister'.

The curse did not stop there. Mary had remarried, to a grandson of the sixth Earl of Galloway, who took the name Stewart-Mackenzie. He sold the ancient Mackenzie holdings on Lewis to another family, the Mathesons. And though later James Stewart-Mackenzie, great-grandson of Francis, was made Baron Seaforth of Brahan, in 1923 this new Brahan laird died without issue. The estate went to a nephew, Francis. He and his brother Michael died within a day of each other, both victims of the Second World War.

After the war the old house, now riddled with dry rot, was demolished by the new owners. Today, there is only a green lawn, surrounded by old trees on the slope above the Conon, to suggest that Brahan Castle ever existed. The curse has come full circle. 'Of the great house of Brahan not a stone shall remain.'

Indeed, today, there is not so much as a stone. Only grass.

As for the four deformed lairds, there is good evidence that this part of the prophecy was commonly known throughout the Highlands, though in varying forms, in the years preceding fulfilment of the curse.

Elizabeth Grant of Rothiemurchus, in her *Memoirs of a Highland Lady*, writes in her diary for 1815 how at the Northern Meeting in Inverness she met Seaforth's surviving son, William Mackenzie of Applecross, the MP for Ross, 'looking extremely ill'. She says: '. . . he had a buck tooth to which someone had called attention, and it was soon the only topic spoken about, for an old prophecy ran that whenever a mad Lovat, a childless —, and an Applecross with a buck tooth met, there would be an end of Seaforth. The buck tooth all could see, the mad Lovat was equally conspicuous, and though Mrs — had two handsome sons born after several years of childless wedlock, nobody ever thought of fathering them on her husband.'

A month or so later, William Mackenzie was dead.

Lockhart, in his *Life of Sir Walter Scott* (1839) asserts that the curse was 'quoted in the Highlands [when] Lord Seaforth had two sons alive and in good health, and that it was certainly not made after the event'.

Duncan Davidson, Lord Lieutenant of Ross, also asserted in writing that the predictions were known before their fulfilment and that, as a frequent visitor to Brahan in his youth (before these events came to pass), he had often heard members of the family refer to the prophesied doom.

So the curse existed before the event . . . but who laid it? There is no good written evidence that anyone called Coinneach Odhar Fiosaiche, the hero – or villain – of the legend, was born in Lewis, lived at Brahan, and died at the hands of Isabella Mackenzie during the reign of Charles II.

However, there *was* a historical Coinneach. In October 1577, the Sheriff of Cromarty and other local Ross-shire justices were ordered by a Commission of Justice seated at Holyroodhouse in Edinburgh to arrest six men and twenty-six women charged with 'the diabolical practices of magic, enchantment, murder, homicide and other offences' within the area. The last name on the list of the accused is that of 'Keanoch Ower' (Coinneach Odhar, as spelt by a clerk without Gaelic); who is described as 'leading or principal enchantress', 'enchantress' again probably due to the clerk's inability to tell between a male and female Gaelic name. An earlier commission, dated January 1577, likewise demands the arrest and trial of 'Kennoth, alias Kennoch Owir, principal or leader in the art of magic'.[2]

These actions arose out of accusations made by her step-family against Catherine Ross, sister of the notorious Earl George of Caithness, that she had hired witches and warlocks to kill her three stepsons by magic so that her own son George might inherit. The outcome of this true story is very complex, but it led at least two of the accused, Christian Ross and Thomas Mackean, to be burned to death at Chanonry in November 1577.

Because the documents are lost it is not known whether Coinneach, 'leader in the art of magic', was likewise caught. If so, he certainly suffered the same fate as the legendary Coinneach, though almost a century earlier, for different reasons, and at different hands. It seems probable that he was caught, that he did die, and that distorted folk-memory of the event was in retrospect transposed to the 1660s, further to blacken the sourly remembered name of Lady Isabella Mackenzie. It also seems likely that the reputation of this historic sorcerer was so powerful in the Highlands that later his name became a nexus for many floating prophecies, each in origin mouthed by now-forgotten seers, all later subsumed in the mythical identity of Coinneach Odhar – just as, earlier and elsewhere, the figures of Merlin, King Arthur and Robin Hood had come to epitomise entire mythologies passed over the centuries from mouth to mouth, heart to heart, mind to mind.

10   English Curses

Though more famously practised by the Gaels, the fine art of cursing was common among the Saxons too. Not a day went by through all the centuries of Merrie Olde Englande without someone somewhere cursing someone else, and for many reasons. Until 1534 the Church in particular claimed the right to use God's Curse as a sanction against wrongdoing. Priests cursed folk who were late paying their tithes; librarians attached anathemas to books as a warning to thieves or careless borrowers; charters and deeds often ended with a curse on their violators; and papal bulls carried a curse on all ignoring their contents. Late in the fifteenth century, when Thomas Perne of Gilden Morden in Cambridgeshire was robbed, he told his vicar, who publicly threatened to curse the thieves if they did not hand back the goods. Four times annually all thieves, murderers and enemies of the Church were formally cursed by bell, book and candle. Even secular folk could use God's Curse, as in 1521 when the Mayor of Lincoln publicly cursed whoever had stolen Common Council books. But Protestants rejected this magical manipulation of divine power, so that, when the Reformation reached England in 1534, everyone was banned from calling down God's wrath on their enemies.

Not that this ended the practice or common belief in its power. 'When God bids curse, there is cause to fear cursing,' someone wrote in 1659.[1] It was long widely held that, though unprovoked curses rebounded on their authors, the more justified the anger leading to the curse, the more likely the curse would work. And given that cursing was among the few weapons the poor had against the rich and powerful, it was no more likely then than now that they would stop cursing their enemies. In fact, the curses of the poor and injured were thought especially likely to work. 'If anyone's curse can effect damnation it is not that of the Pope but that of the poor,' wrote William Shenstone in the eighteenth century; and as late as the nineteenth century some folk believed in the Beggar's Curse on those refusing to give alms.[2]

Curses were often delivered in public, ritually, on the knees in street or churchyard. The boundary between curse and prayer was narrow. In 1598 in Herefordshire, John Smyth cursed William Walton of Yarpole, 'kneeling on his knees in the churchyard there and praying to God that a heavy vengeance and a heavy plague might light on him and all his cattle'.[3] In 1614, also in Hereford, Catherine Mason accused Robert Davies of killing her husband, and 'prayed to God that his house, children and all that he had, were one wild fire'. So too ('a thing of too common example', declared John Gaule in 1646) parents not only blessed but sometimes cursed unruly children, as at a Hereford wedding in 1655 when Rachel Dewsall 'pulled up her clothes and kneeled down upon her bare knees and cursed her son and her daughter and wished they might never prosper'.[4] This caused terror: the parental curse was a formidable thing which might so obsess the child that death was the result.

Apparently most potent of all and certainly most memorable were the curses said to have been laid by dispossessed monks after 1536 when Henry VIII, eager to grab the monasteries' wealth, dissolved them and sold off monastic land to new private owners. The idea that a divine curse lay on these new owners arose not only from the monks' prophecies of retribution, but also out of belief that the sale of monastic lands was sacrilege; that ill-gotten goods never prospered, and that guilt was inheritable, the curse remaining on the family even after the death of the original evil-doer. By 1600 it was widely put about that families which had acquired monastic land would die out after the third generation. But belief in the 'infelicity of meddling with sacred places' was most encouraged by Sir Henry Spelman, who in his *History and Fate of Sacrilege* (1647) analysed the fate of the owners of all former monastic estates within twelve miles of Rougham, Norfolk. In less than a century, he wrote, 'the monasteries had flung out their owners with their names and families (all of them save two) thrice at least, and some of them four or five or six times, not only by fail of issue, or ordinary sale, but very often by grievous accidents or misfortunes'.[5] In addition, nobody else had dared to build on these otherwise attractive sites 'for dread of infelicity that pursueth them'. In 1895, the authors of the fourth edition of Spelman's book calculated that the families of over 600 of the original 630 grantees had paid for their sacrilege by the nineteenth century – an impressive strike-rate.[6]

Of the many families by then extinguished by their sacrilege (or by other causes), one which endured longer than most was named Browne. Owners of Cowdray Castle and also of Battle Abbey in Leicestershire, they were afflicted by one of the best-known monastic curses.

Restored in recent times by Sir Weetman Dickinson Pearson, first Viscount Cowdray, Cowdray Castle lies near Medhurst in Sussex, and is reached from Medhurst's High Street by a causeway crossing fields.

The estate is ancient. After the Norman Conquest it was owned by the De Bohuns, who built a castle, replacing it with a bigger castle during the reign of Edward III (1272–1307). The estate changed hands several times, and early in the sixteenth century was owned by the Earl of Southampton, who started building a third, even bigger edifice. When he died in 1543 his half-brother, Sir Anthony Browne, inherited both the estate and the still unfinished pile.

Master of the Horse and Chief Standard Bearer in Henry VIII's court, Sir Anthony survived Henry's ire when acting as proxy in arranging his marriage with Anne of Cleves. Betrothed without even meeting the prospective bride and on the sole basis of a portrait, Henry was not happy when he met the 'Flemish Mare' in person. Meanwhile, having broken with Rome, not because he was a convinced Protestant but because he wanted to divorce his first wife and marry Anne Boleyn, in 1536 Henry had dissolved the monasteries in order to grab their wealth. Whatever he thought of his Chief Standard Bearer's eye for feminine beauty, he did not forget Sir Anthony when rewarding his cronies with the plunder. Though Browne was apparently still a Catholic, he was nevertheless fast off the mark when Henry gave him the building and lands of Battle Abbey. Within three months he was living in the Abbey, busy converting it into an opulent private residence with all the latest Tudor conveniences, such as chimneys.

With the work at last done, Sir Anthony and Lady Geraldine his wife held a great house-warming party in the Abbot's hall. During the revelry, with the banquet in full swing, uninvited into the hall strode a furious monk. Forcing his way through the crowd to the platform where Sir Anthony sat he met milord straight in the eye and, grim with rage, loudly cursed him for his sacrilege. Foretelling calamity for the Browne family as long as it lasted, he concluded by prophesying: 'By fire and water thy line shall come to an end, and it shall perish out of the land.'

No other part of the curse has been preserved verbatim, nor was the monk's identity ever clear.

For a long time, however, the worst that happened to the Brownes is that they stayed rich in gold and royal favour. Executor of Henry's will, and guardian to Prince Edward and Princess Elizabeth, Sir Anthony died a wealthy old man. His son, made Viscount Montague by Queen Mary, not only survived Elizabeth's reign despite voting against abolition of the Papal Supremacy, but prospered. Retaining his head, his religion, and most importantly his property, Montague was delighted to spend a fortune entertaining the queen at Cowdray, where she hunted his deer.

The second Viscount, having squandered most of the family fortune by living less wisely than well, got involved in the Gunpowder Plot of 1605, when several Catholic dissidents almost blew up Parliament with King James in it, and was jailed in the Tower of London. Even so, he left a substantial fortune to his heir, the third Lord Montague who, taking the king's side in the Civil War of the 1640s, had his estates confiscated by the victorious Cromwellian Commonwealth. Cowdray was converted into a barracks, and many of its treasures were sold to benefit the new regime. When in 1660 the monarchy was restored, he got back his lands, but not his lost wealth, so that for the next century the family slowly declined. The sixth Viscount had to sell Battle Abbey; the seventh could not even afford to continue living at Cowdray.

Not much sign of a curse here. Many other uncursed families had done much worse. Had the monk got it wrong?

In 1793, the eighth Viscount Montague decided on a jaunt through Germany and Switzerland with a friend, Sedley Burdett. Travelling up the Rhine, at Lauffenburg the two young men decided to try shooting the Schaffhausen Falls – a drop of sixty feet – in a small flat-bottomed boat. Hearing of this insane scheme, the local magistrate posted guards by the river to stop them trying it, but Montague and Burdett launched their boat. They passed the first fall, but at the second went under the roaring white torrent and were never seen again.

'By fire and water thy line shall come to an end, and it shall perish out of the land.'

So that was the water. As for the fire, that had happened already, a week earlier. A workman at Cowdray had carelessly let a fire take hold. The castle had burned to the ground. Treasures including the sword of William the Conqueror were lost. A letter telling Montague of the catastrophe apparently reached his hotel just after he had left it to meet his own appointment with death.

The monk had been patient. It had taken two and a half centuries before both prophesied fates struck, almost simultaneously.

The estates went to Montague's sister; the title to a distant relative who died childless in 1797. So the male line of the Brownes ended, more abruptly than any but believers in the curse could have envisaged.[7]

The Curse of Grayrigg Hall in Cumbria is another family curse calling down the wrath of God. This one was delivered late in the seventeenth century by Francis Howgill, a contentious Cumbrian Quaker who, preaching in the south, caused a riot in Bristol. He fled north, but his reputation preceded him. He was arrested and ordered by the justices at Kendal to take the oath of allegiance, which he refused to do and so he was lodged in Appleby Gaol. Offered his freedom if he promised to behave, he persisted in being awkward. Nevertheless, the authorities released him for a few days to visit his home, Grayrigg, to take care of some 'private affairs'.

Arriving there, he promptly visited Justice Duckett of Grayrigg Hall. This persecutor of Quakers was among those who had committed Howgill to jail and was surprised to see the man free. 'What is your wish now, Francis?' he asked. 'I thought you had been in Appleby Gaol.'

To which (according to Thistleton Dyer in *Strange Pages from Family Papers*) Howgill righteously replied: 'No, I am not, but I am come with a message from the Lord. Thou hast persecutest the Lord's people, but his hand is now against thee, and he will send a blast upon all that thou hast, and thy name shall rot out of the earth, and this thy dwelling shall become desolate, and a habitation for owls and jack-daws.'

Taken aback by this biblical outpouring, Duckett asked: 'Francis, are you in earnest?'

'Yes, I am in earnest,' Howgill assured him. 'It is the word of the Lord to thee, and there are many living now who will see it.'

So they did. During the next few years all Duckett's children died childless, so that Grayrigg Hall went to the Lowthers, who let it fall into a ruin fit only for 'owls and jackdaws'. A century later the remaining foundations were cleared away, and a farmhouse was built on the site.

Howgill the Quaker was not alone among radical Protestants of the time in being quick on the draw with his curses. Of many examples, notable is the 'divine commission' to issue curses on the ungodly claimed during the Commonwealth (1649–60) by John Reeve and the extravagantly named Lodowick Muggleton. The latter loved issuing curses, in person or by letter. 'It did him more good than if a man had given him forty shillings,' it is said. And whether through the power of fear and auto-suggestion, or through the benevolence of God, several of his victims are said to have died rapidly. When the Ranter John Robins was damned by Muggleton, he felt a 'burning in his throat', but must have been impressed by such signs of godly power, because before too long he started issuing similar curses himself.[8]

Another curse from the same part of the world was attached to Levens Hall, in what was Westmoreland and is now Cumbria. Sited by the River Kent, this old tower was converted into a manor house during Elizabeth's reign, additions being made in the seventeenth century by Sir James Bellingham.

The origins of the curse, of which local tradition persists well into modern times, are vague. According to the legend, centuries ago, an unidentified man cursed the owners of Levens for reasons unknown, predicting that strangers would inherit their lands and that no son would ever inherit until a white doe was born in the park and the waters of the Kent were still.

It is a matter of record that the estate went from father to brother, nephew or cousin, or through the female line, being owned by the Redmaynes, Grahames and Howards, until at last it came into the hands of the Bagots. The rule held with them until, just before the First World War, Mr (later Sir) Alan Bagot inherited Levens from his father. That same year a white doe was born in the park and the Kent froze over.[9]

As told by the nineteenth-century author Bernard Burke in his *Rise of Great Families*, another noteworthy curse originated at the other end of the realm, on Jersey in the Channel Isles. When after the Civil War the royal cause collapsed, King Charles I's young sons Charles and James were sent for safety to Jersey. Here they often saw a certain Colonel Payne, one of their father's most loyal supporters, who was newly married. James Duke of York (later James II) became attached to the older man, and promised that if the colonel's first child should be a son, James would be the godfather. This flattering offer so overwhelmed the colonel that when his wife bore him a daughter his disappointment knew no bounds. Giving vent to his rage he loudly cursed, and consigned himself, his wife, his daughter, his property and the entire world to the devil. No doubt soon enough he calmed down, but among those who heard his oaths was the hereditary midwife, Douce Vardon, whose family had served the Paynes for over three centuries. Believed to own the second sight, severely shocked by what she had heard, she retired to bed that night full of foreboding. As she tossed and turned, the ancient ghost of Duke Rollo of Normandy appeared to her, ordering her to inform the colonel that heaven was so displeased by his oaths that not only would his daughter die young, but that no daughters would ever again be born to his family.

Naturally afraid to speak, for some days the midwife kept quiet, but at the christening she summoned her courage and delivered the message, doing so with such conviction that all present believed her. It became an issue that nobody with any sense ever spoke about in the hearing of a Payne.

The daughter soon died and, though later Mrs Payne had a son which James godfathered as promised, she never had any more daughters. Nor were any daughters born in any of the next six generations, so that the Paynes, utterly convinced that the curse was inexorable, whenever a child was conceived, chose his male names for him months before his birth.

Commenting on Burke's account, Lockhart said in 1938 that he had not been able to find out what had happened to the Paynes, and so could not tell if the curse still held.[10]

Well known due to the publicity attending a famous trial in 1869, the Curse of Tichborne in Hampshire dates from the reign of Henry II in the twelfth century.

Lady Mabell of Tichborne was a woman famed for her charity. Feeling the approach of death after having been bedridden for years, she begged her husband Sir Roger to allow her the means to endow an annual dole of bread to succour the poor. But Sir Roger, who had probably been fuming for years as she gave his money to all and sundry, had no intention of letting her go on doing so even after she died, and so set her what seemed impossible conditions. One account says he promised her the produce of as much of his land as she could walk over; another says he took a brand from the fire, saying she could have as much of the estate as she could circle while it still burned. Either way, all were amazed to see her find the strength to crawl round twenty-three acres, known even now as 'The Crawls'. Enraged by her husband's meanness, she returned to her bed, summoned the family, and told them of the curse that would strike, if and when the dole were ever suspended. This, she prophesied, was sure to happen, but only after a Tichborne had had seven sons and his eldest son seven daughters. After that spate of prodigality, the family would die out, and the estates pass from the male line.

For six centuries the family obeyed Lady Mabell's bequest, annually on 25 March, Lady's Day, handing out nineteen hundred small loaves of bread to the poor. But, with pieces of the bread superstitiously treasured as a cure for all ills, in time the fame of the dole meant that for days before the neighbourhood swarmed with vagabonds converging on Tichborne. Sir Henry Tichborne's neighbours began muttering to the magistrates that something must be done. Sir Henry, who had seven sons, decided to abolish the dole, though he preserved its spirit by giving an equivalent sum of money to the poor. However, when his successor, the eighth baronet, had seven daughters and no son, it seemed that the curse was about to strike.

So it did, but not instantly, nor even according to the strict terms of the prediction. Tichborne went from the eighth baronet to his brother, Sir Edward Doughty, who had assumed that name according to the terms of his inheritance of another property elsewhere.

What *did* happen was more extraordinary than anything predicted by the curse. In 1865 the dowager Lady Tichborne, living in Paris, got a letter from Australia. It purported to be from her son, Sir Roger, the eleventh baronet. He had been lost at sea in 1854 en route from Rio de Janeiro to Kingston, Jamaica. Refusing to give up hope, she had placed advertisements in newspapers in South America and Australia. One was read by Arthur Orton, a ne'er-do-well drifter originally from London's East End. Though barely literate, he wrote to Lady Tichborne from Wagga Wagga in Australia, where he worked as a cattle slaughterer. Her response was so encouraging that in 1866, having raised about £20,000 on the strength of his 'expectations', with his wife and baby daughter he sailed to England, then ventured into Hampshire.

Nobody believed him. 'If you are [Sir Roger], you've changed from a racehorse to a carthorse!' jeered the village blacksmith, pointing out that Sir Roger, weighing under nine stone, had a long sallow face with straight black hair, and had a tattoo on his left arm. Orton weighed twenty-four stone, had a large round face with wavy hair, and no tattoo.

Even so, in January 1867 Orton met Lady Tichborne in Paris, in his hotel room – darkened, he claimed, because he was ill. His blunders were glaring, yet the grieving old woman – by now her husband, two daughters, and her other son had also died – accepted him as her son, making him an allowance of £1,000 a year. Emboldened, Orton now began a legal action to claim the Tichborne estates. Though his case was weakened by Lady Tichborne's sudden death, he produced over a hundred witnesses to testify for him against the seventeen family members and friends who denounced him as a fraud.

Lasting 102 days, the case cost the Tichborne family £90,000. Damned by his rough speech ('I would have won if only I could have kept my mouth shut', he said) and charged with perjury, Orton was jailed for fourteen years. Released after ten, he appeared as a music-hall turn and sold his 'confession' to *The People* for £3,000, but died penniless.

Meanwhile, the Tichbornes decided to placate the ghost of Lady Mabell by resuming the dole of bread every Lady's Day, a practice continuing into the twentieth century.[11]

Human skulls have always played an important role in witchcraft and black magic because they are widely regarded as the seat of the soul. Headhunters kept the skulls of their fallen enemies as trophies. Berserk Norse warriors drank from the skulls of slain enemies to acquire their valour. And sometimes, it is said, the skull of a person whose dying wish had been denied retains a malignant power to disturb the living.

In Britain, where in 1612 Anne Chattox, head of a Lancashire witches coven, was hanged for allegedly digging up skulls from a graveyard for use in demonic rituals, there are many tales of skulls that scream.

At Wardley Hall in Lancashire, the skull of an Elizabethan Catholic martyr, Father Ambrose Barlow, still sits atop the main staircase, because an old legend warns that it will emit terrible screams if moved at all.

And when Anne Griffiths of Burton Agnes Hall in Yorkshire was attacked and badly beaten by footpads three centuries ago, she managed before she died to ask to be buried in the house she loved. However, she was buried instead in the village churchyard. The Hall began echoing to the sound of awful groans, slamming doors and mysterious crashes. Only when her head was exhumed and bricked up in the staircase wall did peace return.

The oddest British skull legend comes from Dorset. It concerns the screaming skull of Bettiscombe Manor, ancestral home of the Pinney family.

The first owner of the manor was the Rev. John Pinney. Socially prominent and a committed Puritan, when the monarchy was restored in 1660 he maintained his faith, so forfeiting living and house. Fleeing persecution, he was in Ireland when in 1685 his sons John and Azariah were sentenced to death at the notorious 'Bloody Assizes' of Judge Jeffreys for joining Monmouth's rebellion against the Catholic King James II. John died, but Azariah's sentence was commuted to slavery in the West Indies. He gained his freedom and made his fortune on Nevis, and only years later, during the reign of George I, returned to Bettiscombe, which had been restored to the Pinneys at the fall of James II and the Stuart dynasty in 1688. With him, as his personal property, he brought a black slave. This was perfectly legal. Not until 1772 did Lord Mansfield legislate that from thenceforth every slave was set free simply by landing on English soil.

The slave did not live long. His heart soon broke under the endless derision of the superstitious Dorset peasants, who called him Satan's black minion. England's climate also contributed to his fatal illness. Before he died, he asked to be buried in the West Indies, threatening to haunt his master's house forever if this were not done. As with Anne Griffiths, he was buried in the local churchyard. Soon violent disturbances broke out. The doors and windows of the house rattled and creaked; terrible screams came from the grave. The skeleton was exhumed, and though no move was made to return it to Nevis, peace reigned until a new attempt was made to bury it. Some versions say that later most of the skeleton disappeared, leaving only the skull which, if ever removed from the house, emitted bloodcurdling shrieks. Finally it was left in the house, in peace – and peace came to Bettiscombe, even though the slave's dying wish had not been fulfilled.

In August 1883, Sir Richard Garnett of the British Museum visited Bettiscombe with his daughter to view the skull. Though reticent about it, the new owner agreed to show it to them, while refusing to so much as move it, far less rebury it in the churchyard. Garnett's daughter wrote:

> We persuaded her to allow us to see it and we tramped up the fine old staircase till we reached the top of the house. Then, opening a cupboard door, she showed us a steep winding staircase leading to the roof. From one of the steps the skull sat grinning at us. It was very old and weatherbeaten and certainly human. The lower jaw was missing and the forehead was very low and badly proportioned.[12]

Today, the Pinneys of Bettiscombe deride any idea that the skull houses a malign spirit. They believe that the slave's body was returned to Nevis, and that the legend was invented by a nineteenth-century antiquarian, Judge J. S. Udall. Visiting Nevis in 1897, Udall heard of the slave who had gone to England and, assuming that the Bettiscombe skull was the slave's, on his return read a paper to this effect to the local antiquarian society.

Expert opinion on the skull's origins remains divided. Though some physiologists accept that it is negroid and male, at least one expert has insisted that it is female, and some 2,000 years old.[13]

Whatever the truth, the belief lingers that if it is ever removed from the house it will scream, and the person removing it will die within a year.

Another kind of curse afflicts the ghosts of those who, suffering a violent or unjust death, can never rest in peace. Britain, as haunted a land as any, boasts thousands of tales of cursed spectres, among them three of the unlucky wives of King Henry VIII, second monarch of a dynasty cursed in more ways than one.

One night in 1864 Major General J. D. Dundas of the 60th Rifles, billeted in the Tower of London, where so many victims of royal wrath had spent their final hours, looked out of a window in the Bloody Tower. Opposite him he saw the guard at the door of the Lieutenant's Lodgings, under the window of the oak-beamed room where Queen Anne Boleyn had awaited her execution on 19 June 1536. Suddenly, Dundas saw a white-swathed figure materialise out of the mist and glide towards the sentry. His challenge ignored, the sentry charged with fixed bayonet and, on meeting only thin air, fainted clean away. He was found apparently asleep at his post. At the ensuing court-martial his story of the wraith would have met with ridicule, but Dundas corroborated every detail; and another senior officer, Field Marshal Lord Grenfell, said that he too had seen the wraith on other occasions. The sentry was acquitted.

In *The Tower from Within*, Major General George Younghusband, Keeper of the Crown Jewels, tells how he occupied a room over Traitor's Gate through which both Anne Boleyn and Catherine Howard had passed on their way to the block. Three times in the first fortnight of his long stay in the Tower, he reports, his securely shut door was opened then shut as if by invisible hands. Others have told how, on certain nights, the Tower's chapel is lit by a ghostly glow, revealing a procession of richly dressed Tudor ladies and gentlemen, at their head a young woman in brocaded robes, her chestnut hair adorned with jewels. A sentry who saw the procession said the woman looked like portraits of Anne Boleyn that he had seen in the Tower.

Anne Boleyn was unjustly executed by Henry on charges of adultery and high treason, though her real crime was her failure to bear him the son he so desperately wanted. Every year on the anniversary of her execution Anne's ghost visits Bickley Hall in Norfolk, where she spent happy days as a child. Her spectral coach, drawn by four headless horsemen and guided by a headless coachman, drives slowly up the avenue and vanishes as it reaches the front door.

After Anne Boleyn came Jane Seymour, daughter of a Wiltshire squire. She died in 1537 at Hampton Court Palace after bearing Henry's one and only son, the short-lived Edward VI. Later her ghost caused such disturbance that the staircase to her room was bricked up.

The distraught spectre of Catherine Howard, Henry's fifth wife, also haunts Hampton Court. Accused of entertaining her lover Thomas Culpepper in her room while Lady Rochford stood guard, she was executed on 13 February 1542. On learning her death was imminent she escaped her heavily guarded room and rushed screaming down the gallery to a door beyond which Henry was hearing Mass. He never turned from his prayers as, uttering piercing shrieks, she was dragged away.

On stormy nights her ghost used to be seen gliding down Hampton Court's Haunted Gallery. As it reached the door of the Royal Closet it would turn away, garments billowing, face utterly hopeless and, shrieking, it vanished through a door at the far end of the gallery. In his *History of Hampton Court Palace*, Ernest Law tells how, occupying a room by the Haunted Gallery, Mrs Cavendish Boyle was roused from deep sleep by terrible screams. Later her friend, Lady Eastlake, said she too had heard the screams during an earlier visit to Hampton Court, but had kept it to herself out of fear of ridicule.

On Tuesday 18 November 1952, an unexplained fire broke out in the Clock Tower of the palace. Several Tudor apartments were damaged, the burned-out area including the Haunted Gallery; and some forty years later the palace was ravaged by an even worse fire.

Not only Henry's unproductive wives but the Tudor dynasty as a whole seems to have been cursed. The Welshman Henry VII, who had seized power by dubious means and with dubious legitimacy in 1485, had two sons. The elder, Arthur, died young; the younger became Henry VIII, who married his brother's widow, Catherine of Aragon. In 1516 she bore a daughter, Mary. That was all. When Rome would not let him divorce her, Henry took England into the Protestant camp and plundered the monasteries, leading to ecclesiastical curses being laid on the impious new owners.

Then came Anne Boleyn, who bore Elizabeth, and was beheaded for not producing a son. Jane Seymour died producing a son, sickly Edward, who died in 1553. None of Henry's last three wives, including Catherine Howard, had a child. By then syphilitic, gross and riddled with worms, he was probably impotent. And after he died in agony in 1547, none of his three children – Edward, Mary, and Elizabeth – had any children at all. Edward, without a healthy day in his life, died aged sixteen. Barren Mary, crowned queen in 1553, was half-mad with sadness that no man wanted her, especially not her husband, King Philip of Spain, who wanted England, not her. In the five years of her reign more than 300 Protestant clergy and laymen died at the stake: thus her name, Bloody Mary. She even lost Calais to the French. Her successor, Elizabeth, lucky to be still alive, never married during the forty-five years of her reign, though some say her rumoured affair with the Earl of Leicester produced a son, Francis Bacon, later Lord Chancellor of England. Others say this was impossible; she was so ambiguously sexed that she could never have had a child. She too suffered perpetual ill-health, and like her father died in agony. The Tudor line was extinct after just 118 years in power.

Like the Kennedy dynasty in the USA today (see chapter 17), the Tudors were cursed not by some malevolent wizard, but by their own ambition.

One ecclesiastical curse originates in the late eleventh century with Osmund, a Norman knight who followed William the Conqueror. Rewarded for his part in the 1066 invasion with the castle and barony of Sherborne, near the end of his life Osmund took holy orders to save his soul. Obtaining the bishopric of Salisbury, he gave it estates including Sherborne Castle, but on condition that 'whosoever shall take these lands from the bishopric, or diminish them in great or small, shall be accursed, not only in this world, but in the world to come, unless in his lifetime he makes restitution thereof'.

The curse was probably uttered in Latin. Nobody spoke English like that for centuries to come.

His successor lost the lands to King Stephen, one of the unluckiest of English kings. The new owners, the Montacutes, soon died out, whereupon a new Bishop of Salisbury challenged the Earl of Salisbury to a battle to decide title. In the event, a more pacific solution was found, the bishop paying the earl two thousand five hundred marks for Sherborne Castle.

Centuries later, in the reign of Edward VI (1547–53), the bishop gave the estate to the Duke of Somerset who, indicted for high treason, promptly lost his head on Tower Hill. Queen Elizabeth gave the land to Sir Walter Raleigh, her favourite, who under James I spent years in the Tower before in 1616 following Somerset to the block. He left Sherborne to his son, but a flaw in the deeds led Robert Carr, favourite of the homosexual James, to seek its ownership. 'I maun hae the land,' James told the protesting Lady Raleigh, 'I maun hae it for Carr.' He paid Lady Raleigh and her son £8,000 plus an annuity of £400 for the estate, but she cursed both him and Carr to their faces. Soon, with James now wanting the land for his son Henry, Carr sold it back to him for £20,000, but Henry died. Carr bought the land back for £25,000, leaving James richer by £5,000. Before long Carr, involved in the Overbury murder scandal, forfeited Sherborne to the

Crown. James made another £10,000 selling the estate to the Digbys who, as Earls of Bristol, behaved so well that James, 'the wisest fool in Christendom', could find no excuse to deprive them of it and add more profit to the royal exchequer.

James himself had done well out of the curse, but maybe only because, as a believer in the powers of witchcraft and malediction, he stayed clear of the place himself. Or did he pass the curse of his own excesses on to his son, Charles I, whose provocation of and defeat in the Civil War led him to the block on 30 January 1649?

During the war, with Lord Bristol a zealous Royalist, Sherborne was twice besieged then taken, damaged and confiscated; but when the monarchy returned in 1660, Bristol recovered the estate. Thereafter the curse was dormant, no visits to the block being asked of any later owners.[14]

11 The Hapsburg Ravens and the Lady in White

For centuries the Hapsburgs were Europe's premier dynasty. At one time they ruled Austria, Hungary, the Tyrol and Bohemia, parts of Germany, the Netherlands, southern Italy, Sicily, Sardinia and Spain, plus holdings in North Africa and a vast empire in the New World. The old joke about this so-called Holy Roman Empire is that it was not Holy, Roman, or even an Empire, but just a motley collection of separated lands conjoined by clever dynastic marriages. Maybe so, but the Hapsburgs struggled on in power for seven or eight hundred years, marrying or killing their competitors and sacking Rome once in a while if the Pope became overly arrogant. Skeletons abounded in their dynastic closet, yet they remained so far above ordinary mortals for so long that perhaps the only thing rendering them human in the common eye was that they were haunted by the *Turnfalken* – supernatural ravens whose every appearance presaged doom to members of the imperial family.

Their last, most disastrous sighting was days before the Archduke Franz Ferdinand, heir to the Austro-Hungarian Empire, toured the turbulent Bosnian city of Sarajevo. The date was 28 June 1914. His wife Sophie failed to dissuade him from the dangerous trip just because the *Turnfalken* had been seen. She went with him, and died with him. Their assassination triggered the First World War and the end of the Hapsburg empire – save in the form of the red limousine in which they were shot, which continued (see chapter 19) on a very odd twenty-year career of its own.

The connection between the ravens and the Hapsburgs apparently began in the eleventh century, when an ancestor of the dynasty, the nobleman Count von Altenbourg, also known as Gontran-le-Riche, held land near where the Aar joins the Rhine. Out hunting in the forest one day he was attacked so viciously by a flock of vultures that he would have died if not for the odd, sudden intervention of a squalling flock of ravens. Owing them his life, he protected and fed them thereafter, and on a rocky promontory built a watch-tower which he called *Habichtsburg* (Vulture Castle). Thus the name of the dynasty he founded, Hapsburg or Habsburg.

Though named after the vulture, the family took the eagle as their crest, and at first had the raven as their friend – until they denied it.

This happened a century after Gontran died. The ravens had done well, building nests everywhere, when Gontran's remote tower came to be owned by his descendants, the arch-abbot Werner and his brother Radbot. Both were ambitious men. Soon the ravens' watchtower became a great castle, Schloss Hapsburg, its battlements dominating the endless mountain forests.

The Hapsburgs were on the up and up, but the ravens, driven from their retreats and no longer fed, so resented the broken bargain that they turned violently on the castle and those in it. So the Hapsburgs began killing them. This war the ravens lost: two centuries later there were no more of them at Schloss Hapsburg. They had been exterminated – physically. But out of flesh is not out of mind. They refused to go away. They kept appearing so vividly and to so many people over so many centuries that no Hapsburg could doubt their reality. Uncannily yet persistently, their every appearance presaged disaster . . .

Black as night, the raven with his glittering eye is known in folklore the world over as an intelligent 'talking' bird, also as a symbol of death and ill-omened prophecy. The species is plentiful; ravens are never far away. And they are carrion birds, unlikely to shy away from the banquet potentially available when folk kill folk bloodily, publicly, and in the open. So cynics may say that it is no surprise that the *Turnfalken* were seen at every Austrian defeat in battle, or that they swooped above Marie Antoinette, Queen of France and ill-fated daughter of Hapsburg Empress Maria Theresa, when in 1793 she was taken to be guillotined.

As if the *Turnfalken* were not enough, there was also a White Lady, the family ghost, 'a Court lady who never did anything to anyone', as Countess Wrbna put it after seeing the apparition in 1807.

Hapsburgs of one generation after another saw this elegant lady glide by like a Snow Queen in her veil and pristine robes, imperiously beautiful, looking ahead, saying nothing, offering no harm – yet invariably presaging disaster or death. Her origin was a mystery, though perhaps she was the same White Lady who haunted the German house of Hohenzollern.

The emperor Francis saw her twice before his first wife Elizabeth died, and again the following day, when the emperor Josef, his father, breathed his last.

Even weirder was the prophesied fate of Francis' second wife, Maria Theresa who, as a girl in Naples, had been told by a fortune-teller she would marry a widower and die at thirty-four. She married a widower. In 1806, as her thirty-fourth birthday loomed, she fell ill. Self-fulfilling prophecy? With Napoleon's armies threatening, she had to be moved from the castle at Olmutz. Everyone thought she was dying, but then she rallied, improving so remarkably that by the end of December she joined Francis at

Holitsch, there safely celebrating her thirty-fourth birthday.
In March the emperor went to war, leaving her behind expecting their eleventh child. At the imperial palace of Schönbrunn on the night of 5 April 1807, the White Lady was seen by several people, including Countess Wrbna, Maria Theresa herself, and her five-year-old daughter Marie-Louise. The empress fell ill the following day and died a week later, just two days after the birth of a daughter.
Which came first, the ghost, or the expectation of the ghost? Childbirth was frequently fatal in those days, and Maria Theresa had been weakened not only by having to endure the fear of a prophecy that she would die before she was thirty-four, but by having already borne ten children.

An even stranger saga began in 1854, with the old empire nearing its end. Up mountain roads from Munich to Ischl one day came a carriage with three women in it, a mother and her two daughters. The archduchess Ludovica, aunt of the emperor Franz Josef I and sister of Bavaria's eccentric Ludwig I, was escorting her elder daughter, Helene, to be married to her imperial cousin. All the way Helene had grumbled. She had had no say in the arrangement and was not looking forward to being empress of the Austro-Hungarian empire.
This did not disturb the archduchess. What the girl wanted or did not want mattered less than the fact that she had to do as she was told. Not that Ludovica was wildly enthusiastic about the marriage herself. It had been engineered by the archduchess Sophia, her nephew's scheming wife, who had also enforced the abdication of Ferdinand, Franz's senile old uncle. On that occasion, Ludovica knew, the *Turnfalken* had been seen over the fortress of Olmutz. She hoped they would keep away from Ischl.
Still, the match made sense, maintaining ties between Wittelsbach and Vienna in a time when, everyone knew, the empire was creaking at the seams. How to rule eight million Germans, twice as many Slavs of one nationality or another, five million Hungarians, five million Italians, two million Romanians – it was more impossible every year. The Napoleonic Wars and the 1848 Year of Revolution had left the empire almost bankrupt. An uneasy new world was dawning. The empire's unity mattered more than Helene's sulks.
But as for Sisi, her young daughter. *Elizabeth* . . .
Ludovica felt sudden apprehension. *Why did I bring her?* she wondered. For sixteen-year-old Sisi was becoming more vibrant and excited the higher they went. She loved this beautiful freedom from the plains, and her smile grew brighter as Helene sank deeper into gloom. One sulking with downcast eyes, the other so full of herself and her joy at being alive! Sensing her mother's gaze, Sisi turned and gave her such a beautiful tomboy look as the carriage lurched round

another bend that Ludovica had to smile too.

When they reached Ischl, however, Ludovica's apprehension proved to be well-founded. The moment His Apostolic and Imperial Majesty set eyes on cousin Sisi he fell for her, hook, line and sinker – and for the first time in his life ignored his mother. The archduchess Sophia was furious, but there was nothing she could do. Franz and Sisi were married at Saint Augustine's in Vienna on 24 April 1854.

Overnight Sisi became the empress Elizabeth of Austria, consort of the ruler of Europe's largest, oldest empire. But Sophia was determined to destroy the marriage, doing all she could to make Sisi miserable, removing her babies at birth so that they might be 'suitably reared', encouraging the loveliest ladies at court to play with her son. And Franz, a Hapsburg to the core, was not slow to accept their invitations. Sisi grew miserable and isolated, ignoring the rumours passing from courtly mouth to courtly ear, that both the White Lady and the *Turnfalken* had lately been seen.

Just about her only friend was Marguerite Cunliffe-Owen, a member of her inner circle, whose anonymous biographies of Franz and Elizabeth, *A Keystone of Empire* and *The Martyrdom of an Empress*, later became world-famous.

Marguerite describes how one autumn they spent several weeks holidaying in Brittany, far from the gossip and misery of court. Everyone knew about Franz's affairs and, though he had remained considerate and kind, Elizabeth's pride could not stomach the endless humiliation. For the rest of her life she travelled Europe relentlessly, always incognita, always shadowed by the Austrian Imperial Police, and later by M. Paoli of the French Sûreté.

Anarchy was in the air, and no crowned head was safe.

Her protectors failed in their duty only once.

On this occasion in Brittany, when the empress was recalled to Vienna, Marguerite stayed behind to finish her holiday. One November afternoon she was out riding on the desolate Quiberon peninsula when, outlined against the sunset, she saw a white figure swaying back and forth on the edge of a rocky precipice. She checked her horse so sharply that it reared: by the time she had it under control and looked again, the figure had vanished.

She went to bed later than usual that night because of a ball held at the *château*, and was wakened in the small hours by what she thought was the chiming of her bedside clock. Then a slight rustle alerted her, followed by quiet, rapid footsteps . . . The moonlight filtering through the window showed her the same phantom she had seen that afternoon, only more clearly, and now she recognised the empress! Aghast, she watched the phantom sadly point at its breast, and saw several drops of blood ooze from a small, triangular wound.

She telegraphed the empress immediately. Elizabeth replied saying she was in good health. On returning to Vienna, Marguerite said nothing about the shocking apparitions. Others attached to Elizabeth's suite also often saw both White Lady and *Turnfalken* during the years of her endless European travels.

But fatal tragedy struck Elizabeth's only son before it struck her. Prince Rudolf had grown up unsettled and unstable – not surprising, given his upbringing and genetic background. On the night of 30 January 1889 he met his lover, Countess Maria Vetsera, in a hunting lodge deep in Mayerling forest. They knew they could never marry. She was a countess, but nevertheless still a commoner. They agreed there was only one solution.

That evening the *Turnfalken* were seen and heard, flying screaming out of a blood-red sunset before wheeling to the south towards the forest. That the White Lady was also seen is a matter of official record.

A few hours later, the news was out. It caused international horror. Rudolf had shot Maria, then himself. Both were dead.

Now Elizabeth travelled more relentlessly than ever, but the White Lady was never far away. On the night of Elizabeth's forty-fourth wedding anniversary in 1898, in the Hofburg Palace next to the church where she and Franz had married, a sentry saw and challenged a woman in filmy white who carried a lighted taper. She turned, retracing her steps. He followed her down the corridor to the chapel, which she entered. He alerted the other guards. The entire building was searched, but the lady in white had vanished. The sentry, a Styrian peasant, only learned of the White Lady and her doom-laden history when he talked over the event with his fellows. His experience went on the record. Then it emerged that sentries at Schönbrunn had also seen the phantom there, that same night, but an hour later.

One Friday morning five months later, Elizabeth was relaxing on the balcony at the Grand Hotel in Caux, Switzerland, when below her she saw a woman in white, staring up so malevolently that she called for help. The grounds were thoroughly searched, but nobody was found. Again that evening the empress was out on the balcony when a lady in white appeared and sat nearby. The hostility of her stare became so unnerving that the empress once again called for help. But, as before, by then the phantom lady had vanished, and no trace of her was found.

Some days later, on 9 September, at Territet in the Alps, Elizabeth sat on a viewpoint with her English reader, Mr Barker, who had brought along a basket of fruit. He began reading *Corleone*, a novel by Francis Marion Crawford, which concerned the Mafia, and their assassinations of royalty. She was about to hand Barker half a peach when from a nearby pine tree a large raven flew down and round about her head. The tip of its wing knocked the fruit out of her hand and touched her on the forehead. Barker was terrified. He knew what it meant.

At noon the following day Elizabeth left her hotel in Geneva with her lady-in-waiting, Countess Sztaray, to board a steamer to take them up Lake Geneva to Mont de Caux. They were near the quay when the countess heard the clanging of the ship's bell. She went quickly ahead, signalling to the crew not to raise the gangplank before they got there. Briefly Elizabeth was exposed. Luigi Luccheni, an Italian anarchist, ran forward to drive a shoemaker's awl into her heart. He was gone before anyone knew what had happened, though he was soon caught. As Elizabeth was helped to her feet she thought she had been attacked by a pickpocket. She managed to get on board but then fainted. Though the ship put back to shore, the doctors could do nothing and Sisi, once so bright and full of life, died of an internal haemorrhage without regaining consciousness.

The awl had caused a tiny triangular wound from which oozed just a few drops of blood – exactly the wound that Marguerite Cunliffe-Owen had seen disfiguring the phantom of the empress in Brittany years earlier. The *Turnfalken* and the White Lady had done their job.

The ravens had also appeared before Elizabeth's sister, Duchess of Alençon, died in a fire at a Paris charity bazaar, and before Archduke Albrecht's daughter died similarly at Schönbrunn. On the latter occasion the White Lady had been seen as well, though not at the same time.

When Franz Josef's younger brother Maximilian was about to leave Europe with his wife Charlotte to rule Mexico, a raven settled on the roof of his wife's train. In 1867 the White Lady again appeared at the palace of Schönbrunn. Soon the news came from Mexico that Maximilian had been shot by a firing squad. The Mexican people had not liked his rule. Charlotte, meanwhile, had gone mad after trying and failing to save his life.

These tragedies, though, were as nothing compared with the rich raven-pickings yet to come . . .

In 1894, Franz Josef's young nephew Franz Ferdinand fell in love with a Bohemian countess, Sophie Chotek, and though she was as blue-blooded as they come, to the rarefied Hapsburgs she was just another commoner – and Hapsburgs could not marry commoners.

Screaming flocks of *Turnfalken* blackened the skies over the palaces of Hofburg and Schönbrunn at the time, following the imperial suite wherever it went. That they had something to crow about would soon be proved. For, though Franz Ferdinand was sent on a six-year trip round the world, he could not forget the lovely Sophie. At last the emperor, who had once, briefly, been similarly enthralled with Sisi before his mother had put things straight, agreed to allow the lovers a morganatic marriage, which meant that their children would have no hereditary rights at all.

And though the *Turnfalken* were again seen and heard, Franz

Ferdinand and Sophie were married on 1 July 1900, and found what Sisi had not found with Franz Josef: happiness. At least, for fourteen years.

One June day in 1914 Sophie was motoring in Vienna when excitement and upturned eyes amid the crowds along the street made her look up too, and she saw them. The *Turnfalken*, wheeling above in great flocks! Abandoning her plans, she rushed to Konopischt in Bohemia. Bursting into the military conference her husband had convened there, she said the ravens had been seen, and pleaded with him to cancel his trip to Sarajevo.

He would not. Bosnia was in revolt. He had to show himself to rally support before everything was lost there. Besides, he did not believe in the *Turnfalken* and, anyway, he had a bulletproof vest.

Sophie could not dissuade him. So she went with him. In their bright-red open touring car they entered Sarajevo, to drive through the streets. As soon as they started off, a revolutionary threw a bomb. It did no harm.

Though shocked, they carried on towards Rudolph Street. Pistol shots rang out. Both were hit. Both collapsed, dying.

The killing by a student anarchist, Gavril Princip, had been planned in Belgrade. The Serbian press boasted about it. The Austrians, egged on by Germany, declared war on Serbia.

Soon the world was engulfed in war. Millions of people died. As for the Hapsburg empire, it was over. The White Lady and the *Turnfalken* had done their job . . .[1,2]

12   Boning, Taboo and Oriental Curses

A giant leap to the other side of the world, to the Far East and the Pacific, where from India to Japan, Polynesia to Australia, there are tales of curse and taboo; their power or potent belief in their power in many cases established beyond reasonable doubt.

In Australia Dr Herbert Basedow saw a man being 'boned' – having a bone pointed at him as a sign of his approaching death.

> He stands aghast, with his eyes staring at the treacherous pointer, and with his hands lifted as though to warn off the fatal medium, which he imagines is pouring into his body. His cheeks blench and his eyes become glassy, and the expression of his face becomes horribly distorted. He attempts to shriek but usually the sound chokes in his throat, and all that one might see is froth at his mouth. His body begins to tremble and the muscles twist involuntarily. He sways backwards and falls, and after a short time appears to be in a swoon, but soon after he writhes as if in mortal agony and, covering his face with his hands, begins to moan.
>
> After a while he becomes very composed and crawls to his wurley. From this time on he sickens and frets, refusing to eat and keeping aloof from the daily affairs of his tribe.[1]

The only way to avoid sure death is to persuade the shaman responsible to withdraw the curse. Rob, a missionary's assistant in Queensland, was boned by Nebo, an aboriginal sorcerer. Dr S. M. Lambert of the Rockefeller Foundation examined Rob, finding him seriously ill, but with no physical symptoms. Lambert and the missionary went to Nebo and threatened to stop food supplies to his tribe if the boning were not immediately lifted. Nebo went back with them and simply told Rob that the boning had been a mistake. Rob was fully fit and back at work that same evening.

Only suggestion? But, as other cases included here *suggest*, just because it is all in the mind does not make cursing less effective. It is exactly because it *is* all in the mind that cursing or blessing *can* work, and doubtless many a curse is sustained entirely by popular fear of it. Take the Curse of Uluru.

Uluru is the aboriginal name for Ayers Rock, a unique hump-backed oval dome of scarred ancient rock heaving itself, 1,100 feet out of an endlessly flat, arid plain in Australia's remote Northern Territory. A hundred miles south of Alice Springs, it lies right in the middle of Australia, its geographic navel. Local aborigines attribute spirits to various of Uluru's different features, but say these are mostly friendly. They deny there is any curse.

Yet lately tourists have been returning pieces of rock taken from Uluru as souvenirs, asking Alice Springs National Park rangers to return them to their original position, to end the bad luck that owning the stones has brought them. They had been coming back in ones and twos annually, until in spring 1993 the rate of return suddenly surged. One Arizona man sent back a stone with a note: 'Please return it to its place of rest as I have suffered a lot of sickness since I removed it.' He had taken the stone from near a spot where five tourists had fallen to their deaths in the previous fifteen years. And an Australian woman attributes giving birth to a stillborn baby and becoming diabetic to her removal of a stone from Uluru in 1968.[2]

In such cases (see next chapter for the identical Curse of Pele from Hawaii) perhaps knowing of the curse plus feeling guilty at removing stones despite it, is enough to trigger subconsciously self-inflicted bad luck. Perhaps. Yet that theory does not explain the following strange case, involving the Japanese God of Good Luck, Ho-Tei.

As he described in his book *Together We Wandered*, in 1928 C. J. Lambert and his wife Marie saw a statuette of Ho-Tei in a junk shop in Kobe. It was ivory, but they were charged a pittance. Leaving for Manila next day, Mrs Lambert was seized by agonising toothache that lasted throughout the fortnight-long voyage. En route to Australia the statuette was now in Mr Lambert's bags, and he had the toothache. In Sydney, the luggage now in bond, it stopped. With the luggage back in their cabin, it began again, but stopped when the luggage was put in the hold. Back in the USA they gave Ho-Tei to Lambert's mother. Toothache struck her, until she gave it back to them. Only then did they wonder whether the statuette was to blame. They found out it was made from the base of an elephant's tusk, with a tiny hole where the nerve had ended.

A Japanese art expert in London said it may have come from a temple, and have been given a 'soul', in the form of a medallion hidden inside it. An ivory plug in the base of the figure made this seem likely. They left Ho-Tei in a shrine in the shop, no wiser as to how toothache struck whoever happened to carry Ho-Tei – who certainly had not brought them good luck.

They had no idea what they had bought, nor that it caused their toothaches, so suggestion is ruled out. Even odder is how the pain struck only the statuette's owner or carrier, and then only when he or she was near it.

Commenting on the statuette's seeming ability to choose its victim, Colin Wilson mentions the Tibetan belief that objects can be animated by the thoughts of living people.[3]

Another tale that seemingly rules out the possibility of suggestion alone as the active force involved in successful cursing is the story of Raku-nene.

Taken from his *A Pattern of Islands* (1952), and as given in *Fate* (September 1953), it concerns Arthur Grimble, an official in the British colonial service stationed on the central Gilbert Island in the Pacific. At his desk one sultry day he heard an eerie, high-pitched cry, 'a changeless, reedy note of insufferable dreariness'. It seemed to come through the palms from the direction of the lagoon. Following the sound through the jungle, he found a girl of about seventeen outside the native constable's hut. Sitting stiffly upright, her naked body swollen like 'taut silk', she sat staring vacantly into space, the pupils of her eyes hugely dilated. From her mouth, seemingly frozen open, came the eerie, endless moaning. Learning from her family that the swelling had begun just before dawn, Grimble asked in amazement why they hadn't gone for help.

The girl's father shook his head. 'We knew it was useless. Nothing can stop the work of Raku-nene.'

Grimble pressed for information. Reluctantly they told him that Raku-nene, once a mortal man, had since his death become the helping spirit for men seeking the love of women. His speciality was the avenging of rejected suitors, who had to follow a prescribed rite to gain his aid. The angry man had first to get a single strand of the woman's hair, and bind it round his thigh for three days. Then on the fourth day he'd remove it and burn it in a fire of leaves, meanwhile invoking Raku-nene's spirit.

Raku-nene would visit the doomed woman that night in a dream. By dawn her body would begin to swell and she would complain of continual nightmares. Falling silent, she would refuse to wear clothes, then begin to moan, quietly at first but with increasing strength and violence. By the sixth day after the casting of the curse she would have gone totally mad, tearing at her flesh and biting at all who came near. At last, on the seventh day, suddenly she would cry out several times, 'Raku-nene! Raku-nene!' Falling silent then, she would become utterly rigid and die.

Wholly sceptical, Grimble gave the girl a sedative. 'You can't fight a spirit with medicine,' the villagers said, amazed at his ignorance.

The sedative had no effect. Helplessly during the next twenty-four hours Grimble watched as the girl went through every stage described to him. Another day dawned, and the girl screamed out 'Raku-nene!'

– then fell dead. Within ten minutes the body had resumed its former shape, but a look of terror remained fixed on the face.

Grimble witnessed so many other similar cases in the Gilberts that he called the disease 'Raku-nene madness'. Time and again the curse seemed to work. Reluctantly he began to wonder if more than superstition or auto-suggestion was involved. He had to ask himself if indeed the madness might be 'induced by some malicious external agency, working from a distance with the aid of a strand of hair, and an incantation'.

The possibility of auto-suggestion or prior knowledge causing not only the physical disfigurement but the death of the victims seemed to be ruled out by another experience. One year he witnessed the terrible death of a Monouti woman struck down by Raku-nene. About a year later an acquaintance of hers, a man, fell fatally ill. On his death-bed he confessed that he had worked the spell which had killed her. He described how he had fallen in love with her, but she had rejected all his advances, so angering him that, after obtaining a hair from her head, he had performed the rite. Within five days she had died. Firmly insisting to his confessor that she had known nothing about it, he died professing Christianity and believing that he had had to confess his crime for the peace of his soul.[4]

Another tale of a revenge curse (also in *Fate*, December 1962) comes from Indonesia. In 1948 Robert Pierson, a vice consul with the US Foreign Service, was posted as a political and language officer to Indonesia. The political climate was explosive. Guerrilla bands were ravaging the countryside so that few crops could be planted or tended. Starvation and disease were rife.

Pierson and his young wife found a small house in the town of Bogor, one of the worst-hit areas. It lay some ten miles south of the capital city, Jakarta, on the mountain range forming Java's backbone.

It was the Indonesian custom for well-off households to support many servants, from gardeners at the bottom of the pecking-order, to washing and cleaning women, then the cook, and, at the top, the Number One boy, a position which commanded considerable local respect.

Pierson and his wife had already realised that the local people, though outwardly Muslim, still secretly practised their old magical faith, when one day a ragged beggar came knocking at the door, asking for food. Aged about thirty, his name was Djam Hari. Taking pity on him, Mrs Pierson hired him as a gardener at the standard rate: food and wages worth about five dollars a month. For the next two years Djam Hari worked hard so that, by the time the Piersons were posted elsewhere, he had risen up the hierarchy to the position of Number Two boy.

In 1954 the Piersons were recalled to Jakarta. During their absence

Djam Hari had worked for Americans, who had just been posted elsewhere. The Piersons were glad to hire him again, but had problems in finding somewhere to live. They were still looking for a house when a friend fell ill and had to leave. He offered them his house on condition that they take on his servants. They agreed, bringing Djam Hari with them – but only, to his disappointment, as Number Two boy. The existing Number One boy, an old man called Maroen, had a considerable reputation and to have downgraded or dismissed him would have been unthinkable.

Djam Hari and Maroen did not get on well. For the most part they kept their arguments to themselves, but occasionally the Piersons heard through another servant that the two men had been fighting again.

About this time a routine medical check-up showed that the Piersons' three-year-old son had contracted tuberculosis. Their doctor at the Bogor clinic soon learned that Maroen was suffering from the disease, and that what Maroen had called 'flu' in his family was TB. His six-year-old daughter, who had died not long before, was exhumed: the autopsy proved it. Releasing him from his domestic duties, the Piersons sent him to a tuberculosis sanatorium.

Within a month he was back, demanding his old job. The Piersons phoned the clinic, and learned that Maroen had refused all treatment, and could not live more than six months without it. They told him sympathetically that they could not possibly retain him; their own son remained very ill. They begged him to return to the sanatorium. He showed no emotion, but his agitation was plain. They could see his heart pounding through his light cotton shirt as he told Pierson it was all the fault of Djam Hari who, he claimed, had hired one of the area's most powerful *dukans* to kill him, so that he, Djam Hari, could take over the job of Number One boy.

Knowing that *dukan* meant sorcerer, Pierson carefully told Maroen that as soon as the sanatorium said he was cured, he could have his job back. Maroen would have none of it. Declaring that what he needed was the help of the most powerful sorcerer in Java, and that the man he had in mind lived in his own village, he bowed deferentially then strode out.

So, by default, Djam Hari became Number One boy. Weeks went by, and nothing was seen of Maroen. The doctor, still trying to check the disease, learned that Maroen and his family had left Bogor. Later, one of the servant girls said he had gone back to his home village, in the Bantam region of West Java, and that he had hired a sorcerer to curse and kill Djam Hari. Perhaps she did not like Djam Hari who, though working flat out organising the diplomatic entertaining the Piersons had to do, had given none of the other servants his old Number Two position – he wanted to do it all himself.

About six months later an Indonesian police officer stopped by to tell the Piersons that he had seen Maroen in Bantam. Rumour had it that the old man was working with a sorcerer, and had been boasting about how soon he would be back with the Piersons, in his old position.

Soon afterwards, after organising a full round of cocktail parties, Djam Hari approached Pierson. He looked exhausted. He said the last few days his strength had been failing and that he had to rest.

'You've been working too hard. Take two weeks off and rest up,' said Pierson, adding that really he should let some of the other servants take over some of his responsibilities.

'It's not the cocktail parties,' Djam Hari said. 'It's my resistance to . . . to other things.' He looked Pierson in the eye and added. 'It's my resistance to Maroen's *dukan* that's wearing me down.'

Incredulous, Pierson heard his Number One boy tell him how in the past few weeks Maroen's spell had begun to work. Djam Hari had told his own sorcerer, who had begun working against the other *dukan*, but if Djam Hari was to survive, he would have to go away and undertake certain protective rituals.

Two weeks later Djam Hari turned up for his wages. Pierson was shocked by his condition. His eyes were sunken, his skin sallow; he was emaciated. Pierson took him to the Bogor clinic, to learn that he was in good physical condition, but highly disturbed emotionally. Acute fear was killing him.

A fortnight later, too weak to pick up his wages, he sent his brother instead. Pierson called the doctor and sent round his own car to take Djam Hari to the hospital. He learned that Djam Hari now weighed only seventy pounds, and was so weak he could consume only liquids. No physical disease was apparent. The prognosis was not good.

That evening Maroen visited, as sallow as ever, with a rasping cough, to tell Pierson he had recovered and would soon be able to take up his post again. Pierson reckoned that the tuberculosis had strengthened its hold.

Two days later Djam Hari's wife paid a visit. She showed no emotion. Her husband was dead. 'Djam Hari wants only to rest in peace,' she said quietly. 'May I please have the money to bury him?'

In his account, Pierson does not say if Maroen recovered, or if there was any evidence that Djam Hari had brought his own fate on himself by hiring a *dukan* to work against Maroen. Djam Hari did know of Maroen's curse, so that the cause of death may be ascribed to a continual, exhausting state of pure terror – which is not to say that no magic was involved as well.[5]

Another odd tale from the Pacific concerns Barney Duffy, an Irish convict imprisoned a century or so ago by the British on Norfolk Island. Some four hundred miles to the north-west of New Zealand's North Cape, this island, though among the most beautiful in the world, has a violent past. The descendants of the *Bounty* mutineers settled there after outgrowing Pitcairn Island; later the British moved rebellious Irish convicts there from Botany Bay. Many of its present residents claim to have seen ghosts, both of the descendants of the mutineers, and of Irishmen hanged by the British.

Barney Duffy was by all accounts a giant of a man. The nature of his crime is unknown, but he suffered along with the other convicts. Singing or possessing tobacco earned a whipping, food was eaten with the fingers, water was drunk from buckets. The only way out was to die.

Duffy managed to escape from the settlement but not from the island, so for some time he hid out in a hollow pine in the jungle, by night emerging to raid the settlement's vegetable gardens. He survived, barely, in rags, with long, matted hair and beard, until one day two young English soldiers out fishing came upon him by the hollow pine. He towered over them, but they covered him with their muskets, and he knew he did not have a chance. Before they took him in to be hanged he cursed them both, predicting they would both meet a violent death before his corpse had been hanging a week on King's Town gallows.

Ignoring this, they arrested him, and he was duly hanged. Two days later they went back to fish at the same place near the hollow pine. They did not return. A search party found their battered bodies drifting in the tide nearby. Who or what had killed them was never known, but even today Norfolk Island maps mark *Barney Duffy Gully*.[6]

A system of magical prohibition which, though found in early cultures the world over, is today generally described by its Polynesian name *tabu*, anglicised as 'taboo', refers to a quality making certain conditions or classes of people, animals, objects, acts or words untouchable or unmentionable. Taboo requires avoidance or performance of specific acts, either because of their inherently sacred quality, or through fear of incurring divine or magical wrath. Certain individuals might be taboo, either all their life (royalty, priests), or for a period (royal barbers, menstruating women, hunters) during which they cleansed themselves of blood or sacrilege. Objects made of iron, or body-parts like the head and hair, were also widely taboo. The idea was that some people or objects have a power that makes them spiritually dangerous to themselves or others, so they must be secluded or insulated. In effect, such people or objects are socially cursed, and have to behave as taboo prescribes for the safety of themselves and everyone else.

So, before and during the chase, hunters or fishermen the world over observed taboos and abstinences lest they offend or scare off the prey. The act of killing incurred further taboos, so as not to anger the ghost of the slain. When the Kayans of Borneo shot a panther they so feared its soul-curse that they would step eight times over its carcass saying, 'Panther, thy soul under my soul.' Returning home they would smear themselves, their dogs and their weapons with the blood of fowls, to calm their souls and stop them running away, and for eight days afterwards had to bathe by day and by night before going out hunting again. During the fishing season the fishermen of the Caroline Isles, whenever on shore, had to spend all their time in the men's clubhouse, and under no circumstances visit their homes or even look at their wives or any other women, or else flying fish would inevitably bore out their eyes at night. They could not even join in song and dance with the other men, but had to remain in silent isolation.[7]

The head and hair were especially taboo and remain so to Buddhists today. From Cambodia to Malaysia, Java to the Marquesas, it was an offence to touch anyone's head. Javanese houses were only one storey high, so that nobody would walk over another's head. A Marquesan father could not step over the head of his sleeping child, women could not touch anything that had hung over the head of their father or husband. When an emey sprinkled water on the head of a son of a Marquesan priest, the boy rolled on the ground in rage and despair, begging to be killed because he had been desecrated and deprived of his divinity. A Maori chief's head was so sacred that if he even touched it, he had to put his fingers to his nose, and snuff up the power they had acquired, so returning it to its source. Hair-cutting was especially complicated, due to the danger of disturbing or hurting the spirit of the head, or of the shorn locks falling into the hands of a sorcerer. When the chief of Namosi in Fiji needed a hair-cut, he had to eat a man first to avert evil. In New Zealand, after a Maori had a hair-cut he had to seclude himself for several days; royal barbers, having touched the sacred head, could not touch food for a day: someone else fed them. A Maori sorcerer would chant a curse over a tress of his victim's hair then bury it. As it decayed the victim wasted away. An Australian aborigine might cut a lock of his unfaithful wife's hair as she slept, tie it to his spear-thrower, and give both to a friend in a neighbouring tribe. Nightly the friend would stick the spear-thrower in the ground before the camp-fire. When it fell down, it meant she was dead. A man of the Wirajuri tribe stated that when a sorcerer 'gets hold of something belonging to a man and roasts it with things, and sings over it, the fire catches hold of the smell of the man, and that settles the poor fellow'.[8]

Taboo was also a way to control the over-mighty, by constricting them with magical prohibitions and ritual. Royalty in particular was hedged by rules amplifying its divine status and emphasising its magical, social and ritual functions. The Mikado of Japan was shamefully degraded if his feet ever touched the ground; so he was carried everywhere on men's shoulders. He could never expose himself to open air; cut his hair, beard or nails; or even clean himself, but was washed at night when asleep. Every morning he had to sit for hours on his throne as still as a statue; his stillness being thought to preserve peace and tranquillity in the realm.

Atop Mount Ago in Togo in the Pacific lived the priest of a wind-spirit called Bagba. Bagba could control rainfall and the winds, which his priest kept bottled in huge jars. Yet, as Bagba's power was so vast, his priest had to spend his whole life on the mountain-top. Only once a year could he descend to market to get supplies, on condition that he entered no house and was back on the mountain-top again the same day.[9]

Such priests and kings were too important and too dangerous to society to be allowed free rein. If they failed in their ritual duties, the land was cursed. Crops would wither, babies die, enemies invade. So too their royal person was taboo. Nobody might touch the body of a king or queen of Tahiti. Even to pass one's hand over the royal head was to risk execution. It was death to touch the king of Siam. When in 1874 the king of Cambodia was thrown from his carriage none of his attendants dared touch him even though he lay injured and unconscious. Royal blood could not be spilled on the ground. In 1688 the deposed king of Siam was executed by being put into an iron cauldron and pounded to death with wooden pestles. Kublai Khan executed his uncle Nayan by wrapping him in a carpet and having him thrown violently about until he died.

As for the taboo on iron, when in 1800 King Tsieng-tsong-tai-oang of Korea lay dying of a tumour in the back, no one thought for a moment of using the iron lancet which might have saved his life. Better that the king die than that taboo be broken.[10]

13   The Kahuna Death-prayer

The mountainous Hawaiian Isles are about as far from anywhere else in the world as you can get. Verdant, actively volcanic, they lie in the Pacific some 2,700 miles southwest of San Francisco, 4,000 northeast of Australia, and nearly 6,000 east of Taiwan and form the northern boundary of the vast Oceanic region of Polynesia. Though far from the Americas, Hawaii is today an American state, rich with the benefits of modern civilisation and Christianity.

Before Europeans 'discovered' Hawaii in 1549, before the missionaries landed in 1820, the Hawaiians infused nature with magic. Their gods might appear as human beings, animals, birds, fish or meteors; live in stones, or take form as ogres, demons and monsters. Their chief god, Kane (the 'Thunderer'), required no human sacrifices, life being sacred to him, but others were less particular. The wizard-god Kahoali enjoyed the eyeball of fish or of man; the evil-smelling squid-god Kanaloa was Lord of the Dead; while Maui the Trickster was entertaining but could not be trusted.

Most violent and unpredictable of all was Pele, fire-goddess and protectress of the volcano Mauna Loa. Pele remains active today. She not only erupts, but curses and afflicts tourists who ignore the local warnings not to take stones from her slopes as souvenirs. If they knew more about her famously bad temper and what happens to those angering her, they would not risk it.

In summer 1977 airline vice president Ralph Loffert of Buffalo, New York, returned home not only with his wife and four children, but with stones from Mauna Loa. Soon after, Mauna Loa erupted. One Loffert boy, Todd, developed appendicitis, had knee surgery, and broke his wrist; another, Mark, sprained his ankle and broke an arm; the third son caught an eye infection, and the daughter lost teeth in a fall. In July 1978 – by now thoroughly alarmed, belatedly believing the warning – Ralph Loffert sent the stones back to Hawaii. Yet the disasters continued . . . until Mark admitted he still had three stones. Once these were returned, the trouble ended.

Allison Raymond of Ontario, Canada, also took stones from Mauna Loa. Her husband soon died in a car crash, her mother died of cancer, her son broke a leg. Back went the stones and that was the end of the problem.

Naturalist John Erickson of Hawaii's Volcanoes National Park says that daily he receives up to forty packages of stones sent back by tourists who laughed at the tale of Pele's curse – before realising that she always gets the last laugh.

But Pele is not the only angry Hawaiian goddess to cast a curse. There is another, and her curse became active only this century . . .

An old Hawaiian legend tells how once a Hawaiian youth saved the life of the Shark God, who gratefully promised that, as long as Hawaiians remained at peace, no shark would ever harm a human being in the local waters.

In time the Shark God fell in love with a beautiful girl who lived on the shores of Wai Momi, the waters of pearl. Changing her into a shark, he crowned her queen of a certain natural harbour. As Shark Goddess, she too now promised to protect people, as long as they remained at peace.

For centuries peace prevailed. Then in 1909 American warships came and violated the tranquil waters. Hawaiians recalling the old pact feared the revenge of the Shark Goddess, but the US Navy, preparing the harbour for its future role as America's Pacific fortress, was not impressed.

One day an old fisherman came with fresh-caught fish as an offering to the Shark Goddess. Diving underwater, he left his offering in the crevice of a submerged rock – her home, he claimed. Talking to the sailors, he heard to his horror that the Americans were going to build a dry dock.

'Shark Goddess get angry!' he warned them. 'Bring plenty trouble!'

They jeered at him, then ignored him, and went on ignoring him. Every day for four years he came with his offerings and warnings. At last, with the dry dock almost ready for testing, he stopped coming. Came the day the pumps began to empty millions of gallons of water. With only a few feet of water left, a huge crowd invaded the dry-dock floor, trying to catch the gasping fish left behind. Suddenly came the sound of cracking cement.

Folk fled as the walls collapsed. In just four minutes, nothing was left of the dry dock but a huge pile of rubble.

The Shark Goddess? Nonsense, said the Navy, and began all over again. Ten years later the new dry dock was ready to be dedicated. The Governor of Hawaii suggested inviting one of the Kahunas, the mysterious priests who had ruled the isles before the missionaries came. It would be courteous, at least. A *kahuna wahini*, or priestess, agreed to attend. As the hour of the ceremony approached, she had still not arrived. An ensign was sent to her home in Waikiki to fetch her. Suddenly, without warning a geyser shot up from the rock where the old fisherman had said the Shark Goddess lived, the rock where daily he had left his offering. It abated, but now the crowd was worried. When the *kahuna wahini* arrived, she knelt down and, tossing crumbs and ashes on the water, chanted ancient incantations. When she was done, she said the Shark Goddess was placated and there would be no more trouble. But still not everyone was so sure.

This time, however, when the pumps had done their work, the dock held.

Then came a collective gasp of astonishment. At the very spot where the old fisherman had so often dived to leave his offering, and from which the geyser had lately spouted, everyone could see the skeleton of a shark.

As for the revenge of the Shark Goddess, this is a matter of history. On 7 December 1941, the Japanese bombed Pearl Harbor. Many ships were sunk, many men died. The war in the Pacific erupted. The pact had been broken . . . and older Hawaiians still claim that true peace will never return to the Pacific until Pearl Harbor is demilitarised.[1]

As for the Kahunas, there are none left.

Many fascinating tales from Hawaii involve the Kahunas (meaning 'Keepers of the Secret'). The Kahunas were the once-dominant magician-priests of the Huna ('Secret') religion, as mysterious in their origin as in their powers, but believed by some to have originated in North Africa, and have had ancient connections with the Berbers of Morocco. The philosophy of these healers, prophets and masters of the death-prayer was profound. Westerners recording their myths soon noticed fascinating parallels with biblical lore. Their Creation myth, for example, told of three gods or principles, Kane, Ku and Lono (Sunlight, Substance and Sound), who shattered space by an act of will to form three heavens. The lowest of these, earth, formed their footstool. On earth, out of spit and red earth, they made Man in the image of Kane, and Woman out of Man's rib as he slept. As biblically complementary was their tale of the Deluge, *Kaiakahinalii*. In it, all men died but for Nuu, (or Nana-nuu) who with his family survived in an ark. When the flood abated, the ark came to rest on Hawaii's highest mountain, Mauna Kea.

How could they have known about Adam and Noah? Because the missionaries told Bible stories which the locals gratefully and promptly adopted, abandoning their own traditions just like that?

Hardly. First, the old legends were '. . . told to the missionaries before the Bible was translated into the Hawaiian tongue . . .'[2] Second, the Kahunas despised Christianity. In 1820 the high priest Hewahewa, far-seeing the approach of what he thought was a band of white magicians, welcomed the first missionaries from New England. Soon he realised their ignorance. He helped them build a temple of cut stone, but still they could not heal or raise the dead, as they said Christ had done.

Outlawed by the Church, the Kahunas spurned this weak, inconsistent faith. It spoke of a Trinity but knew nothing of the Three Souls! Why give up their own superior, ancient tradition, one that conferred real power?

The reality of their power is plain. Into modern times they used their traditional magic. No sane Hawaiian policeman or magistrate dared stop it. Even after the First World War, Queen's Hospital in Honolulu annually admitted many victims of the 'death-prayer'. All died, whatever was done. One Christian minister fought back when his congregation was being prayed to death, one by one. He learned and used the death-prayer to kill his Kahuna enemy. The magician died, the minister's flock returned, but for fighting fire with fire he was cast out of the Church. The Hawaiians understood, however, and gave him land.[3]

This tale is recorded as fact by Max Freedom Long, an American teacher who came to Hawaii in 1917 and died in 1971. Without his work, little now would be known about the Kahunas, by then already in terminal decline, and nothing would be known about the working of the death-prayer.

Max Long was a Baptist and had a degree in psychology. He went to Hawaii to teach but soon after his arrival he grew curious about the Kahunas. Though often rebuffed, he persisted in his inquiry, to hear of gods and goddesses walking among people, such as Pele, who would appear as an odd old woman somewhere she had never been seen before, demanding tobacco which was never refused. He heard of magical healings and deaths; of the future investigated and altered. Though sceptical, he was intrigued, especially by the Kahunas' belief that man has three souls. Long was versed in the early work of Freud and Jung and realised that Kahuna psychology, which had seemed incomprehensible to self-righteous missionaries, not only predated modern psychology by perhaps millennia, but seemingly was more sophisticated.

He learned of the Kahuna belief in *Unihipli* and *Uhane*, a pair of spirits closely united in a physical body. The body was controlled by the stubborn, contrary, grieving *Unihipli* which, acting secretly and silently at an animal level of mind, controlled the body's vital force (*mana*) and also acted as a repository of memories. *Uhane*, the 'talking' spirit, represented the rational, self-conscious ('human') mind or soul. At death, the two spirits separated. Sometimes the unlucky *Unihipli* would be caught by a Kahuna to work against enemies, being sent out to invade the body and suck dry the life force of a victim being prayed to death.

Though the Kahunas believed that man cannot know God any more than a fish can know man, they hypothesised many levels of consciousness above man, particularly the 'high self', *Aumakua*, meaning

'Older, parental, trustworthy spirit'. Through *Aumakua* they claimed that man may command powers like firewalking, prophecy or casting the death prayer.

Long was fascinated. Kahuna lore tied up with Western occult speculation about the physical, astral and etheric bodies. How odd to run into such a similar but ancient system at the far end of the world! And how disturbing, in the questions it raised.

How long ago, and where, had they learned their lore? And did their magic really work? Still without answers after four years, his curiosity led him to Honolulu's Bishop Museum. Here he met the curator, William Tufts Brigham. A polymath with an entry in the American *Who's Who*, this bald, bearded old man of eighty-two heard Long's urgent questions patiently. Then he said that for forty years he had studied the Kahunas to find answers to Long's questions. He insisted that they 'do use what you call magic. They do heal. They do kill. They do look into the future and change it for their clients. Many were imposters, but some were genuine. Some even used this magic to fire-walk across lava barely cooled enough to carry the weight of a man.'[4]

He told Long that he personally had fire-walked under Kahuna protection, but had no idea how it had been done. The boots he had insisted on wearing while fearfully running over a freshly hardened lava-flow had burned right off his feet – but his feet had not even been blistered. The Kahunas who had protected and led him safely across had thought his boots a great joke, a sacrifice to the gods. Long naturally doubted this tale – as Brigham had doubted the evidence of his own experience – but later research convinced him that fire-walking is a fact, though inexplicable by materialistic dogmas alone, being a case of mind over matter.

Warming to Max Long, Brigham admitted how little he knew. He said that Kahuna power was waning; the old knowledge was no longer being passed from father to son. The missionaries, advance guard of the West's materialist flood, had done their work. Even so, he was bewildered by the abrupt and total collapse since 1900 of a philosophical and magical system which was, he was sure, thousands of years old. In the last four years of his life Brigham told Long all he knew about the Kahunas, though he confessed he still had no idea how they worked their magic, save in the matter of the death-prayer (*anana*) which, he said casually, he had successfully practised himself.

Brigham said that to master it, a Kahuna had to inherit from another Kahuna one or more ghostly *unihipili* – subconscious spirits. Or he had to locate such spirits, then use hypnosis to capture and enslave them. In early Hawaii, prisoners of war or criminals about to be executed had sometimes first been hypnotised so that, after death, their *unihipili* separated from their *uhane*, to remain as a ghostly guard at Kahuna temples, or to serve in death-prayer magic.

When, for whatever reason, a person was to be prayed to death, the Kahuna called up his spirits (*kala*) and ordered them to absorb vital force (*mana*) from food, drink and ceremonial objects charged with his own *mana*. He ordered the spirits to catch the scent from clothes or hair taken from the victim, then track the unfortunate.

When they found him, the spirits shocked him with their *mana*, entered him and sucked the vital force from him. This caused an increasing numbness that climbed the body, in three days reaching and stopping the heart.

The Kahunas said the success of such an attack relied on whether or not the victim had a guilt complex over wrongs done to others. Without a sense of guilt, the victim's subconscious mind would beat off the attacking spirits.

If the attack succeeded, the spirits, charged with the *mana* of the dead man, returned to their master, who had ritually cleansed himself to protect against the risk that another Kahuna might not only have saved the victim, but hypnotically ordered the returning spirits to attack their master. Or the Kahuna might simply name the person who had hired him to send the death-prayer as the one responsible, so averting any attack on himself.[5]

Brigham knew of a case in which a Kahuna sending out a death-prayer had neglected to take ritual precautions, so that when a rival sorcerer saved the intended victim by sending back the spirits, the Kahuna died. The rival sorcerer in this case had been Brigham himself.

It had happened, Brigham said, during a plant-collecting expedition on Mauna Loa. He hired guides and animals at a village called Napoopoo and set out with four men and eight horses and mules. But in barren land above the rain forest, near the summit crater of Mauna Loa, one of the guides, a youth of twenty, became ill. Thinking it was altitude sickness, Brigham left him with one man and went on with the other to the summit. Returning at sunset, he found the youth much sicker, too weak to rise. One of the older men told Brigham he thought the boy was being prayed to death. Asked if he thought this was the case, the youth was instantly terrified, denying it. Examining him, Brigham found the usual symptoms of the death-prayer: slow paralysis of the lower limbs and incipient general collapse. One of the guides questioning the youth learned he came from a tiny, out of the way village where the old Kahuna had ordered the people to have no dealings with the *haoles* (whites) under penalty of being prayed to death. The youth had left his village some while back and had all but forgotten the order. In any case, he had assumed that the command held good only in the village.

By joining Brigham, he had brought the death-prayer on himself.

The old Kahuna was apparently powerful enough to have seen at a distance that his command had been disobeyed, and so had sent out the *anana*.

Convinced of it, yet enraged by this vicious attack, Brigham listened when the old guide came to speak. The old man suggested the obvious solution: since everyone knew Brigham was a Kahuna and even a fire-walker, he should save the youth by praying the village Kahuna to death.

Cornered, Brigham realised he had to try it or lose face. All he had to do, he told himself, was to talk the idiot spirits on to his side and get them to attack the priest. Trying to convince himself that it should not be too hard, since the boy was guilty of nothing, he decided to try persuading the spirits that their master must be evil to send them to attack one so pure and innocent. Maybe the Kahuna had cleansed himself lest the death-prayer be returned, but this seemed unlikely; Brigham doubted if the magician had even heard of him. Steeling himself, he stood. 'You all know I am a very powerful Kahuna,' he told the men. They all agreed. 'Then watch me,' he growled.

Standing over the boy he began flattering the spirits, telling them how clever they were, and how sad it was that a Kahuna had enslaved them rather than let them go to heaven as they deserved. He explained to them how good the boy was, and how vile the sorcerer. Finally, ready to command them to go and tear the Kahuna limb from limb, he threw back his head and roared his command so loudly that the pack animals were frightened and even his guides drew back. Three times he bellowed his order. Though exhausted by the mental effort, as he sat down by the boy he kept his mind fixed on the task. For over an hour as the stars came out he continually willed the spirits to obey him. Round about, the air seemed to tremble with furious unseen conflict.

At last, suddenly, he felt the tension dissipate . . . and a few minutes later the youth whispered, '*Wawae . . . maikai*' ('Legs . . . good').

Brigham had succeeded. He wanted to shout with triumph. His legs massaged back to life, soon the youth was up, health and appetite restored.

That was not the end of it. Curious to learn what had happened to the Kahuna, Brigham had travelled for days through the mountains to find the youth's remote seaside village. At last, he told Long, he and his guides reached a valley where an old woman and a girl worked a *taro* patch. Taking one look at Brigham and the boy, they fled, screaming. Entering the empty village, Brigham waited before the big hut where the magician had lived. Soon the youth, sent to call the frightened people back, returned with the tale of what had happened the night Brigham sent back the death-prayer.

The old man, asleep in his hut, had awoken screaming. Rushing out for *ti* leaves, he had begun fanning himself to fight off the enraged spirits. Gasping, he told the people he had neglected to cleanse (*kala*) himself, and that the white magician had got the better of him. Soon, falling to the ground, he lay frothing and groaning. By dawn he was dead.

The youth told Brigham his people feared that the white Kahuna had come to kill them all. Brigham promised them he had already taken his revenge and that, if they behaved, they were his friends. Led by their head man, they emerged from hiding, scared and uncertain, but he reassured them so successfully that for the next few days they fêted him as an honoured guest.

None of them resented his killing their Kahuna. A rebounding death-prayer was one of the occupational hazards of being a magician. Indeed, by the time he left, they had made him their blood brother. Perhaps they were glad he had rid them of the tyrannical old sorcerer.

The one thing he could never understand, he told Long, was why, since by psychic means the Kahuna knew he had hired the boy, the old man had not realised that Brigham was returning the death-prayer. The only explanation was that the priest, unable to read the future, had gone to sleep before Brigham had begun his own magic on the slopes of Mauna Loa.[6]

Brigham rejected all the usual explanations of death caused by curse or similar means, such as the use of an unknown poison (see chapter 15), or that the victims died of superstitious fear. He explained that, at least in Hawaii, the victim rarely if ever knew that he was about to be killed by magic. To illustrate this, he told Long the case of a young red-haired Irishman who came to Honolulu and began working as a taxi-driver.

Not long after his arrival, this Irishman took up with a Hawaiian girl who was soon so much in love with him that she broke off her engagement to a local man. Her grandmother, sure the Irishman was up to no good, tried to break up the affair, threatening that heaven would punish him if he did not leave her alone. But he was a sceptic who feared nobody and believed in nothing and just laughed at her. One day, though, his feet 'went to sleep'. Slowly, during the course of a day in which he was seen by two doctors and ended up in the hospital, the prickling numbness crept up his legs. No cause was found and no treatment worked: after fifty hours the prickling had reached his waist. Several doctors, including a friend of Brigham's, began to suspect that in this mystery illness there was more than met the eye of science, so an old doctor was called in, and he at once recognised the symptoms of the death-prayer.

Questioning the victim closely, the old man learned about the girl, and also about the grandmother's threats, which the Irishman still regarded as nonsense and superstition, and nothing at all to do with his weird illness.

The doctor went to visit the old lady. 'I know you are not a Kahuna and have had nothing to do with this case, Grandma,' he told her. 'But, just as a friend, will you tell me if anything could be done to save the man?'

Agreeing that she knew nothing and that, as he said, she was no Kahuna, she said she thought that if the man would promise to take the next ship to America and never return or even write, he might get better.

The doctor guaranteed all this. The old woman agreed.

At first the paralysed victim did not believe a word of it. Only when it was finally explained to him that he was being prayed to death and had less than twenty-four hours to live, did it sink in.

Now terrified, he agreed to leave Hawaii immediately. That was in the early afternoon. By that evening he was on his feet again. That night he caught a Japanese ship to the USA . . . and presumably never came within three thousand miles of Hawaii again . . .[7]

Though now accepting the truth of Kahuna power and knowledge, Long still did not understand their origin. Conventional wisdom said the eleven Polynesian tribes, each speaking dialects of the same tongue, were once a fisher folk driven out of southern China by stronger inland tribes. They had migrated southeast over the ocean to find their scattered island homes.

This did not explain how, when Polynesians were first 'discovered', they had customs and beliefs also followed in India; or why Polynesian words are found from Japan to Madagascar, and perhaps even further afield. The solution Long came up with seemed too bizarre.

A year after publishing his first book about the Kahunas,[8] Long received a letter from a retired English journalist, William ·Reginald Stewart, who thirty years earlier had travelled widely in North Africa, where he had heard of a Berber tribe in the Atlas mountains that practised magic, and especially of one woman, Lucchi, who maintained the old traditions.

Seeking her out, he persuaded her to teach him the secret wisdom.

In Berber, an adept in this wisdom was a *quahuna*. A female adept (in Hawaiian, *kahuna wahini*), was (in Berber) a *quahini*.

Lucchi told him how once twelve tribes had lived in the Sahara when it was still fertile. But the rains failed and the rivers dried up, so eleven of the tribes had moved east, to the Nile Valley where, Lucchi claimed, they ruled Egypt, using *quahuna* magic to build the Great Pyramid. They foresaw a dark time coming, one in which the secret magic might die. To preserve it, they decided to find isolated lands, and using their far sight, they located the empty isles of the Pacific. Setting out from the 'Red Sea of Kane', soon they had vanished. The

Berbers had no idea what had happened to them.

Now only Lucchi understood the old magic language. Studying with her, Stewart learned many of the same things that Brigham learned in Hawaii. He learned how to store vital force in stone, wood, water and the human body; and in the invisible body of a 'ghost'; also how such force could be used to move heavy objects. He learned about potent elemental spirits inimical to man, and the careful ritual needed to avoid harm in dealing with such spirits. But one day Lucchi was shot and killed during a fight between two raiding parties and Stewart had to give up his apprenticeship.

Thirty years later he read Long's book, in it recognising many terms as being the same as in Berber, but for dialect differences.

Hawaiian lore tells how once, in a land far away, by psychic sight the Kahunas saw Hawaii, and set out to find it. From the Red Sea of Kane they left in large double canoes, progressing from land to land until at last their scouts reached Hawaii. Bringing with them trees, plants and animals, the rest followed. For centuries the secret lore was preserved in its pure state. When the royal blood line ran out, a voyage was made to the other islands to find and bring back a prince of the old lineage. He brought with him a Kahuna who introduced a regressive belief which commanded idol worship and temple building. This contaminated form persisted until the coming of the *haoles*. Even so, the old practical magic had been preserved, including the knowledge of the death-prayer.

14 Africa: The Tale of Isaiah Oke

It is now widely agreed that the human species originated in the south and east of Africa, the so-called dark continent, somewhat more than one and a half million years ago. Today this vast continent, with over a thousand different languages (not counting dialects) and many religions and beliefs, remains bewildering in its cultural diversity. The Western image of Africa is still confused.

Africa seems, even today, to be a continent full of ancestor-worship, magic, witchcraft and witch doctors, sorcery and evil spirits; of curse, charm and fetishism; of ancient superstitions only barely overlaid by a thin veneer of nineteenth-century European colonial attitudes, modern American Coca-Cola imperialism, and the influence of Islam and Christianity. But Africa is where we all began, and thus where we might expect to find many of the oldest beliefs that characterise human culture.

There are specific African belief-systems concerning sorcery and magic not found anywhere else, such as the concept of *mangu*, found in Zaire and the Sudan. It is said to be a phosphorescent witchcraft substance that kills, and exists as an organ or liquid located somewhere in a man's upper abdomen near the bile tract. It is physical in itself but has a spiritual component which the sorcerer, while asleep himself, may send out to devour and vampirise the spirit of an enemy.

There is no English word for such a concept or organ.[1]

The procedures of death-curse do not appear to vary much from continent to continent. From Kenya in East Africa comes a tale which has been recorded by the psychiatrist Dr John C. Barker, which concerns the senior dresser at a medical centre. He learned that one of his staff at an outlying station was selling off the centre's supplies for personal profit and disciplined the culprit, but soon after found himself bewitched. He told the centre's doctor his strength was failing. The doctor found himself helpless, until one day the victim came to him with a bundle of sticks and leaves.

'This he informed me was the witch doctor's spell and he said that if it were opened there would be found in it some object that at some time had been part of his body: hair, nail-clippings or even a tooth extracted years before. The little bundle had been found over the entrance to his hut. Every time he passed under it the spell would exert its baleful influence.'

Barker does not describe what body part was in the bundle but tells how, summoning all the dressers from the outlying stations, the doctor first threatened them, then cajoled them, but to no effect. So he went to his dispensary and prepared a revolting, evil-smelling, but otherwise harmless concoction. He then told the dressers they must all take the medicine. It would not harm the innocent, but the guilty one would be struck down dead. Only one man refused to take it. 'I then told him I was going to make him take the medicine by force and that it would undoubtedly kill him.'

At this the man confessed. He was given twenty-four hours to arrange for the witchdoctor he had employed to remove the spell, and did so without delay. Thereupon the senior dresser, who had been growing obviously weaker day by day, began to recover immediately, and was soon well again.[2]

Another tale, from Zambia, as told to the Christian evangelist Derek Prince by a missionary friend of his who had lived all his life in central Africa, concerns a General Conference of Christians held in a remote rural area. After one particular service an elder from a local village church came forward in tears, trembling all over, confessing to the sin of killing a fellow elder by witchcraft. He explained that for years he had been fighting this man, who was senior to him. At length the situation had got so bad that he had gone to a witchdoctor and asked him to curse the senior elder. Having demanded and received a large down-payment, the witchdoctor had told the elder to come back the next day. The elder had done so, and found the witchdoctor sitting under a tree with a mirror in his hand and a bowl of witchcraft medicine on the ground before him. Sponging the medicine all over the mirror, the sorcerer had asked the elder to look carefully at the mirror and describe what he could see. The elder was startled to see the face of his enemy; it was quite clear. At this the witchdoctor took a razor blade and cut across the throat of the face reflected in the mirror.

Horrified, the elder saw blood instantly cover the mirror. 'You have killed him!' he cried out. 'I only asked you to curse him.'

The witchdoctor laughed. 'I thought I would do the job properly while I was at it.'

Hurrying home, the elder found, to his shame, that his fellow elder had just collapsed and died, of an inexplicable haemorrhage.

Terrified by what he had done, the elder had kept quiet about his crime until, at the church service, his conscience would not allow him to remain silent any longer, and he had come forward and confessed his sin.[3]

White people, supposedly not superstitious, have also been the victims of inexplicable sorcery, which seems to negate the insistence that curses work only because they create a self-fulfilling death-wish.

In 1949 in Rhodesia (now Zimbabwe), a witchdoctor was sentenced by the High Court in Salisbury to be jailed for two years for illegally practising his craft. At this he just shrugged, but when the judge ordered that all his charms and medicines be destroyed, he lost his temper, screaming out a curse that lions would return to the streets of this modern city, in which lions had not been seen for half a century. Just three weeks later, a pride of lions – an adult male, an adult female and three almost fully grown cubs – were seen crossing a street just two miles from the city centre. Some days later, in full view of a horrified family on the verandah of their house just a mile from the centre, the pride attacked and killed a tame goat.

This was just the start. After dogs and cattle had been slaughtered, a hunt was launched, and poison was put down, but with no success. The lions moved away, and were next seen sixteen miles away at Mazoe, where they made two kills at a farm. The two hunters waiting up for them only managed to kill, by mistake, a pedigree bull which had wandered over to investigate the bleating of a goat staked out as bait. After this the lions were never seen again.

Even stranger was the case involving Adrian Brooks, a young graduate who in 1942 was appointed Government District Officer at Kasama in Northern Rhodesia (now Zambia). Kasama was the administrative headquarters for the Wemba tribe. Brooks learned from a tribesman of the existence of a sacred burial ground, which no white man had ever visited, where Wemba chieftains were interred. The ancient rite involved placing the chief's body in a royal hut, where it was watched until the flesh rotted from its bones. The skeleton was then buried in a seated position, a hand sticking out of the ground and held upright by a forked stick so that passers-by could shake it and greet the dead chief.

The sacred grove was guarded by two old witchdoctors, but Brooks, a keen amateur photographer, brushed aside their angry protests and started taking photographs, showing such lack of reverence that he irritated the guardians. As he left they told him he had angered the spirits and would soon be dead. Unworried, when he got back to Kasama, Brooks joked about the curse. But three days later he was standing outside his office when the flagpole crashed down and killed him. The official report said that termites had eaten away the base of the pole, which fell just as Brooks happened to be standing under it.[4]

One of the most fascinating modern accounts of African sorcery, published in 1989, is given in the ghost-written (or maybe ghost-*ridden* would be more appropriate) autobiography of Isaiah Oke, a Yoruba *babalawo* or juju priest from Ghana in West Africa. He was born in a mining camp in the 1930s, when Ghana was still called the Gold Coast, and was initiated into the inner secrets of the juju religion at an early age. The word *juju* may come from the creole French *joujou*, 'toy', inferring amulets worn to protect against evil spirits, or from the Hausa spirit *jigo* or *jugu*, the 'father of the hunters'. Either way, as Oke explains, the essence of juju is ritual blood sacrifice or killing, to appease or gain the aid of ferocious spirits, the *Orishas*, who 'ride' their human 'mounts' until ecstatic collapse results.

Oke insists that the higher juju spirits demand the blood not just of animals but of human beings; that human sacrifice persists in Africa – he describes participating in such a ritual, Death by the 'Two Hundred Cuts' – and that this practice, of gaining spirit-power by shedding and drinking human blood, has spread to the USA. He gives graphic examples, and blames the spread of AIDS on such practices.

Unfortunately, his claims appear to be not so fantastic, but are supported by other evidence.

Describing how many Africans, though nominally Muslim or Christian (thus his own first name, Isaiah), still secretly believe in juju, Oke tells how, as soon as he had been baptised, his father took him to the local *babalawo* for juju ritual. A *babalawo* is a junior priest who can lay curses and cast spells, but who cannot, unlike a *babalorisha* or high priest, speak directly to the *Orishas*, who number four hundred and one.

The *babalawo* to whom he was taken was a friend of his grandfather, Awore Oke, who was a *babalorisha*, chosen by the *Orishas* themselves.

Inspecting the infant Isaiah, the *babalawo* concluded excitedly that an important demi-god, Orisha-Oko, said to be the ancestor of the Oke clan, had been incarnated in the boy. Isaiah's father was stunned. His grandfather recognised that it was the will of the spirits that Isaiah would be the clan's next *babalorisha*.

Throughout his early years Isaiah enjoyed the fearful respect awarded to an infant *babalorisha*. When he was five he went to Nigeria, to the Yoruba village of Inese-Ile, to live with old Awore Oke. He never again saw his father, who had always been terrified that his son, the infant god, would curse him. But life was not easy. Because Isaiah was his grandfather's heir, he was hated by his cousin Joshua who, as a seventh son of a seventh son, had expected to become a *babalorisha* himself.

Joshua, who was five years older, tried to hex him. Isaiah fell ill and nearly died. Everyone said Joshua, already strong with juju, had been responsible.

When Isaiah recovered, his grandfather decided he must learn to read and write, so that in time he would record on paper the whole of juju knowledge. So Oke learned to make the 'talking leaves'.

Years passed. When he was thirteen and having already received his secret name at birth, he underwent his initiation. For days and nights, secluded in a hut, he was kept awake and terrified. A python was thrown on to him, then a net was pegged over both snake and youth. For six hours he endured this ordeal. He drank rooster's blood and met the spirits, the *Orishas*, both light and dark. He drank more blood, and was fitted round the loins with the blood-soaked *ibante*, or power-garment. This he would have to wear for the rest of his life, in the utmost secrecy. He would be cursed if he undressed in front of anyone, even a doctor, or if he undressed, even alone, in the light. When in time he married and coupled with his wife, she would have to wear a hood, so as not to see his power-garment.

His initiation complete, he returned to Inesi-Ile armed with the power of his new knowledge. Now he had defences against the evils of life; now he was a man, and was greeted as such. For the first time, amid dancing and feasting, he slept with a woman, Rebecca Abanogu. Next day, she did not recognise him: she had lain with a 'spirit-man', not Isaiah Oke. Grandfather told him that any woman would be honoured to give herself to *Orisha-Oko* and this Isaiah soon found to be correct. But his cousin Joshua was jealous of Isaiah's new power, and that night at the festival a remarkable thing happened.

Joshua became possessed by an *Orisha*. He turned into a feeble old man. He broke sticks from a tree and made them into crutches. His back became hunched. He hobbled. With every step he seemed to grow older. A mangy dog jumped round him, eyeing the sticks as if expecting a game of 'fetch'.

Everyone recognised what had happened. Babalu-Aye, the father of all the *Orishas*, was riding the youth. Grandfather greeted him fearfully. 'Great Babalu-Aye, how can we appease you? Is our ceremony not pleasant to you? Are the animals we sacrificed not . . .'

Amid the public circle, Babalu-Aye said he approved of the ceremony, but that he had curses to cast on some people present. He turned slowly, sweeping his crutch. People cringed as it passed them. It came to rest, pointing at a blacksmith from whom Joshua had bought some pots, only later to complain about their poor quality.

'That one,' said Babalu-Aye. 'That one is a cheat. His right arm will wither up and will no longer know its former cunning with metals.'

The blacksmith fainted. Nobody went to help him.

'That one.' Now the crutch pointed at an old woman who sat on her porch all day insulting passers-by. 'That one's tongue has condemned her. She will die. Tonight. Even before the moon rises.'

Next, the crutch stopped at Rebecca Abanogu.

'That one is a harlot. She dishonours the people of Inesi-Ile. She too will die.' Rebecca started crying. People moved away from her. 'But first, her beauty will decay. She will become a hive of open sores, so that no man can look upon her and hold his eyes open. Flies will breed in her body and fly out into the world through her sores. And when the flies have consumed all of her that they wish, then she will die.'

Then Babalu-Aye, alias the jealous Joshua, turned to Isaiah. 'And *that* one . . .', he shrieked, 'THAT one . . .'

At that moment the mangy dog grabbed one of the crutches. The *Orisha* tumbled into the fire, which all *Orishas* hate. And it was Joshua who leapt out, howling. Nobody paid Joshua any more attention. The *Orisha* was gone and Joshua was just Joshua again. The joy had gone out of the festival. Rebecca Abanogu and the blacksmith were helped home. The old woman stayed, but suddenly shrieked, and fell stone dead. The festival was halted.

Grandfather Aworo Oke dealt with the curse on the blacksmith with the paralysed arm. Calling on *Ogun*, the god of metals, to observe the cure, he laid three copper coins on the blacksmith's paralysed arm, lit a white candle and waved it over the arm, then walked round the victim nine times, and finally asked the blacksmith to extinguish the candle by spitting on it. 'As you have extinguished this flame, so I extinguish your pain,' he declared, then spat on the blacksmith's arm, pronouncing him cured.

Rebecca Abanogu's condition was more problematic. Within weeks she had lost weight and was disfigured by festering sores. Grandfather made Isaiah poke at one of the sores until it burst. He saw a swarm of flies buzz out and managed not to faint.

'This is serious,' said Grandfather. 'An evil spirit of extraordinary power and malignancy is inside her: she has been possessed.'

The complex cure required the sacrifice of a billy goat. Its blood, mixed with green juju-water, was poured into Rebecca's sores and rubbed into her body. Taken into the juju shrine, she writhed and exposed herself.

'She is with her "heaven husband" now,' said Grandfather calmly. 'What you see now is "spirit rape" – what we call "*oko-orun*".'

Grandfather decided that the spirit possessing Rebecca was Esu, closest of the *Orisha* spirits to the Christian Satan. Esu was sought out for help in all evil purposes, such as calling down an *epe* (curse) on a neighbour. As the old man chanted and shook his rattle, Isaiah felt the shrine grow cold. He heard a man's deep voice demand to be left alone. The exorcism proceeded until Esu acknowledged his name. Isaiah saw and felt a freezing vapour emerge from Rebecca's mouth. Growing scared as the argument between the *babalorisha* and the evil spirit continued, Isaiah fled the shrine, which was only a hut. The exorcism took four days. Voices of men and animals were heard screaming and shouting.

At length the old man and the young woman emerged from the hut. They supported each other, exhausted. Rebecca had recovered, but she was no longer young. She looked sixty, not twenty. Her hair had fallen out, her once-firm breasts sagged, she was dumb and never spoke again. But the sores were gone and she lived for another ten years.

As for Grandfather, after the battle with Esu he was never the same again. He aged rapidly. Later it became obvious he had the 'slim disease' – the African name for what in the West is called AIDS.

Isaiah's education continued. For the first time (he was fifteen now) his tutor, Mr Olungwe, introduced him to the Bible and the Koran. But Grandfather had other forms of instruction in mind. One day the old man told him that, if ever he were to be a *babalorisha*, it was time he learned more. So he was to go to the big city, Lagos, to study with Doctor Drago, the famous 'devil doctor of Lagos'. It was said that Doctor Drago did not only speak to the spirits, he *commanded* them, and he was believed to be the incarnation of Esu. So Isaiah caught the bus to the big city.

At least three million people lived in Lagos. Isaiah had never seen anything like it. Doctor Drago's house was huge and white, with glass in every window. After his first-ever hot bath, Isaiah met the wealthy 'devil doctor', who was elegant, bespectacled, and wore Western clothes.

For two months Isaiah studied and ate well. He worked in Drago's *ile-agbara*, his specially built Power House, labouring over the sacrificial killing table. Made of stainless steel and imported from Sheffield in England, it had little gutters cut in it so that blood and other bodily fluids could drain away. A lot of blood flowed down those gutters, but all of it was animal blood – until one day a motorcade arrived in the compound.

Jeeps full of armed, uniformed soldiers flanked a huge black American limousine. Bringing up the rear was a white ambulance, red crosses on its sides. Out of the limousine stepped a vast man in military uniform, his chest full of medals. His uniform was not of the Nigerian army. Isaiah was surprised to see that Doctor Drago, who called the giant 'Colonel', seemed humbled. The Colonel spoke in English as men in white suits removed from the ambulance a body strapped to a stretcher. The body was hidden by a sheet, but Isaiah saw movement under it, and heard muffled noises.

Two hours later Isaiah was called to the Power House. Drago and the Colonel were already there, two soldiers behind them; both visiting dignitaries wore white, the juju ritual killing colour. 'You will do the killing, Isaiah,' Doctor Drago told him, adding casually that this ritual was called *iko-awo*, meaning 'spirit-slave'.

Isaiah had never heard of it. Then he saw, tied to the killing table behind them, a skinny, naked white man, gagged by a tennis ball stuffed in his mouth. He had been kidnapped by the Colonel's men.

The ritual, the 'Two Hundred Cuts', was meant to be as brutal and inhumane as possible – the greater the pain, the greater the power attracted. And so the *Orishas* would bring the Colonel wealth and political power.

Only the last cut, the two-hundred-and-first, would kill.

At the scalpel's first touch, the white man urinated on himself. But this touch of the blade was just to cut the thong holding the tennis ball in his mouth. The captive did not realise that this was so that his screams of pain and fear should attract the curiosity of the *Orishas*. The greater his pain, the more receptive his body would be to the spirits.

'Yes,' Doctor Drago gleefully told the white man. 'I think you will make a very strong messenger for the Colonel. You will go to the spirits in pain. They will hear you above all others because your pain will be so great. You will plead for good fortune for the Colonel.'

The torture began. Very, very slowly, the white man was skinned alive. Isaiah vomited when told to grasp a cut flap of flesh and pull it off. The white man kept fainting, but each time smelling salts revived him. For three hours the doctor cut, Isaiah pulled, and the white man screamed, even as the Colonel kept telling his hapless victim that the purpose of the ritual was to ensure the *Orishas* would help him to take control of his country. He knew it would take ten years but he was ready to wait. He kept repeating this so that the white man should remember it and tell the spirits.

So the white man become the Colonel's *iko-awa*. Isaiah was told to make the final cut, across the throat. Afterwards, he always told himself that by then the white man was already dead. The entrails were discarded, save for the liver, which the Colonel put in a plastic box, which had a blue flower on its side and a matching top.

The skinned corpse, with a big iron hook through its back, was hung up in a sky-blue wardrobe and taken out to the ambulance. Isaiah carried the carton of herbs and spices that the Colonel would apply weekly to the carcass until, in about a year, it would be fully ripe.

Then the Colonel's motorcade left for the airport and the trip back to a land in the east. In due course he became the dictator of that land. In his account Isaiah does not say who the Colonel was, but perhaps, just perhaps, the land in the east was Uganda.

Isaiah was ill after that; he could not keep his food down. He began to have doubts. He remembered the Bible and the Koran and the Western books his teacher, Mr Olungwe, had shown him back in Inesi-Ile. He began to feel guilty, especially after another human sacrifice that involved a new-born child. Perhaps Doctor Drago, who seemed to see such rituals as chores, not atrocities, really was an incarnation of Esu. Isaiah said he wanted to leave and Doctor Drago agreed. Isaiah went back to Inesi-Ile. He was a man of knowledge now. He had been away four months and hundreds turned out to welcome him home, but he did not stay long. Grandfather Awore Oke, who seemed much older and skinnier than ever, declared that Doctor Drago had recommended that Isaiah learn more about Western ways. He was now to be sent to the Normal College at Oyo, to learn about the white man's juju.

The dilapidated, prefabricated college which had opened just after the Second World War at least offered the chance of a formal education. Isaiah shared a mobile home with seven others. As soon as he got there he let it be known that he was a powerful *babalawo* who could manufacture charms that guaranteed good grades, success with women, and money from home by the next post. He even restored the potency of one of his professors, the ancient Honourable Omo. For nearly three years he was the campus celebrity, but soon after he began his last term an event occurred that opened his eyes – and which, incidentally, provides one of the few moments of light relief in this entire dark tale.

One evening in the cafeteria he and his friends were teasing freshmen, insulting the youngsters, especially the women, with juju signs and curses. Most of the newcomers were frightened, but one of the girls looked scornful, not scared. She glared and spoke without being spoken to, in English but with an odd accent.

'Woman, you forget yourself!' said Isaiah.

'Stop calling me "Woman"!' she demanded.

It turned out that her name was Janet, and that she was American. She was offensive, not respectful, and kept interrupting shamelessly. Isaiah ordered her to apologise for her behaviour.

'Drop dead, creep!' she said, and then left.

His friend Simon squeezed his arm in fear. 'You heard her? "Drop dead," she said. It is an *epe*, a curse on you!' Simon urged him to turn this American girl's curse back on her.

The first curse Isaiah put on her was only a mild one. Calling on *Olofin-Aye*, the *Orisha* controlling famine and food, he sacrificed a pigeon, thrust two needles into its stomach, transferred one pin to a piece of fruit, buried the carcass, and left the fruit on the burial spot to rot.

This 'belly curse' was meant to produce the symptoms of food poisoning, but after some weeks Janet, who lived not on campus but in town with her father, still seemed well enough. When Isaiah and Simon next saw her in town, Simon went up to her. This time she not only told Simon to 'Drop dead', she also shook her finger in his face. Simon, fearing what might happen to him, asked Isaiah for protection against this American juju.

Isaiah laid a more powerful curse on the girl, and this time let her know what he had done. A monkey was sacrificed, and its bloody paw tied to the doorknob of her house. It was meant to make Janet go blind.

It did not work, it only made her angry. She confronted him with the monkey's paw. 'Is this your idea of a joke, you creep?' She shook it in his face. 'I've asked around and they tell me it's more of your stupid juju.' Throwing it in his face Janet went on: 'I don't want any more of your juju junk. I'm a good Christian girl, so save it for somebody who believes in it, okay?'

For the first time in his life, Isaiah says, he saw the power of courage that comes from an independent will. The girl did not fear him because she did not fear his gods. On the contrary, he had begun to fear her. It was not that he feared she might turn his curses back on him; more that he had begun to fear that none of them might work.

He decided it was time to use the power that frightened even him. He went back to Inesi-Ile in secret. Hiding in the woods near Grandfather's shrine, he fasted and prayed for three days then, fearfully, went to the mahogany grove where his special spirit, his power, lived inside a hollow tree which, though struck by lightning, still survived.

Climbing inside it, he whispered his secret name, then called on the power of the tree. And he called for hours, but heard no voice in his mind. At last the sun rose; the effects of the narcotic *iboga* root wore off and, for the first time, he saw that the mystical home of the terrible power was just an old, hollow tree.

Isaiah lost his faith in juju. Perhaps he was not a *babalawo* after all, not a god or even a son of the gods.

He returned to the college to find he had been expelled for going absent without leave. He threw out all his juju – it now seemed more like junk than juju – then went looking for Janet.

He found her in the college cafeteria. 'Please,' he said, 'sell me your gods. I will worship them vigorously; I will feed them all their favourite foods.'

She rolled her eyes impatiently. 'There are no gods to "buy",' she said. 'Christians pray to Christ. And Christ is free.'

'Free?' Isaiah was confused. 'Ah! Then he, too, must be an American, this Christ fellow. Is it not so?'

Janet laughed, then advised him to go and talk to a Christian priest called Dr Osborn. And that is what Isaiah did.

He avoided expulsion, studied Christianity and graduated. He returned to Inesi-Ile with apprehension. How to tell Grandfather that he was no longer a jujuman? But it seemed Grandfather already knew. The old man was sad and angry at this betrayal of the ancestors, of the *Orishas*. Isaiah explained his new faith as best he could. Shocked, Grandfather placed him under obligation to go through the entire

village, telling everyone to make ready for a sacrifice the following day
at dawn.

What did he mean? What – or who – was going to be sacrificed?
There was only one possible conclusion.

Fearfully Isaiah started round the village. His old enemy, cousin
Joshua, followed him with a machete, taunting him, making sure he
visited every house. Grandfather had sent him to make sure Isaiah did
as he had been told. At length, Isaiah had taken enough. 'Now
Joshua,' he said, 'prepare for your end. Today may be your last day.'

Joshua just laughed at him. Could Isaiah overcome the best warrior
in Inesi-Ile, outrun the fastest legs, prevail against the strongest arms?

'No, Joshua.' Isaiah shut one eye, looking through the other. 'But
can you stand against the power of . . . *my eye?*'

Suddenly terrified, Joshua dropped the machete, threw one arm
over his eyes, and with the other made the universal sign of protection
against the evil eye. Isaiah hit him in the stomach, then on the jaw,
and knocked him down. He grabbed Joshua's machete, and his
money, and ran for his life. He fled Inesi-Ile and did not return for
years.

Reaching Port Harcourt in south-east Nigeria, he thought of getting
a job as an accountant, but he had left his college diploma back in
Inesi-Ile. Soon he was reduced to begging. For a week he tried and
failed to get work on the waterfront. At last he got a day's work,
scrubbing out the hold of a big cattle barge. Then he got regular work,
as a clerk, and was able to rent a house. He spent two years in Port
Harcourt. He began to forget the past . . . until one day he found a
monkey's paw tied to the doorknob of his house. Someone was trying
to curse him with the same type of curse he had tried to use against
Janet. It was supposed to cause a slow deterioration of the brain,
leading to death. His enemies had found him. He was caught up in a
juju feud again.

When Isaiah got home that night he found blood smeared on his
porch, and the head of a small dog on his sleeping mat. His
employer, who had seemed so modern and sceptical of the old
beliefs, heard about this. Isaiah was fired. He left Port Harcourt
and went inland to the town of Enugu, where nobody knew him.
Months passed. One morning he awoke to find blood and tadpoles
in his water pitcher.

He fled again, north, to the edge of the Sahara, then returned south,
hoping to lose himself in the anonymity of Lagos. Again his enemies
caught up with him. After a day in the factory where he worked he
came back to his room one night to find a dead dog just inside the
door, a rusty iron pipe thrust right through it, in at the anus and out at
the mouth.

At last one day he caught his tormentor at it, casting spells in his
room. It was Joshua! But he was sick. His cheeks were hollow, his

eyes fevered. He had lost weight. He had the 'slim disease'. Isaiah, however, was no longer scared. His old enemy looked ridiculous, laden down by the weight of all his juju: stacks of iron bracelets, a heavy iron necklace, an iron chest-plate – all necessary for the 'iron ritual', in which the essence of the god *Ogun* would be focused in the *ida-agbara*, or 'sword of power'.

Joshua had this sword with him. It was old and rusty. He struck at Isaiah, but only succeeded in burying the blade in the door-frame. When he tried to free it, the blade snapped. Then suddenly Joshua collapsed. Either it was the disease catching up with him, or hysteria caused by the breaking of the sacred juju relic but, whatever the cause, his lungs stopped working. He lay there, gasping. He took several minutes to die, starving for oxygen.

Taken before the magistrate, still in shock, Isaiah was fined ten *kobo* – about the same penalty as for a parking ticket. Everyone understood what had been going on. Later, word reached him that Grandfather had died, with a juju curse for Isaiah on his lips.

It was a year before Isaiah dared go back to Inesi-Ile. The place had changed during the years of his absence. There were strangers. There was prostitution and public drunkenness. The slim disease had spread. Theft was now common. Even his own mother, whom he had not seen in years, blamed Isaiah for the new confusion, saying it was his denial of the ancestors, of the *Orishas*, of juju, which had brought all the misfortune.

He had, after all, once been regarded as a god. His apostasy, which he had seen as a personal matter, had affected many more people than just himself. In losing his own faith in juju, he had damaged the faith of many others. He was publicly accused of theft. 'Theft of *what?*' he demanded.

'Of our juju,' the furious villagers told him.

He was lucky to escape being lynched. He realised, though, that the charge was true. He admitted it: he wasn't a god, just another poor, struggling mortal.

The old ways of blood-rite and juju could not be brought back. Or could they?

Isaiah's subsequent travels in the West led him to a controversial conclusion.

Isaiah believes that the AIDS virus, prevalent among both women and men throughout Africa, is spread by exposure to raw blood. He notes that men, women and even children in Africa drink blood – human as well as animal – as casually as Westerners drink cola. He claims that Western doctors and scientists refuse to acknowledge the possibility that juju blood rituals are responsible for the pattern and frequency of AIDS in Africa, 'because they refuse to accept that human sacrifice is as common in Africa as I say it is'.[5]

Describing how heated Western liberals become at the notion that he might be telling the truth, Isaiah asks why Haitians – who practise voodoo, the New World offshoot of juju – are so susceptible to AIDS. He offers several recent examples of ritual killings as reported in the Nigerian press during 1987 and 1988, and warns that such practices have begun to spread among the urban populations of America and other Western lands.

He tells how, on 6 October 1988, in the USA, he watched a television chat-show, chaired by Geraldo Rivera, on which self-confessed satanists – all white, educated, middle-class young Americans – admitted proudly and in public to the practice of rituals that involve blood sacrifice and the consumption of human flesh and blood, in order to gain magical power.

Certainly, the interest in such rites is increasing in the West, as the lurid 1991 bestseller by American novelist Bret Easton Ellis, *American Psycho*, suggests all too horribly.

15 Voodoo, Fugu and Zombie Resurrection

Voodoo. The very term conjures up vivid images of secret midnight rites conducted in tangled groves deep in the hills of the West Indian republic of Haiti; of devotees possessed by spirits dancing to the rhythms of endless drumming; of unfortunate victims cursed and killed by sorcery, then resurrected from their graves as shambling, soulless 'zombies', and set to work as slave-labour by those responsible for their dreadful fate.

The reality is both more and less fantastic. Voodoo is not just an isolated cult, but a system of beliefs embracing the relationship between nature, man and the unseen forces that order the cosmos. Its devotees ask for the satisfaction of basic needs, a remedy for ills, and hope of survival.[1] As such it is the popular religion not just of Haiti's rural peasantry, but of the urban population up to the highest levels. The late Haitian dictator, François Duvalier ('Papa Doc') wrote a serious study of voodoo, and it was rumoured that he used black magic against his enemies. Certainly it was used against him, as his father's skeleton was once stolen from its grave.

But nowadays the practice of voodoo is not limited to Haiti. Call it voodoo or juju, or (as Isaiah Oke defines it: 'The religion that is believed to give power through blood'), its darker elements appear to be spreading in the USA, imported initially by Haitian refugees congregating in Brooklyn and Miami, and since taken up by other groups as black magic or satanism.

On 1 September 1988, the Cable News Network reported that the remains of sixteen animals had been found in plastic bags in a park in Newark, New Jersey. The remains included chickens, dogs and a goat – minus its head. A few days earlier the Chicago television station WGN reported that an apartment in the city had been used as a 'holding pen' for sacrificial animals. Dozens of animals including pigs, goats, dogs and chickens were kept there in their own filth until sold to jujumen or voodoo *houngans* (priests) for sacrifice.[2]

More horrific yet, on 11 April 1989 in Matamoros, Mexico, Mexican and US officials found thirteen human bodies in nine crude graves on a ranch near the US border. They included the mutilated corpse of Mark Kilroy, a twenty-one-year-old University of Texas student who had vanished a month earlier from the border town of Matamoros. The other bodies had also been mutilated. Fingers, limbs and genitals had been severed. Faces had been disfigured, and brains scooped from skulls. They had been killed by a drug gang led by twenty-six-year-old Adolfo de Jesus Constanzo, alias 'El Padrino', the Godfather.

Constanzo had been born in Miami to Cuban expatriates, though his father soon abandoned his mother Delia. The daughter of a Cuban priestess of Palo Mayombe, the dark side of the old Cuban slave religion called Santeria, she had turned to the old magic to make a living. In 1983 she moved with her son to Mexico City. Working as a male model, the handsome youth studied under a major *santero*, learning the rituals of human sacrifice. Entering the drug trade and gaining control of his own gang, Constanzo viewed such sacrifice as 'a magical shield' to protect him from the police. Extending his operation into the US, he had ordered the kidnap and sacrifice of an 'Anglo', the spilling of *white* blood supposedly offering better protection against *white* policemen.

So Mark Kilroy was kidnapped and ritually slain. After the bodies were found Constanzo fled with his 'high priestess' Sara Maria Aldrete and other followers. Cornered three weeks later by police in a Mexico City apartment, Constanzo screamed 'Let's all die!' as he burned wads of money on the gas stove, then persuaded his lieutenant Alvaro de Leon Valdez to shoot him and his lover Martin Quintana. 'I think they must have been possessed by the devil,' said Mark Kilroy's Irish Catholic mother Helen. 'That is the only explanation for what they did. I pray for all of them.'[3]

This insane tale makes Isaiah Oke's account of Doctor Drago's gruesome *iko-awo* rite (see previous chapter) more comprehensible – or does it?

On 29 January 1978 in Youngstown, Ohio, Alice Hicks, said by neighbours to have been a 'witch', died in unexplained circumstances. Detective Mike Gilboy removed from her house a six-inch doll wrapped in ribbon. Its head was turned backwards, a thorn pierced its back, and there was a two-inch needle through its chest. The accidents started to come thick and fast.

The day that Detective Tony Cafaro put a piece of paper in Gilboy's desk, where the doll was kept, he slipped on icy steps and suffered spinal injury. Detective Joseph Fajack, who rode to work with Gilboy, fell sick for the first time in twelve years. Detective Clarence Greene went down with pneumonia. Lieutenant Don Malleske caught flu for the first time in twenty years. And Patrolman Sam DuBose, who had taken home some of Mrs Hicks's voodoo books, contracted a dental infection, and had to have all his top teeth removed.

As for Gilboy, a week after taking the doll he almost choked to death on a pepper seed. The following day he pulled a shoulder muscle; a month later he suffered a double hernia and a torn groin muscle. In March he caught Russian flu. Finally he was pushed into a swimming pool and broke his neck and back.

On 10 June Detective Steve Krispli moved the doll from Gilboy's desk to an evidence locker. Four days later he was hospitalised with severe chest pains. Finally, Lieutenant Sabatino burned the doll on 16 June 1979.

'My feeling was that this had gone on long enough,' he said.[4]

These events happened not in Africa or Haiti, but in the heartlands of the Midwest; not to 'superstitious primitives', but to American cops.

Lethal voodoo also seems to have developed an extensive hold not only in the big cities but throughout the American South. The first report detailing the research into voodoo deaths conducted by Professor Kenneth M. Golden of Little Rock, Arkansas appeared in *The American Journal of Psychiatry* in 1977. By 1982 he had amassed more than a dozen cases of voodoo hexing, several fatal.

One involved a thirty-three-year-old man caught up in a love triangle. 'He was confused, agitated, and almost delirious on the ward,' Golden reported, 'necessitating bed restraint and large doses of chlorpromazine. All neurological findings, including a brain scan, proved normal. The patient died two weeks later of cardiac arrest. The autopsy provided no basis for the failure.' His wife said the 'other woman', who was known to cast spells, had hexed him.

Another man, aged thirty-six, whose wife had 'throwed at him' when he left her for another woman, became 'emaciated, dehydrated, apprehensive, unshaven, his hair long and matted'. This case, though, Golden managed to cure by giving the man a placebo, at the same time telling him emphatically that it would work. In effect, Golden countered black magic with white magic.[5]

Such cases once again seem to prove that 'it is all in the mind' – which only shows just how strange, vulnerable, imaginative and powerful is this invisible entity the very existence of which behaviourists deny.

One case from North America involves a black woman aged twenty-two who, in Baltimore City Hospital in August 1966, gave birth to a baby girl, then went into a steady decline which doctors from John Hopkins University could not understand. She was overweight but seemed perfectly healthy. Then, three days before her twenty-third birthday, she told her doctor the story of her birth, in a remote area of the Okefenokee Swamp in Georgia. On the day she had been born – Friday the 13th – the local midwife had delivered three baby girls, then told the mothers that all three girls were hexed.

The first would die before she was sixteen, the second before she was twenty-one, and the third before she was twenty-three. As predicted, the first died the day before her sixteenth birthday, in an accident. The second, thoroughly relieved to get to twenty-one without disaster, went out to a saloon to celebrate . . . but as she walked through the door she had been hit and killed by a stray bullet.

After telling this story to Dr Gottlieb Friesinger and his colleagues, the third girl developed a galloping pulse and heart irregularities. There was nothing they could do. The day before her twenty-third birthday, convinced she was doomed, she began to sweat profusely. By nightfall she was dead.[6]

It is all further proof, if further proof is needed, that blood-rites are less uncommon in the 'civilised' West than one might hope, and that in many a case of hex-death the fear of the victim is enough to *kill.

But, yet again, sometimes there is more to it than that. For the rest of this chapter we follow the strange adventures and remarkable discoveries made in Haiti in 1982 by a young American ethnobotanist, Wade Davis.

Before narrating his tale, however, some background . . .

Voodoo is associated with trance-inducing dance and chant bringing about ecstatic states and possession by the *loa* (voodoo deities), and is notoriously connected with the use of sorcery to curse and kill enemies, and especially with the macabre creation of *zombies*, the walking dead, whose master is the sinister Ghede (or Baron Samedi), lord of cemeteries and black magic. Wearing a black top hat, a long black tailcoat, and dark glasses, he waits at crossroads to guide souls to *guinée*, land of the dead. His chief ceremony, on All Souls' Day, provides protection from creatures like the *loup-garou* (a red-haired female vampire that makes incisions between the victim's toes), and the *baka* – sorcerers who take on animal form and prowl by night, seeking victims to devour.

Ghede is also God of Love, and thus partner of Erzulie, the love goddess. Powdered, perfumed, fabulously rich and generous with her gifts, she weeps for the brevity of life and love.

In 1947 US film-maker Maya Deren, working for *Life* magazine, joined in a voodoo dance and was possessed by Erzulie. She felt a numbness creep up her legs: what she called 'a white darkness – its whiteness a glory and its darkness a terror'. Flooding her body, it threatened to explode in her skull. Inwardly begging for mercy, she heard a shrill chorus crying 'Erzulie' in her mind even as she fainted. Later the *houngan* told her she had been 'mounted by Erzulie'. Deren came to see voodoo as an authentic religion with its own ethical values. In *Divine Horsemen: the Living Gods of Haiti* (1953), she insists that voodoo differs from other religions in that, in trance, the voodoo devotee *becomes* a god or goddess. Each devotee not only has direct contact with the spirits, but actually receives them into his or her body.[7] As Wade Davis points out, voodoo is a 'quintessentially democratic faith'.[8]

The Catholic Church has failed to persuade voodoo devotees that voodoo and Catholicism are not complementary. 'The things of the Church are always affairs of magic,' one devotee told an anthropologist, unanswerably.[9] Yet at least one aspect of voodoo practice has always excited both the horror and disbelief of Christians who assume the higher morality of their own faith. No matter that Christians assert the resurrection of the flesh or that once the Church burned thousands of women alive at the stake – the belief that voodoo sorcerers can reanimate the newly dead, turning them into soulless slaves called zombies, still retains its power to shock.

The term 'zombie' comes from the African *zumbi*, which in the Congo means 'fetish' or 'enslaved spirit'. It refers to individuals who, though physically alive, have lost their souls, or had them 'caught' by a magician, and who thus cannot distinguish between good and evil. Such loss is usually seen as the result of sorcery. The Zulus of Natal, saying such people *walk zombe*, tell of two brothers, Sipo and Vamba. Vamba became sick and aged prematurely, and soon died. Sipo buried him, though his body was still pliable; a proof of sorcery. Next morning the grave was open and the body gone. Sipo tracked down the sorcerer and came to a farm where men worked without song or animation. Among them was Vamba, grey-faced and mute, his tongue slit. Sipo took him home, but soon he died, and this time *rigor mortis* did set in.[10]

Among the Fon of Dahomey zombie also refers to the python-god Da. In modern voodoo usage the *loa* Damballah is called on to animate the corpse. To prevent this, and also because of the common ancient fear of premature burial, the relatives of a newly dead person may 'kill' the body a second time, by knifing the heart or severing the head.

How to be sure if a person is dead or not? Two millennia ago the Roman senate banned burial until the eighth day after death. In the nineteenth century, the Russian Count Karnice-Karnicki was at a funeral when screams arose from the coffin as the first spadefuls of earth landed on it. Terrified of this happening to him, he invented a device to prevent such a fate. It involved a large glass ball being placed on the chest of the 'dead' person. If this ball was moved by the 'corpse' breathing, a spring was released and the coffin lid flew open. If the coffin was already buried, a flag sprang up above the box, a bell began to ring, and a lamp ignited, while a tube admitted oxygen into the coffin. This apparatus was hailed as a technological breakthrough.

The Victorian fear of premature burial was intense, due not only to the difficulties of diagnosing death, but to a growing realisation that certain drugs or techniques may induce a state of suspended animation indistinguishable from death.

Wade Davis went to Haiti in search of such drugs or techniques. What he found, however, was more ambiguous and less clear-cut than he had hoped.

In *The Serpent and the Rainbow* (1985) Davis tells how in 1972 he came to Harvard University to study anthropology. In 1974, bored with academia, he decided to collect plants in the Amazon, and sought the aid of Professor Richard Evans Schultes, an ethnobotanist who had spent thirteen years in Amazonia, studying the Indian lore of medicinal plants. Schultes advised him to undertake a similar expedition and, before Davis left, suggested that in the jungle he should experiment with *ayahuasca*, a hallucinogenic plant. Arriving in Colombia, Davis joined an expedition to cross the Darian Gap: 250 miles of roadless rain forest separating Colombia from Panama. Led by the British aristocrat Sebastian Snow, who had just walked the length of South America, this rainy season expedition almost ended in disaster. The Kuna guides lost their way, Snow twisted an ankle, they ran out of food, and grew totally exhausted. In a delirium one morning, Davis saw a jaguar leap from the jungle before him. Following the direction in which the jaguar vanished, the exhausted men soon stumbled across a trail leading to the Pan-American Highway and to safety. For Davis, this chance meeting with the jaguar seemed to affirm nature's benevolence.

After further travels in South America and northern Canada, Davis graduated in anthropology and in 1977 Davis returned to Harvard to work with Schultes.

Early in 1982 Schultes asked Davis if he could leave for Haiti in a fortnight and referred him to Dr Nathan S. Kline, a pioneer in the field of psychopharmacology, the study of the effects of drugs on the mind. Kline's research had led to the development of reserpine, a tranquilliser derived from snakeroot, a plant used in Vedic Indian medicine for millennia.

In his Manhattan apartment Kline told Davis of cases of people in Haiti who, though their death certificates existed, were known without doubt to be still alive. One such was a man called Clairvius Narcisse, who had died officially in 1962, but who now was back with his family in the Artibonite Valley in central Haiti. Narcisse and his family, Kline explained, claimed that he had been a victim of the voodoo cult and that, immediately after he had been buried, he had been removed from his grave as a zombie.

In spring 1962 he had entered the emergency ward of the Albert Schweitzer Hospital at Deschapelles in the Artibonite Valley. Complaining of fever, he was spitting blood. On 2 May he was pronounced dead by two doctors, one American. His sister Angelina notified his family; an elder sister, Marie Claire, had arrived to witness his death.

Clairvius had been buried the following day in a cemetery near his village of L'Estère. Ten days later his family had erected a concrete memorial slab over his grave.

Eighteen years later a man walked into the L'Estère marketplace and, approaching Angelina, introduced himself by a boyhood nickname known only to Narcisse's immediate family. Claiming to be Clairvius, he said he had been made a zombie by his brother due to a land dispute. Resurrected from the grave, he had been beaten and bound, then led away north by a team of men. For two years he had worked with other zombies until, the zombie master being killed, the slaves had dispersed. He had wandered the land for sixteen years until at last, hearing his brother was dead, he had returned home.

This case, Davis learned, had become famous via a BBC documentary based on Clairvius' story. Davis was sceptical. Kline suggested that a drug had caused the apparent death, and that this drug had so reduced the victim's metabolic activity that, once buried, he had survived without oxygen until exhumed and enslaved, even though by then the higher brain functions controlling character and will had largely been destroyed. Kline said he had failed to obtain such a drug, but a BBC correspondent had given him a brown powder of unknown composition which reduced metabolic activity in rhesus monkeys.

Davis at last realised what was being asked of him: to discover the formula of the poison that creates zombies. But what he found out was not so simple or scientific . . .

What sort of poison might it be, he wondered, and how was it applied? The BBC had suggested a powder sprinkled at the threshold of a door and absorbed by the feet. Whatever it was, it had to be incredibly potent, the first dose being capable of causing catalepsy. Also, its source had to be a plant or animal found in Haiti. The only such plant he could think of was one neither he nor Schultes had dared try – datura, 'the holy flower of the North Star'.

He knew that Yaqui sorcerers of Sonora in north-west Mexico (see next chapter) sometimes anointed their feet, legs and genitals with a salve of crushed datura leaves, so achieving the sensation of flight.

And once, in Peru, he had watched a *curandero*, a healer, drink a decoction of *cimora* (the 'tree of the evil eagle', datura's closest botanical relative). He had seen the man foam at the mouth, start convulsing, and wail in agony before collapsing. Davis did not feel like trying it himself.

Before going to Haiti he heard of three kinds of datura growing there. One of them, *Datura stramonium*, the Haitians called *concombre zombi*: the 'zombie's cucumber'. He also heard that West African women breed beetles, feed them *Datura stramonium*, then use the faeces to kill unfaithful lovers; also that an antidote to datura poisoning, physostigmine, comes from the Calabar bean, a climbing vine native to just those swampy coastal regions from which the Haitians' eighteenth-century ancestors had been sold to European slavers by the brutal Efik tribe of traders.

The Efik had been ruled by a Leopard Society, which had judged criminal cases by making the accused drink a potion of eight Calabar beans ground in water. Sedating the spinal cord thus causing muscular collapse, this decoction kills by asphyxiation. When the accused were visibly affected by the poison, they were told to walk to a line on the ground ten feet away. If they vomited before reaching it, they were innocent. If they got to the line, they were likewise innocent, and given an antidote made of excrement mixed with water used to wash the genitalia of a female. More usually, they convulsed and died horribly. Many slaves who later reached Haiti had been imprisoned by the Efik, and would have known of the ordeal of the Calabar bean.

It all seemed to add up. In April 1982 Davis flew to the Haitian capital, Port-au-Prince, armed with Kline's introduction to Lamarque Douyon, the psychiatrist who had the reputed ex-zombie Clairvius Narcisse in his care, and with the names of two contacts given him by the BBC: Max Beauvoir, a Haitian intellectual and noted authority on voodoo, and Marcel Pierre, the voodoo *houngan* from whom the BBC had got their sample of the reputed zombie poison, and whom one of their correspondents had called the 'incarnation of evil'.

Tall, debonair, and fluent in several languages, Max Beauvoir met Davis at the airport of Port-au-Prince, a poor, semi-tropical sprawl.

After questioning Davis closely about his previous work and background, the first thing Beauvoir explained was that the making of a zombie lies not in the poison but in the power of the *bokor*, or sorcerer. 'This is a land where things are not the way they seem,' he added cryptically.

That first night in Haiti, Davis attended a commercial voodoo ceremony in Beauvoir's *hounfour* (temple). For ten dollars anyone could attend. The drumming began; the *hounsis*, or initiates, responded, bodies twisting and swaying. In time the big drum, the *maman*, broke the rhythm, then returned in jazzy counterpoint. Amid waves of sound Davis saw a tiny woman, one of the *hounsis*, thrashing desperately to retain the rhythm. He saw her look up to the sky; he saw the moment the *loa* possessed her; with his own eyes he saw her race round the temple and swing large men off their feet as if they weighed nothing. He saw her swallow glass and tear a live dove to pieces with her teeth. He saw other *hounsis* likewise possessed.

He had never witnessed anything so raw and powerful. For half an hour there was pandemonium, until the *loas* departed and the *hounsis* collapsed.

This, Beauvoir told him, was the ritual of the *Rada*; friendly domestic gods, the old gods of Africa. But now came the *Petro*, a new race of gods reflecting all the fury and violence by which the Haitians had thrown off slavery and seized their freedom from the Europeans. This dance sent one of the *hounsis* rushing into a fire at the base of the *poteau mitan*, the centrepost of the temple. For what seemed ages she lay on the fire, but then burst away, screeching like a raven. Lasciviously she licked a burning faggot, then took a red-hot coal between her lips, spinning about the *poteau mitan* three times before collapsing, the red-hot coal still in her mouth.

The ceremony over, Beauvoir's sixteen-year-old daughter Rachel, one of the *hounsis*, white dress wet with sweat, came up to Davis. In perfect English she said: 'The *loa* are strong. Fire cannot harm them.'

Next day she took him north to the town of Saint Marc. Here he found the *houngan*, Marcel Pierre, a tall and intimidating voodoo priest who had built his *hounfour* behind the bar he owned. Davis was taken into the *bagi* (inner sanctum) and shown a sample of the reputed zombie poison, a coarse, light brown powder. Davis bargained a price for it, so long as he could see it being made, and could collect raw samples of each ingredient. He watched Marcel grind up the ingredients, which included a human skull. Davis paid the agreed sum, and left with a powder he was sure was useless. But he was also convinced that Marcel Pierre knew how to make the real poison.

The uselessness of the powder was confirmed that night by Max Beauvoir and four other *houngans* in Port-au-Prince.

Finding a species of datura planted as an ornamental tree in the hills above Port-au-Prince, Davis visited Lamarque Douyon, the psychiatrist who had publicised the case of Clairvius Narcisse. Douyon, who had graduated from Canada's McGill University in the 1950s, thought datura the basis of the poison, applied as a powder scattered by the threshold of a door, and absorbed through the victim's feet. Davis wondered how the *bokor* ensured that only the intended victim suffered. Also, while respecting Douyon's definition of a zombie as someone who, having been poisoned, buried alive, then revived, manifested symptoms of incoherence and catalepsy, he wondered why they became victims in the first place. Psychiatric definitions did not explain the social background leading to the creation of zombies. Douyon blamed random criminal activity, but Davis doubted this, especially after hearing about and meeting Francina Illeus, a zombified woman known as 'Ti Femme'.

Declared dead in 1976 after a short illness, in 1979 she had been found in the market at Ennery by a Baptist missionary, Jay Ausherman, who had sent her to Douyon. Malnourished and mute, she had made a partial recovery, but her family would not accept her when Douyon had tried to return her to her home village. Douyon said this was because they could not afford to feed a useless person, yet Davis had already seen how Haitians cared for their old and sick. Francina meant more to her family than another mouth to feed.

Why had she and Clairvius been turned into zombies? Davis knew now that in voodoo society there are no accidents. The *bokors* and *houngans* exercised power, but were not irresponsible. As moral and religious leaders who guaranteed a philosophy regulating social order, they could not afford to be capricious, or act without ethical purpose. Nobody else would put up with that.

Davis interviewed Clairvius Narcisse, who seemed alert and physically fit. The elderly and white-haired Narcisse explained how in 1962 he had argued with one of his brothers, a *bokor* who coveted land he had been working. He said his brother had passed the magic to him one Sunday, and that by Wednesday he was dying. Denying the use of poison, he insisted that the *bokor* had sent for his soul. Conscious throughout the ordeal, he recalled his sister weeping as the doctor pronounced him dead. During and after burial, he had seemed to float above the grave. Disinterred, beaten, gagged and bound he had been led north to a sugar plantation. Here with other zombies he had worked daily from sunrise to sunset, pausing only for a single meal. Salt was prohibited. Though aware of his predicament and missing his family, he had existed in a dreamlike state, without will or conscious purpose. Until one day another zombie, enraged at being beaten for rebelling, had killed their master with a hoe. Thus set free, Narcisse had stayed in the north. Letters to his family had gone unanswered, and only when his brother died had he dared return to his home village of L'Estère. There he had been taunted and threatened. Jailed for his own good, he had come to Dr Douyon, and now rarely went home. He showed Davis his tomb in the cemetery at Benetier. Etched into it was his epitaph: *Ici Repose Clairvius Narcisse*.

Davis wondered how, if the zombie state induces total lack of purpose, any zombie could be disobedient, let alone get angry and violent if beaten. Had Clairvius told the *full* truth? His sister Angelina told Davis how Clairvius, though well off, had refused his brother's loans, and denied all responsibility for the children he had fathered by many women. Suggesting that an angry mistress had sold him to a *bokor*, who had sent a *coup l'aire* (curse), she too denied that poison was involved. Increasingly confused, Davis heard how, when Narcisse 'died', the family had taken his fields.

Angelina and another sister still worked them. Seeing him as a dead man who should have stayed dead, they had refused to give him back his land.

Another relative, a cousin, said what had been involved was not a *coup l'aire*, but a *coup poudre* (magic powder). Asked what was in it, the man said he thought maybe a lizard called the *agamont*, and two toads, the *crapaud bouga* and the *crapaud de mer*. Asked how the poison was applied, he denied that poison was involved – if it had been, Clairvius could never have been revived.

Trying to make sense of it all, suddenly Davis realised that for Haitians, what made a zombie was not a drug but a *magical act*. Moreover, neither Ti Femme nor Clairvius had been made zombies at random. Hated by those around them, both had been tried and condemned by the councils of the voodoo secret society, the true masters of Haiti.

When is a poison not a poison? Davis wondered. By now he was totally confused. Was something wrong with his Western world-view? That a zombie poison existed he was sure, just as he was sure that Marcel Pierre knew how to make it. But there was more to it than just a poison. Other, 'magical' factors were involved.

Davis had to revisit Marcel Pierre, though by now he had heard how, in the 1960s, this *bokor*, a follower of the dictator François Duvalier, had been a notorious member of the Ton Ton Macoute, a rural militia used by Duvalier to create a reign of terror. After extorting secrets from traditional *houngans*, Marcel had himself been poisoned, and had barely survived. Now, though some claimed he was a genuine *houngan*, others maintained that he was a charlatan, a *malfacteur*, an evildoer. Yet Davis knew he had to win this man's trust.

Returning to him with Max Beauvoir, Davis told him to his face that the poison he had made was useless. Enraged, Marcel produced a white bottle. Davis grabbed it from him. Pretending to pour the brown powder it contained on to his hand, Davis wiped his hand on his trouser leg.

'Sawdust,' he said contemptuously.

Briefly silent, Marcel fell back, then told Max Beauvoir in a matter of fact way: 'He is a dead man.'

'Tell me, then,' asked Davis, 'when shall I die?'

'A day, a week, a month, a year.' Marcel added, 'You shall die from handling that powder.'

This, Davis later learned, was the true poison. Both to conciliate and tempt the *houngan*, he said he knew Marcel could make the real poison, but that if he went back to New York with a fake, Marcel would lose the chance to get rich. Proving himself unafraid, Davis slowly gained Marcel's respect.

One night, Marcel and his assistants led Davis to a grave on a knoll. From it they dug up the corpse of a baby girl. This, said Marcel, was the poison's vital ingredient. Three nights later, having coated the exposed skin of all present with an oily emulsion, carefully he put the shattered remains of the child's skull in a jar. From his sack he removed two newly killed lizards and a large toad, also recently killed. This Davis recognised as *bufo marinus*, whose glands secrete a potent hallucinogenic poison.

In a mortar Marcel put the fruits of various plants, all toxic. Finally out of the sack came two fish – one of them the highly toxic puffer or blowfish, source of the chemical tetradotoxin, though it was only later that Davis learned about tetradotoxin and its history.

The bones of the child which Marcel had burned almost to charcoal, followed these gruesome ingredients into the mortar.

Marcel's presence, Davis guessed, ensured everyone's safety. He was protecting them not so much from the *physical* danger of the toxins, but from the *spiritual* risk they ran simply by being involved in such ambivalent black magic activity. He was both malevolent sorcerer and benevolent healer; he served both darkness and light – there was ultimately no distinction between the two.

Asked about the poison's reputed antidote, Marcel said that the *bokor* alone revived the dormant zombie, by calling out the victim's name above the grave. Yes, he agreed, there *was* an antidote which, properly prepared and used, counteracted the poison, but the chemicals were only part of the magical process. They could not work outside their social context.

Davis obtained the antidote. Later chemical analysis, however, only deepened the mystery. The antidote consisted mostly of chemically inert ingredients. Also, it was meant to be used according to a specific timetable. If a victim was aware of having been poisoned within the previous few days, the antidote worked simply if rubbed into the skin. But if the attack had occurred more than a fortnight earlier, the antidote had to be augmented by an elaborate ceremonial in which the victim was symbolically buried alive.

Davis the ethnobotanist had work to do. Returning to Harvard with his specimens and ingredients, he had now to decide how they combined, which were the most active, and whether they had to be ingested or would work if applied externally. Soon he ruled out both datura and the Calabar bean – but the toxins from *bufo marinus* and the puffer fish proved essential.

The glands on the back of toads have long been exploited as reservoirs of toxic compounds which may either kill or cure. Roman matrons used toad venom to poison their husbands. The Choco Indians of Colombia milked toads for an arrow-tip poison so potent that even big cats like jaguars survived only ten minutes after being hit. For centuries, Chinese doctors formed this poison into smooth dark discs called *ch'an su*, 'toad venom'. Used to treat many ailments, *ch'an su* was analysed early in the twentieth century and found to contain two heart stimulants, bufogenin and bufotoxin, each fifty times more potent than digitalis which is extracted from foxglove and has been used as a cardiotonic in Europe since the tenth century. As little as half a gram of bufotoxin applied intravenously to a grown man quickly produces massive, fatal heart failure.

Another toxin derived from *bufo marinus*, bufotenine, had long been used as a hallucinogen by New World folk. It produces convulsive muscle spasms and delirium by barring oxygen from the bloodstream. The berserkers, naked warriors of old Norse legend, may also have attained their condition of frenzied battle-fury by ingesting bufotenine.

The symptoms of Clairvius Narcisse at the time of his reported death, Davis noted, included both cyanosis (bluing of the face due to oxygen starvation) and paresthesia (tingling sensations). *Bufo marinus* toxin was certainly a part of the zombie poison. But another compound was also required, one which so reduced the body's metabolic rate that the victim would appear to be dead – and would stay apparently dead – until exhumed and revived.

This turned out to be a nerve poison, tetrodotoxin, extracted from the liver of the *crapaud de mer*, or sea toad, known in English as the blowfish or puffer fish. Five hundred times strong than cyanide, this poison was known to the Egyptians and Chinese almost 5,000 years ago. The poison is concentrated in the fish's liver, its potency varies seasonally, and nothing can save anyone eating the liver or eggs, but by 1596 Chinese sophisticates ate blowfish as a delicacy, despite the risk of paralysis and rapid death.

Even today, the Japanese find the eating of what they call *fugu* the ultimate aesthetic experience. The task of the *fugu* chef is to reduce the concentration of the *fugu* poison while retaining its exhilarating, euphoric after-effects. But sometimes, as with any dangerous drug, things go wrong. The risk is part of the thrill.

Tetrodotoxin (by which, incidentally, James Bond, secret agent 007, is poisoned at the end of *From Russia With Love*) is the core of the zombie poison. Typically, its victims remain fully conscious until shortly before death or apparent death. Seemingly dead, they may be buried for up to seventy-two hours yet still make a full recovery if disinterred.

Those who do recover, like Clairvius Narcisse, or like many *fugu*-eaters in Japan, remember everything that happens after the paralysis sets in. The senses are unimpaired, though life seems to have left the body. In such a state, you might be buried alive, and survive – for a while. In such a state, you might even be resurrected – as a zombie.

Marcel had told Davis that the poison was never put in the victim's food. That way it killed, and quickly. But, if applied to the skin or to open wounds, or if inhaled, it produced catalepsy indistinguishable from death. Those thus cursed and cast out of Haitian society for their crimes remained functional after their revival, but as zombie slaves.

Is it odd to suggest that the voodoo solution to crime fits the society in which the creation of zombies is practised? If Davis is correct, then zombies are people who so offend their society that they are cast out into the ultimate prison, death in life. Then they are 'revived' to work for other people.

Is 'civilised' indignation appropriate? Many prison regimes in the West (and elsewhere), are equally harsh. It is not unknown for convicts, in the USA and elsewhere, to be used as guinea-pigs for new drugs. LSD-25 was unknown in the USA before being tested by prison doctors in the early 1960s. Ironic, that such experimentation backfired. LSD became a 'recreational' drug, now available everywhere, despite its illegality.

Voodoo *bokors* such as Marcel Pierre at least acknowledge the power of the forces they work with; and function in a society acknowledging such power.

If there is a mystery about voodoo, it lies not only in its practices, but in our Western refusal to admit that traditions going back millennia can and do sustain a wealth of practical wisdom not only about matters of life and death, but about the nature of the human will – and imagination.

16 Rosalio Moisés: A Yaqui Life

For centuries the Yaqui people of north-west Mexico have clung to an arid, heat-bleached land between the Gulf of California and the Sierra Madre. Until recently few outside Mexico except anthropologists and historians had ever heard of them, or of their massacre by the Mexican army between 1887 and 1926, or of how the survivors fled over the US border to *barrios* in Tucson, El Paso, and other shantytowns. They were just another lost *indio* tribe; always poor, persecuted first by Spain, then by Mexico.

Yet, though accepting the Jesuit mission system in the seventeenth century, the Yaqui had resisted Mexican culture, sticking to their own language . . . and to a magical world-view that regards sorcery as pragmatically as we regard a trip to the supermarket. They adapted Christianity to their own needs.

Thus it was in Belem (Bethlehem), one of the eight Yaqui *pueblos* (settlements) established by the Jesuits, that Jesus was born, the Yaqui claim. And belief in Christ did not disturb traditional belief in witches and wise men (*sabios*) and healers (*curanderos*); in evil *sierpas* (giant beasts lurking deep underground, once people who committed incest or other sins), or *coludas* (seven-toed coyotes who lead men to buried treasure); or in the premonitory power of visions, omens and dreams; or in the power of curse to inflict death. To see one's shadow cast without a head means death is near; so does to stumble and fall during one of the sacred dances conducted by the many religious societies.

The Yaquis say every event has meaning, nothing is random. They say each person has a candle in heaven, and will live until it burns down.

Their lives are hard, with little room for romance, much for fate.

In the 1960s, a Peruvian anthropology student, Carlos Arana Castaneda, presented his doctoral thesis at the University of California in Los Angeles. It offered a revolutionary approach to field anthropology. Castaneda had not just studied Yaqui magic as a distant scientific observer, he had worked (he claimed) with an irascible old Yaqui *brujo* (shaman), Don Juan, under whose tutelage he had ingested hallucinogens and gained entry to a Yaqui spirit-world of shape-shifting magic.

Not only was his incredible narrative accepted as fact by his examiners, gaining him his PhD, but it became a global bestseller – *The Teachings of Don Juan: A Yaqui Way of Knowledge* – the first of Castaneda's many increasingly fantastic accounts of Yaqui sorcery.[1]

At the time, Castaneda's account of Don Juan's magical assault on his Western material preconceptions seemed as authentic to millions of fans as his description of the *brujo's* rites, pharmacopoeia, and knowledge of the spirit-realms. Never mind if (as Castaneda's witty debunker Richard De Mille later proved beyond reasonable doubt[2]) the entire Don Juan opus is in fact one of the century's most lucrative and devastating literary hoaxes.

It now seems certain that 'Castaneda' never strayed far from the UCLA library in preparing his 'field notes', and that 'Don Juan' exists only in his own imagination. Yet to Castaneda's fans, his mythmaking powers matter more than the historical authenticity of his account. A hoaxer of genius, this brilliant synthesist of shamanic traditions did his magical homework.

Tuning in to New Age longings, offering fantasy as fact, from the start he presented himself as the dull-witted, reluctant pupil of a Yaqui shaman whose knowledge predates but scornfully encompasses modern science. Thus when hallucinogenic drugs were in fashion, 'Don Juan' used peyote, jimson weed, and psilocybin to propel his pupil into the spirit-world. In later books, as Castaneda's encounters with supernatural entities grow ever more fantastic, hallucinogens are abandoned, apparently because, says Don Juan, Carlos the eternal pupil has moved beyond need of chemical props: the magical will alone is enough to fuel more volumes of mystical encounters.

So Castaneda goes his merry way, adapting his imaginary saga to each new twist and turn of New Age mystical fashion. The main problem involved in admiring his work is that it wholly misrepresents Yaqui sorcery as it is actually practised. This is proved beyond reasonable doubt not only by the work of debunkers like De Mille, but by another account of Yaqui life and belief which was published in 1971, within a year of Castaneda's rise to fame. *A Yaqui Life*, by Rosalio Moisés, shows Yaqui belief and sorcery to be quite as odd as anything Castaneda claims, but describes a society so far removed from Castaneda's version as to be unrecognisable as such.

This is unfortunate, at least for Castaneda's fans, since this stark and wholly unromantic account is by a Yaqui.

Born in 1896 during the Yaqui war against the Mexicans, as a boy Rosalio fled with his family over the US border to escape massacre. His father Miguel remained to fight, but Rosalio grew up as an expatriate in Tucson, Arizona.

He was an itinerant labourer in California and elsewhere in the USA before eventually returning to Mexico. Many called him a witch for his public curses (he called them prayers) against anyone offending him, which included his mother-in-law, who sickened and died after he prayed against her.

Always poor, hard-working, and as unlucky in love as in his life as a whole, he was in Sonora, surviving by cutting wood and planting melon, when he met American anthropologist William Curry Holden. Though most Yaqui mistrusted Holden, Rosalio (who spoke Yaqui, Spanish and English) became his interpreter, and later lived on his Texas ranch. Holden persuaded him to write his life-story before he died. He did so, in English, later revising it, aided by Holden's daughter, Jane Holden Kelley.

When he died in 1969, she saw that his account was published, initially under the title of 'The Tall Candle' (University of Nebraska, 1971).[3]

In his autobiography, Rosalio makes no distinctions between 'natural' and 'supernatural'. Hoboing on the railroads, working in one place as a grape-picker and in another as a miner, often absent from his wife and cuckolded by her while earning a meagre living, his account of his endless search for work is as direct as his description of death and life among his people, whether in exile in Arizona or at home on the banks of the Rio Yaqui. Magic is as much a daily part of his tale as the need to earn a living; and much of the magic has to do with the power of the curse.

Rosalio tells how when he was twenty his family in Tucson arranged for him to marry Loreta Sánchez, who was fifteen. The event was organised by his grandmother Maria, who paid for the dancers, the food, drink and firework display at his wedding-feast. Rosalio had no choice in the matter: it was all arranged against his will. But this did not stop him going that night, as usual, to a local pool hall in Sasca, where his 'five Mexican girl friends' were all enraged. They called him crazy, *loco*, for marrying that 'wildcat', that 'alligator'; and one of them said: 'You will not like what happens to you. I will pray to God every night for you to have bad luck.'

At work the following day he fell thirty-five feet from an unloading chute to the ground. Though bleeding from the mouth and with several broken ribs he refused the doctor's attentions and walked the long mile home.

'They told us you would die,' said Loreta. He could not answer. In agony he lay down on his bed. For several days and nights he could not eat or sleep. But, with blood still running from his nose and mouth, at last one night he fell asleep, and dreamed that a beautiful woman dressed in white stood at the foot of his bed, telling him that he would live.

The following day his father sent him to a *curandero*, who placed a poultice of parched cornmeal mixed with herbs on his crushed chest, then made him blow into an empty gallon jar.

Rosalio recovered, but never went back to the pool hall again. Starting work on the railroad, his luck improved. But in 1918 misfortune struck his family. His grandmother died on the evening of 23 December, his father Miguel the following afternoon. The bad luck had begun when on 21 December his father went to a *fiesta* and lost all his money at cards. Standing outside round the big fire, he had been hit on the nape of the neck by a lit cigarette. It was a magic cigarette, which only a witch could use. It meant Miguel was cursed to death. He came home sick, and went to bed. Grandma Maria made medicine, but spilled the cup holding it, making her so sad that she became sick too. She went to bed, crying: 'Something is going to happen to us.' By the following morning she was mute: she would open her mouth, but no sound came out. With his friend Juan Sasueta, Rosalio went looking for a *curandero*, but they were all out at work – it was a Monday. That evening grandmother Maria died. On Tuesday afternoon his father died. Mercifully the deaths were peaceful.

On Wednesday a *sabio* came, but too late. This wise man, himself of the Papago tribe, said: 'I had a dream last night, and I saw it all. They were killed by a Papago witch.'

'Why would the witch men kill them?' Rosalio asked.

'Because your father had enemies among the Yaquis.'

Rosalio knew this was true. Miguel had been active in resisting the Mexicans, and many *torocoyoris* (collaborators) hated him.

Later, Rosalio's witch-friend Pedro Alvarez showed him how to make and use a magic cigarette. A strong local tobacco called *macucho* was wrapped in a cornhusk, making a cigarette six inches long and as thick as a little finger. Pedro prayed to God and a saint, told the cigarette where to go, lit it, and sucked on it three times. Rosalio saw it 'sort of explode', and off it went on its journey. Pedro sent it a few miles away. In about half an hour they saw a faint light far away, then another light closer, then a third light close by, and at last the cigarette came back.

Like a mosquito buzzing it whispered in Pedro's ear, telling him that the place it had been sent was dark and there had been nothing to see.

Pedro warned him that anyone using a magic cigarette must stay awake, for if on returning it finds its 'driver' asleep, it will hit him on the side of the head and kill him. As with the rebounding Kahuna death-prayer (see chapter 13), whoever curses another must ensure that the curse is not bounced back. The energy, once released, must find a victim – *any* victim.

Rosalio decided to stay clear of this sort of magic, but often watched Pedro send off the magic cigarettes.

Pedro knew all sorts of magic. He kept a *chone*, a doll with a scalp attached, able to fly through the air wherever it was sent, to be used as a guide in the mountains, or to warn of approaching danger. *Chones* could be used for good or bad purposes. Everyone feared *chones* sent out by a witch, typically to strangle an enemy by wrapping its scalp hair round the enemy's throat. If folk heard a whispering noise inside a house, they would start looking for a *chone*. If they found it, they would grab it, cast ashes and ground chilli on it, and throw it out. Terrified, the *chone* would fly back to the witch who had sent it, and not come back again.

Rosalio fell sick again, one day when he went out to visit friends. At first there was only a pain in his neck but when he reached his friend Claudio's house, he had to lie down. Hour by hour he felt worse. Devils were pulling at his hair, pinching him, prodding him, spitting on him. That evening he could not eat. Taken home by car, he lay down but could not sleep. His wife thought him drunk, but the driver said he was sick. The following day Rosalio told his wife he had to go into town, but she said: 'How can you go to town looking like that? Your eyes are red and your teeth are dirty.' In a mirror, he saw this was true. Though tired to death, he could not sit, stand or lie down, because whatever he did the devils would come and build fires under him. He began hallucinating. When women came to pin many-coloured ribbons to his chest, he threw them off. These women, he knew in his delirium, were the Virgin Mary and the other Marys, but he had denied them, and they had gone away. Then, on the fifth night since he had last slept, the candle left burning by him began to drip wax on his face. He saw three old devils come in. One said this was his last night on earth. But then came a man to help him. This man wore a red knee-length dress and carried a long sword. Afraid, the devils fled, but when the man left, they came back to taunt him again.
    Then Rosalio's spirit left his body and went underground. The ugly old dead people in that place said he had no hope of returning to life. They showed him his own body: it was red hot, like a stove. He tried to get back into it, but could not. Then he saw it in a long white burial sheet. The ugly people told him that he had to go everywhere he had ever been before in his life, and pick up all of his spit and his sweat. So in his winding sheet he went everywhere he had ever been. He went through California, Arizona, Sonora, meanwhile raving at his wife and the medicine men and women brought in to try and make him sleep.
    By then it was the sixth morning of his madness. Rosalio felt the candle wax still falling on his face, but neither his wife nor anyone else saw it, nor could they understand his raving talk of the devils that came to throw him over a cliff. He hurled his shoes at them, and they ran away.
    'What's wrong with you?' Loreta asked. 'Why throw your shoes away?'

'Two devils came to throw me down that cliff,' he told her. 'See that cliff over there?'

'There is nothing,' she said. 'There are no devils and no cliff.'

Then in his sleepless torment he began thinking about what his grandmother Maria and the *fariseos* (from 'Pharisees': a Yaqui male society that dances during Easter) had said about Jesus Christ, that He would cure anyone who was sick or who had been hurt. Now Rosalio saw his candle of life burning down too fast. In his delirium he begged Christ to give him rest, peace and a longer life. In return he would become a *fariseo*, a masked dancer at the Easter parades. Ending his prayer, he saw a little white fence around him, and two children on either side of him, each with a staff about four feet long in their right hands. With his hands clasped over his chest as if he were dead, he looked from side to side, but saw no devils. They were gone, and the candle wax no longer dripped on his face. Instead, two white-bearded and white-robed old men now stood before him.

One said: 'Is this the man who is going to wear the mask for Jesus Christ?'

The other said: 'Yes, he is the one.'

Women brought food, which he rejected, making them angry. Now he was moving, leaving his bed, folk looking at him over the little white fence. His speed increased, scaring him, but with the children still with him he came out of a forest past rows of lit candles. Nearing the gates of glory he heard folk singing, and big bells ringing, and so he entered that wonderful realm of light reported through the ages by those who appear to have died yet have returned to life. He met Jesus Christ, who said: 'Come and follow me.' So he followed Christ, but from his walk, begun in glory, he found himself cast into a violent, elemental storm. Thunder and lightning broke loose; rocks and trees sailed past, but nothing hit them.

'We will now see the war,' said Christ.

The battle was dreadful, but though the air was filled with bullets and shells and explosions, nothing touched Rosalio. He stayed calm, hands folded together, following Christ through the bursting shells and the rains of blood.

'Now we will go this way,' said Christ, as the war faded away.

They came upon thousands of candles, at one of which Christ stopped.

'This is your candle,' he said. About him were many which had burned down to the ground. 'It is very tall, and it is burning still.'

Then Christ showed him further visions of heaven and hell, and gave him a sign so that in future he might control thunder and lightning. The sign was of the thumb and index finger crossed, on each hand. Later Rosalio often used this sign, to banish storms.

Still with Christ, he entered a church. There he saw his father, who told Christ: 'You had better baptise my son again.' His father went away, then a man had him sit at a table, and took out all his bones and teeth, laying them on the table. Next, the man removed Rosalio's heart, telling a bird to fly with it three times over a lake. Then, with Rosalio lying in his dead, red-hot body, his bones, teeth and heart were returned by this phantom surgeon.

Christ called two angels and told them, 'Now you had better take him down to the earth.'

The return was slow. The little white fence touched the ground, then disappeared. With difficulty re-entering his red-hot body, Rosalio opened up his eyes. It was like looking through smoke. Christ came and told him to get up and walk. He did so, but after one step he fell on to his hands and knees. Christ said: 'This is the way you will come to me.'

So Rosalio awoke back in the real world. He saw many people in the room about him, some awake, some sleeping. He realised that he was lying on a bed beside his wife, who was asleep. Months seemed to have passed.

He woke her up and asked: 'How long have I been on this bed?'

'About two hours,' she said.

It was about three in the morning.

After that he slept peacefully, and when around noon he awoke with a healthy hunger and thirst, he ate and drank everything given to him, then explained to his family what had happened, when they had thought him gone beyond death's door. When he was finished he said: 'Now I have to be a *fariseo* and wear the mask for Jesus Christ every year during Lent.'

Nobody denied his good vision. Everybody accepted that he had been to glory and that he had seen Jesus Christ. He fell asleep again, and dreamed sweetly not of devils but of angels.

He says that after that he dreamed no more and played no more tricks; that he gave up gambling, dicing, and drinking; and that in February 1924 he made his first *fariseo* mask, as a sign that he was no longer cursed, but had received the blessing of Christ.

Even so, his life grew no easier . . .

After first dancing as a *fariseo* at Easter 1924, Rosalio worked for the Water Users Company, then as a cotton picker, and in the Tucson wood yard. At Lent the following year he left work to make a new *fariseo* mask.

That year, as she ran inside the church during the Fiesta de Gloria during Holy Week, his *fariseo* godmother Chepa Armenta stumbled and fell. This meant she would die before next Easter. She lived only another few months. Rosalio says this happened to five of his *fariseo* godparents, and that he knew many others who died within the year after such a fall. He says white people would not believe it, but that it is a sign from God.

All summer he worked in California, sending money to Loreta to help support their children, Marcelina and Salvador. When he came back to Tucson, everyone was talking about Micaela Naponohi, widow of one of the men who had helped pay the Papago witch to kill Rosalio's father. She had spurned a Mayo man who had been courting her, so he had got a witch to give her the stomach of a horse, and she had eaten herself to death.

Worse was Rosalio's discovery that everyone knew Loreta was cheating on him. On his return he had begun working for the gas company, but each evening when he came in she was out, and never came back till late. Pressed, she said she had been with Charla, her mother, but Charla denied this. One night, as he passed a neighbour's house, he heard people inside mention his name. 'That Rosalio really has a fast wife,' he heard someone say.

At last the penny dropped. He wanted to kill her, but thought of the children. When she got home he would not speak to her. A few days later the witch Pedro Alvarez, who had taught him how to make and use the magic cigarette, came by and said: 'Something has happened to you.'

'No. Nothing has happened to me. Why do you say that?'

'Because I saw you in my dream,' said Pedro. 'For sixty dollars I will make an end of your fool wife.'

Rosalio refused. In a quandary, he did nothing about it. Months went by, unhappily. After Easter 1926, when again he danced as a *fariseo*, he returned to California. That year many of the Yaquis in Sonora were killed by the Mexican army. Returning to Tucson that autumn sick with tuberculosis and a bad heart, he let himself into his house to find Loreta out, and only his small daughter Marcelina at home, alone. Loreta returned after dark. Though dressed in black, she denied she was in mourning. The following day she was out again. His cousin Viviana came and told him what was going on.

'She is no good for you. She takes the money you send her and spends it with her friends. You let her go. You can find another wife.'

Viviana added that Loreta was mourning the death of a friend's aunt. That night when Loreta returned, he had fortune-telling cards spread on the table. 'See here,' he told her. 'The cards never tell a lie. From now on you can wear the mourning dress all you like.'

He grew sicker and could not sleep, but Loreta went on doing exactly as she pleased. At last, losing his temper, he threw her to the floor with a knife at her throat. 'If you don't tell the truth, this will be your last night.'

When she told him she was 'just having a little fun', he choked her almost to death. The following day she left early, taking Marcelina.

He went out and came back an hour later to find the house ransacked. Nothing was left but his clothes and an old blanket. Her drunken friends paraded in front of the house, taunting him. He threw a rock at one and broke the man's wrist. They tried to get in at him, but he had locked the door. He was ready to shoot, when at the last moment his cousin Simón Valenzuela came to his rescue and drove the tormentors away.

The following day Rosalio went to see his mother-in-law, Charla, but nobody would speak to him. 'I've come here for my wife,' he shouted. 'I will take her back to help the children. I want to raise my children.'

Charla told him to go away and never come back.

'You hate me,' Rosalio cursed them all. 'But I tell you that you are not going to be happy. Do you think there is no God to see what you do? Every word you say to me is going to bring you bad luck, every one of you. You will not forget what I say.'

They laughed at him as he left. Penniless, he asked his neighbours for food. The first two pretended they did not even see him. The third, though acknowledging him, would not ask him in to eat. But the fourth, Hilario Rodriguez, not only fed him but told him to stay until he got better.

A few days later Rosalio learned Charla was sick. Day by day she got worse. Three times she sent word that she wanted to see him, but he would not go.

'She said for me never to come back,' he told her messenger. 'Go and tell her I haven't forgotten what she told me. I will never go back.'

Within a month of his curse, Charla was dead. He watched the funeral from Hilario's house, and told himself: 'Jesus Christ is answering my prayers.'

Next day Loreta visited Rosalio, with Charla's children as well as Marcelina and Salvador. 'Now I believe what you told me some months ago,' she wept. 'You said I would have the chance to wear mourning all I wanted to.'

'That's right, but it has only started,' he told her. 'Now who do you think is to blame for this, you or me?'

'I blame you. You tried to kill me, and you helped to kill my mother. You put the curse upon her, and you would not come when she sent for you. You did not even go to her funeral. I cannot forget that.'

'So that is the way it is,' Rosalio told his wife. 'And that is the way it will always be. I do not want to hear another word from you. Now get out.'

He spat in her face. She ran from the house with the children. That was the end of their marriage, but whenever he saw her in his dreams after that, Rosalio did the same thing. He spat in her face.

Returning to California, he said goodbye to Marcelina, and did not see her again for nineteen years.

When he was working at the Water Users Company, one day

Rosalio's boss asked him if he knew a man in Tucson called Manuel Salinas.

'Yes,' he said, not saying that Manuel Salinas was his father-in-law, one of the people he had cursed.

'I read in the newspaper that he was killed yesterday,' said the boss. 'He was crossing Meyer Street in Tucson and a car hit him.'

One by one the people Rosalio had cursed all died. Many people said he was a witch, but he denied this, saying that he only believed in Jesus Christ, who had answered his prayers.

Years passed. It was the time of the Great Depression and work was hard to find. Rosalio hoboed all over the United States riding on the freight trains, but any work he got was short lived and any money he made was soon gone. He thought about going to the Rio Yaqui, where his family came from. He had not been there since he was ten, but folk said a man could live there without wages by raising crops.

So in 1932 Rosalio went south, passing through Tucson without stopping, because of his bad memories of what had happened there. In Hermosillo, two hundred miles south of the border, he was advised to avoid the Rio Yaqui. Everyone there was very poor. By contrast, he seemed rich, with new clothes. But by October, when he reached the Rio Yaqui, he had only five *centavos*.

For the first time he met his younger half-brother, Mariano González, from Torim *pueblo*, which had been his father's home. Rosalio planted watermelon by the river but grew very poor. He survived by cutting wood, but he never had enough to eat. One day he visited one of his grandmother's relatives, Gregorio Juárez, the captain at Vicam *pueblo*. Gregorio and his family had beef, cheese, coffee, milk and beans on the table, but they only gave him beans and a tortilla in a dirty plate, and an oil can to sit on.

As he walked back to Torim, Rosalio prayed to God: 'These people hate me. Do not give them good luck.'

Weeks later in Vicam Station he saw Captain Gregorio, pale and thin. Soon Gregorio died, and his wife became very poor.

Early in Lent of 1934 Rosalio had a good dream, of white men coming to the Rio Yaqui from the north, who would help the Yaquis. It reminded him of a prophecy made in his boyhood by the *sabio* José Maria Nóteme, of the hard times to come, and how many Yaquis would flee to the United States when the Mexicans again tried to destroy them. This had happened in 1926. But the *sabio* had also said that then white men would come from the north, and help the Yaqui by recording their history.

Soon Rosalio heard that the white men had arrived, but nobody knew what they wanted. Many Yaquis were fearful. Too many *politicos* had made trouble for them in the past. Rosalio, who spoke English, was sent to interpret, and so he met William Curry Holden, an anthropologist who wanted to write about the lives of the Yaqui. It was the start of a friendship that lasted many years.

Holden told government officials in Mexico City about the poverty of the Yaquis. Blankets, agricultural tools and tractors were sent, but were all stolen by Mexican soldiers and the *torocoyoris*, the rich Yaqui collaborators. Nothing changed for the poor Yaquis.

Later that year Rosalio went with two others to the Bacatete Mountains, drawn by tales of old Spanish gold mines. They found no gold, but saw the lair of a *sierpa*: a big hole in the ground, the soil about it swept clean. Wind strong enough to suck a man down rushed into it, and they saw birds being sucked into it. *Sierpas*, Rosalio explains, were formerly people who sinned by committing incest or other crimes. Almost any animal can be a *sierpa* – rattlesnakes, scorpions, centipedes or fish so huge they can eat an entire cow or deer at one go. In their lairs they eat and get bigger, then one day go down to the sea, tearing up trees and uprooting everything in their path. Once in the sea, they stay there. Those with a white cross on their forehead are harmless; those with no cross are dangerous.

Rosalio had known a man who, while working with another cowboy at a place called Cerro del Tigre, was sucked off his horse by a strong wind and pulled close to a cave. Desperately he hung on to a tree but was about to lose his grip when the other man reached him and, with hat in hand, made the sign of the cross three times. The wind had dropped instantly.

Holden came back with other Americans in 1938 and again in 1940, but many Yaquis hated them, and also hated Rosalio and any other Yaquis who got too friendly with them. Several Yaquis who liked the Americans were murdered. Rosalio's friends and relatives warned him of any plot to ambush him, and he never took the same road twice when walking between Toram and Vicam.

So he lived. He was still chopping wood for a living and in 1939, having remarried, became a father again, but his wife Rosa died two weeks later. His mother came to visit him in his new adobe house in Torim, and stayed five years, looking after his daughter Juana.

In 1943 Rosalio's sister-in-law Anastasia, her daughter Micaela, and Micaela's husband Jaime all fell ill. They had been cursed by a witch, Clara Morales. She was infatuated with Jaime, who had ignored her.

On New Year's Day of 1944 Anastasia was standing close to the adobe wall of her house as the sun rose, but her shadow had no head. She laughed, saying: 'Well, I guess I never will get well. Soon I will die.'

So she did, two weeks later, preceded by Micaela, closely followed by Jaime. Clara Morales left town for a while, as everyone knew she had caused it, but soon came back. She and her sister Anita were well-known witches who caused many deaths. Among their victims was a baker, Pablo Peralez, who could never keep his mouth shut. He went about telling people, Rosalio included, how Clara and Anita made little cloth dolls that they named after a person they did not like, then stuck pins in them and buried them in the cemetery, so that soon the person died. Furious at Pablo, they made a doll of *him*, and buried it. Soon he grew very thin. He knew he was bewitched, but the *curanderos* could not save him. Anita was also blamed for the death in 1942 of her husband, Beto Valencia, who often beat her up. It was said she had ground up the bones of a corpse from the cemetery, added cemetery dirt, and put the mixture in his food. He died within two months.

There were other victims too, but nobody ever took any action against the Morales sisters, who became rich and lived long lives.

Rosalio reports many other cases of death-curses during the years he lived in the Rio Yaqui. He speaks of them as matter-of-factly as he speaks of the hardship of his life, without pity or self-pity.

Another round of fatal cursing began in December 1946, when night after night Rosalio heard buzzards cry 'Manuel' over the house of his neighbours, the Valencia family. Prepared for something bad, he was not surprised when on Christmas Eve his friend, Manuel Valencia, was falsely accused of theft by Juana Chávez, his angry girlfriend. Juana went to her other boyfriend, Victor Palma, Yaqui captain of Torim *pueblo*.

Victor not only had Manuel immediately arrested, but by midnight had called all the Torim officials to sentence him to death. The executioner arrived at 4 a.m. By dawn Manuel was dead. On learning what had happened, his mother, Cornelia Valencia went to a witch, Román Arpero, and asked him to harm everyone involved with her son's death. One by one they all died, except Victor Palma, who only became very ill. The first to die, within a month, was Juana Chávez. Celso Flores, the governor of Torim, followed her a few days later. Five other men present at the sentencing died during the next year or so. Last to die were six members of the Buetemea family.

Captain Rosario Buetemea and Commandant Crecensio Buetemea had both been present at the sentencing. They, Rosario's wife and two sons, and Crecensio's son, Joaquin, all died within a week in 1952.

By then Rosalio had gone to Texas, but a friend wrote and told him all about these final deaths. As to why Victor Palma did not die, this was because Ramón Arpero died, and a *curandero* was able to save Victor when the witchcraft stopped and the death-curse was lifted by Rámon's death.

In 1946 Rosalio got married again, to Pancha Wailika, and for a time he was happy, because she laughed a lot. At the end of 1947 they had a son. But life stayed hard. Nico, the baby, cried all the time with hunger. Rosalio wrote to Dr Holden, begging for clothes, which Holden sent, as well as some money.

Then, early in 1949, the Rio Yaqui flooded. Many folk drowned. Those who lived, including Rosalio and his family, lost their homes and all they had. Food, medicine, money and blankets were sent from the United States but, as usual, few of these supplies ever reached the poor Yaquis.

Pancha fell ill and nearly died. Then, that summer, after watching over their garden to protect the ripening corn and beans from thieves, they returned home to find everything stolen. The thief was Nacho Paroy, an old friend who began resorting to petty crime after the death of his own wife.

Rosalio wrote to Dr Holden in Texas, asking him to arrange a six-month work permit in the USA. Before they could leave, Pancha died after giving birth to a daughter. He persuaded an orphan girl, Chepa Moreno, to come to Torim and look after his son and daughter, and in May 1950 went to Lubbock, Texas. Briefly well off after working five months building a house for Dr Holden, he returned to the Rio Yaqui and to Chepa. Early in 1951 Rosalio's mother died.

Chepa, who had loved his mother, grew sad and never again danced to the radio. In June their hen hatched seventeen chickens, but three were black, which meant bad luck. A fortnight later his half-sister Julia died. Soon the last of his American money ran out. Chepa stopped eating and just lay all day alone in the house. Consumed by *tristeza* (sadness), she took to her bed and died in December. Rosalio's son Nico, who had also fallen ill, died three days later. Only his daughter Tara was left. When he went back to Texas in 1951, she was too sick to travel and had to stay behind. When she was six, she went to live in Tucson with his cousins.

They did not speak Yaqui. So Tara forgot her own language.

Rosalio spent the rest of his life alone on a farm in Lubbock County, raising cotton and doing odd jobs. Every year he saw Salvador his son and Marcelina his daughter. Folk he had known in Tucson still believed he was a witch with the power to lay a death curse, which he denied. Every winter until 1967 he returned to the Rio Yaqui, but that year he could not, due to a witch sickness. It came about, he says, because he had broken a promise to give a gift to a woman, Maria Victoria Tava, who had cured him of illness a year earlier. One day she visited, but he avoided her, and the following day woke up sick. Everything he ate and drank tasted bitter.

'A woman is doing you harm,' a *curandero* said. 'She formed a ball of green *jariondia* leaves inside your stomach, but it will pass any day now.'

Days later, still sick, he vomited up a green, leafy ball. A *curandero* broke an egg into a glass of water, added holy water, and in the mixture he saw Maria Victoria Tava. So Rosalio knew who had harmed him, even though others did not believe it. They lived in the modern United States, and no longer believed in witches. He says he had always known about them, but that this was the only time he was ever harmed by a witch's curse.

Rosalio Moisés died in 1969, aged about seventy-three.

As for Carlos Castaneda, he is a wealthy author, and famous, though what the Yaqui people think of him is not known.

17 The Kennedy Curse

On 22 November 1963 President John F. Kennedy was assassinated in Dallas, Texas. It was the death not just of the era's most prominent American, but of a dream shared by millions. This charismatic young President and his vivacious family had seemed so regal that the White House had become known as Camelot, as if he were King Arthur and his wife Jackie was Guinevere. When Jack's brother Bobby was installed as Attorney-General, the Kennedys, a Boston-Irish clan, were at the height of their power.

But enemies lurked in the wasteland beyond Camelot. That November day, one or more of them shot the President dead. Five years later, Bobby too was slain.

Who killed JFK and why remains unknown. The official Warren Commission version cites but one killer, Lee Harvey Oswald. Yet the testimony of over fifty witnesses (many meeting early deaths) directly contradicts the official version. So who killed him? Were government agencies like the CIA involved? Were the Cubans behind it, or J. Edgar Hoover of the FBI, or the Mafia? All had motives.

In a sense, it hardly matters. JFK's death is only the tip of the iceberg – he was not the first nor the last Kennedy to die violently.

This ambitious clan has had such persistent bad luck since gaining power as to defy the law of probability. Three brothers violently killed, a sister born retarded; another sister, in-laws and friends killed in three plane crashes; a fourth brother, badly injured in a fourth plane crash, driving drunk off a bridge and drowning a 'secretary' . . . And as for the children . . . amputation, arrests, illnesses, drug-deaths, endless publicity. The lost generation, seemingly as doomed as characters in Greek tragedy. A curse?

A century ago the Kennedys were Irish-Bostonian bar-keepers. The ambition of JFK's father, Joe Kennedy, made them rich, powerful and famous. If there is a curse it is rooted in the Kennedy quest for power; in the brutal pressure Joe Kennedy exerted on his sons to succeed.

Karmic retribution? The just desserts of unscrupulous pride? That would be only half the story.

The Kennedy 'curse' also involves a trail of weird events, premoni-tions, and apparent coincidences going back over a century before

JFK died; a trail seemingly originating in the very office of the US Presidency itself.

Between 1840 and 1960, every US President elected in a year ending in a zero either died in office or was assassinated. This bizarre sequence is called the 'Presidential Death Cycle'.
First to go was William Henry Harrison, dead in 1841 after one month as President. Abraham Lincoln, first elected in 1860, was shot down in 1865. Garfield, elected in 1880, was assassinated in office, as was McKinley, re-elected in 1900. Harding, elected in 1920, died in office in 1923, and Franklin D. Roosevelt, elected for the third time in 1940, died in 1945, still in office.
John F. Kennedy, elected in 1960, was thus the seventh President to die in this extraordinary sequence; and Ronald Reagan, elected in 1980, was nearly the eighth, being shot and wounded in his first term of office by would-be assassin John Hinckley.
Whether Reagan's survival means that JFK's death marked the end of the cycle is unclear. The fate of the President elected in AD 2000 will tell us more. The cycle may not be over yet.
By contrast, of the other twenty-nine Presidents *not* elected in the twenty-year cycle since 1840, only one has died in office; none has been assassinated.
As for those elected in 1800 and 1820, both survived their term.
The cycle began in 1840. But why? What causes (or caused) it?
Astrologers point out its coincidence with a Jupiter–Saturn conjunction occurring every 19.85 years, always on the decade-opening election year. Moreover, since 1840 the conjunction has occurred in an earth sign: Taurus, Virgo or Capricorn, and will go on doing so until 2080. There has been one exception: in 1980 Jupiter and Saturn met in an air sign, Libra.
So, before the 1980 election it was widely claimed by astrologers that the new President, who turned out to be Ronald Reagan, would not only live, but would become one of the USA's most popular Presidents.[1]
Both predictions proved correct. Was Reagan 'lucky'? When in 1988 he and his wife Nancy, who consulted astrologers in the White House, retired to Hollywood's 666 Saint Cloud Avenue, they had the number changed to 667 – 666 being viewed by some as the accursed Number of the Beast of the Apocalypse.
Surely it cannot be argued that JFK, like three former assassinated Presidents, was slain not by men but by a recurring conjunction of planets? Maybe not. But there are other odd aspects to his death, including similarities between his murder and that of Abraham Lincoln almost a century earlier.

President Abraham Lincoln was shot to death by John Wilkes Booth (fifteen letters in his name, born in 1839) on Friday, 14 April 1865 in Ford's Theater, Washington DC. John F. Kennedy died, also on a Friday, slain supposedly by Lee Harvey Oswald (fifteen letters, born in 1939). Booth shot Lincoln in a theatre and ran into a warehouse; Oswald supposedly shot Kennedy from a warehouse and ran into a theatre. Both killers were southerners; both were killed before being brought to trial.

The 1960s like the 1860s saw the USA divided on issues of war and civil rights. The 1860s draft riots parallel the 1960s draft resistance movement. Each decade saw three Presidents; in each the first was slain. Lincoln, elected in 1860, had a secretary called Kennedy; Kennedy, elected in 1960, had a secretary called Lincoln. Kennedy was killed in a Lincoln limousine; Lincoln died in Ford's Theater. Both were tall men who lost a child in infancy in the White House; both had their wives with them when they died; their last names both contain seven letters. Their Vice Presidents were both southerners called Johnson. Andrew Johnson was born in 1808, Lyndon Johnson in 1908; their first and last names had the same number of letters. Likewise the first, middle and last names of the third President in each of the two decades (Ulysses Simpson Grant; Richard Milhous Nixon) each had the same number of letters.

All coincidence, of course.

Other parallels between the two assassinations include premonitions of sudden death experienced by both men.

Shortly before his death Lincoln, who told his friend Ward Hill Lamon that his dreams had always suggested he would rise to a great height then suddenly fall, dreamed that in the East Room of the White House he saw a throng of people gazing mournfully at a corpse on a catafalque, its face covered. 'Who is dead in the White House?' he asked one of the soldiers guarding the body. 'The President,' he was told by the soldier, who added, 'He was killed by an assassin.' Then the crowd's grief woke him.

On the last morning of his life he presided sombrely over a cabinet meeting. 'I had a dream, and I have now had the same dream three times,' he said. 'I am on a great, broad, rolling river, and I am in a boat . . . and I drift . . . and I drift . . .' That afternoon, he told his bodyguard William Crook: 'I believe there are men who would want to take my life.' He added, 'And I have no doubt they will do it.' Walking on, he said, almost to himself, 'It would be impossible to prevent it.' A few hours later he was dead.

Early on 22 November 1963, Kennedy said: 'If anyone really wanted to shoot the President of the United States . . . all one has to do is get [into] a high building some day with a telescopic rifle, and there would be nothing anybody could do to defend against such an attempt . . .' Kennedy was aware of the Death Cycle; among his favourite poems was 'I Have a Rendezvous With Death'.

Once, riding in his car with Dr Janet Travell, his personal doctor, they drove past a small boy, who pointed a movie camera at him. Starting nervously, Kennedy took a deep breath and said: 'I will not live in fear. What will be must be.'[2]

An epitaph suitable for the whole Kennedy clan? Ever since they left Ireland and rose to power, their fortunes seem to have been star-crossed.

The 1845 potato crop failure (caused by a fungus from America) brought a million Irish to the New World. Behind them they left another million who, with English-owned granaries locked and guarded, starved to death.

Many never survived the voyage. Packed into 'coffin ships', thousands died of disease. In 1847 an estimated 40,000 perished, twenty per cent of those who had left. Two hundred and fifty thousand packed into Boston's Paddyvilles and Mick Alleys where even more died. By 1850 the 'famine Irish', now a third of Boston's population, worked as coal heavers and longshoremen, 'muckers' and 'blacklegs'. NINA (No Irish Need Apply) signs began to appear. Tension in the city grew.

Patrick Kennedy, third son of a rich Wexford farmer, arrived in 1849. Aged twenty-six, he emigrated not to flee famine but to make his fortune. En route he met Bridget Murphy, also of Wexford, and married her. He worked as a cooper while Bridget bore four children. The last, born in 1858 just before Patrick died of cholera, was their first son, Patrick Joseph, who was greatly pampered by Bridget. At the age of twenty-two this self-confident young man bought a run-down bar and went into business. Handsome and ambitious, he joined a Democratic Club and opened a liquor import business. In 1886 he entered the State Senate and in 1887 married Mary Augusta Hickey, daughter of a prominent businessman. By the early 1900s he was one of four members of the Board of Strategy, Boston's power-centre.

Another was John F. Fitzgerald, a pugnacious philanderer who in 1905 became Boston's first mayor, whose parents had been born in Ireland.

P.J.'s son Joe (born in 1888) grew up immersed in politics. At Harvard he found out that Irish and Jews were equally despised. All his life he was driven by the need to avoid poverty; he refused to be a poor Irishman. Entering banking in 1912, within a year he was the country's youngest bank president, saying: 'I want to be a millionaire by the age of thirty-five.' In 1914 he married Rose, Fitzgerald's eldest daughter. In July 1915 their first son was christened Joseph Patrick Kennedy, Jr.

John Fitzgerald Kennedy, future President, was born two years later. With Joe now general manager of a Bethlehem Steel ship-yard, next came three daughters: Rosemary, Kathleen and Eunice.

Rosemary was retarded: Joe and Rose had her lobotomised and packed off to a convent. Returning to banking in 1922, determined to win at any cost, sharp in deals which others thought shady, by 1924 Joe was a millionaire.

'What is it you really want?' a friend asked, when in 1926 Joe moved his family to New York.

'Everything,' said Joseph Kennedy.

Becoming a movie mogul, he commuted between New York and Hollywood as Rose, despite endless snubs, fought for social acceptance. The Kennedys were, after all, Irish. Yet she persisted, turning a blind eye as Joe romanced actress Gloria Swanson. Rose bore a third son, Robert, then a fourth, Edward, also two more daughters.

Tormented by stomach ulcers, ruthless yet charismatic, Joe held the family together despite his frequent infidelities and absences. To control his unruly children he had only to give them his famous chilly look. They grew up competing for his love, and thus became as unprincipled, arrogant, and reckless as he was. Bravery and daring were demanded. The eldest, Young Joe, often broke bones fighting to defend his father's name. Confident and brash, he was challenged only by Jack, the second son. Smaller and weaker, Jack always lost the fights that left the other children, especially Bobby, shaking. Often bedridden by mysterious illnesses, Jack alone took to books and developed a sense of irony. But the competition with his elder brother grew ever fiercer. Fighting not only for Joe's love but his respect, as they grew the boys' philandering became as obsessive. Women, like the world, they saw solely in terms of conquest.

'I met this extra in Hollywood that is the best-looking thing I have ever seen,' young Jack wrote in a letter to a friend from Los Angeles, adding a tag: 'The Extra's delight, or how I got my tail in Hollywood'.[3]

Twenty years later, while sharing a mistress with Chicago Mafia boss Sam Giancana, he was competing with Bobby for the favours of the actress Marilyn Monroe, whose mysterious death in 1962 is part of this tale.

Joe Kennedy had taught his sons that wealth, women and political power, however acquired, were theirs by right. A curse?

Joe entered politics in 1930, and helped fund Roosevelt's first presidential election campaign. When Roosevelt refused to make him Secretary of the Treasury, he threatened to call in his loans. Profiting from the impending repeal of Prohibition, he became Chairman of the Securities and Exchange Commission. Now he was a Washington 'face', Joe's outspoken opinions made good copy. Twice he made the front page of *Time*. Roosevelt visited the Kennedys; the Kennedys visited the White House. Meanwhile, in Germany, Hitler was on the rampage.

One night Joe told the President's son, Jimmy Roosevelt: 'I'd like to be Ambassador to England.'[4]

FDR almost fell out of his wheelchair laughing when he heard this, but then he thought again. Maybe a boorish Irish Catholic was just the man to cover the Nazi threat without falling prey to Anglophilia. So, early in 1938, Joe became US Ambassador to the Court of St James. The English press were fascinated by this rich Irish-American who called the Queen a 'cute trick'. Playing it up, Joe asserted that he was a politician, not just a diplomat. Opposing the coming war, by now at home he was seen as a future Democratic presidential candidate, and when Young Joe and Jack joined him in London, he groomed them for power. Jack knew Joe Sr pinned his hopes on Young Joe. Yet it was Jack who had the independent and original mind.

With Young Joe in Madrid at the height of the Spanish Civil War, and the rest of the family visiting the Pope in Rome, Joe Sr found his anti-war stance increasingly unpopular with Roosevelt. On 1 September 1939, phoning Roosevelt to say Britain was about to declare war on Germany, he predicted a return of the Dark Ages, his voice shaking. 'It's the end of the world,' he kept saying, 'the end of everything.'

Despised by Churchill, ignored by Roosevelt, and claiming that England would be 'thrashed' by the Nazis, Joe became a pariah, known during the Blitz as 'Jittery Joe', and 'Run, rabbit, run'. Back in the USA in October 1940 to endorse FDR's re-election and claiming that 'Democracy is finished in England', in Hollywood he urged movie-makers to stop using 'Jewish money' to make anti-Hitler films. 'I never want to see that sonofabitch again,' Roosevelt said in fury after a meeting with Joe. 'Get him out of here.'[5]

Young Joe now entered public debate, supporting his father's position. Yet when FDR declared a state of national emergency, Young Joe enlisted as a naval air cadet. The calamity Joe Sr feared was about to erupt. When in December 1941 the Japanese attack on Pearl Harbor dragged the USA into war, privately Joe thought FDR had set up the attack. Realising his own political career was over, he began working on his sons' careers. But first they had to survive the war. Young Joe did not. Jack almost did not.

In 1943 Jack, now in the navy, took command of a torpedo boat, PT109, near Guadalcanal. On 1 August the Japanese destroyer *Amigari* rammed the PT and cut it in half. Jack and other survivors swam three miles to an islet, Jack pulling an injured man by a rope clenched in his teeth. Later he swam far out into the Blackett Strait looking for rescue. It took six days. He should never have let the PT be rammed at all, but his bravery put him on the front page of the *New York Times*. The family was jubilant; but Young Joe, upstaged, was heard raging one night: 'By God I'll show them.'

Soon he got his chance. Joining a naval reconnaissance squadron in

Cornwall, England, during a London furlough he met and fell for Pat Wilson, a married Australian, whose husband was abroad. It was Joe's first serious affair. Perhaps because of it, and despite his squadron's high casualty rate, he volunteered for an extra month's duty before going home. Flying during the D-Day invasion of France in June 1944 he seemed driven, alarming his crew with the risks he took. On leave in London he gambled fanatically. About to return home, he heard of what amounted to a suicide mission: diving a bomber packed with ten tons of TNT into a Nazi buzz-bomb bunker, the crew bailing out at the last moment. Volunteering, he cheerfully told a friend that his chances of survival were no better than fifty-fifty.

'I'm about to go into my act,' he told Lorelle Hearst, wife of the newspaper magnate, on the phone just before take-off, 'and if I don't come back tell my dad – despite our differences – that I love him very much.'

Twenty-eight minutes into the flight, the TNT blew up and the bomber exploded in a huge fireball. Young Joe would never be President. He was the first victim of his father's driving ambition.

Next in line, Jack duly climbed the greasy pole. Sixteen years later, Joe Sr's ambition was realised . . .

The Kennedy presidency was bought, not just in the last days of the 1960 election race against Richard Nixon, but over a period of fifteen years before that.

As soon as the war was over Joe Sr began speaking on national issues, creating a platform for Jack to exploit. Running for Congress as the PT109 war hero, Jack won by a landslide in 1946. A poor dresser and always in bad health, his views were his own, but his father's money was behind him. His sexual appetite remained insatiable, driving him from one chorus girl to the next. Yet when in 1952 he appeared at Eisenhower's inaugural ball, it was with Jacqueline Bouvier – an aloof, wide-eyed debutante. Her sense of irony appealed to him and, though deciding she had a 'father crush', soon he proposed, by telegram. She thought she knew what she was taking on, the young senator (as he now was) being such a famous rake, but was taken aback to find herself stranded at parties while he sneaked out with whoever had caught his eye. She put up with it. She was, after all, a Kennedy wife, and Jack was on the up and up.

So was Jack's brother Bobby, by 1953 working for the McCarthyite Subcommittee of Investigations, his first job being to investigate an alleged homosexual infiltration of the State Department. Bobby, married and soon father of the largest Kennedy family, was the least rampant womaniser among them, and probably the most idealistic, which made his own fate in 1968 all the more painful.

By 1954 Jack's back problems were so bad he could barely walk even with crutches. He almost died undergoing spinal surgery. After several operations he began to recover, and wrote a book lauding senators who had taken stands on controversial issues. Published in 1955, *Profiles in Courage* made him a celebrity, but he failed to gain the nomination for the vice-presidential ticket at the 1956 Democratic Convention. When he was asked why he wanted to be President, he said: 'I guess it's the only thing I can do.'[6] Joe Sr had seen to that.

In 1957, *Profiles in Courage* was awarded the Pulitzer Prize. Meanwhile, Joe Sr was fading from view. 'I don't want them to inherit my enemies,' he said of his sons while still working on their behalf behind the scenes. 'It's tough enough they inherit my friends.'[7]

Not all his sons aided the Kennedy cause. The youngest, Teddy, expelled from Harvard for getting a friend to take his Spanish final exam for him, signed up in the army for four years. Furious, his father pulled strings, cutting the assignment in half. Back at Harvard, then at law school, Teddy drank so heavily and drove so recklessly he became known as Cadillac Eddie. When he married in 1958, however, he seemed ready to settle down. Before long his father saw to it that he too became a senator.

The 1960 campaign was Jack Kennedy's hour. By now he and Jackie were national figures, icons of popular culture on magazine covers and in the popular press. Author Norman Mailer later described it as 'superman coming to the supermarket'. Moving into his new role like a method actor, JFK was acquiring universal appeal as a handsome, glamorous figure; the hope of the future. 'We'll sell him like soap flakes,' said his father.[8] On 2 January 1960, Jack declared he would run for the Democratic presidential nomination.

The family mobilised. Joe Sr poured a fortune into the campaign. Jack's opponent, Hubert Humphrey, began to feel, as he put it, like an independent merchant fighting against a chain store. Jack got the nomination; he was just forty-three years old. Choosing Lyndon Johnson as his running mate, he told doubters who hated the Texan senator: '. . . I'm not going to die in office. So the vice-presidency doesn't mean anything.'[9]

JFK's presidential campaign was won during the TV debates against his opponent Richard Nixon. Good-looking, cool and collected, he was perfect for the new television age; Nixon looked shifty. An overnight star, Jack was mobbed at every campaign stop. Yet the election was the closest call ever in US politics. JFK won by only a few hundred thousand votes nationwide. Rumours about irregularities in the Chicago polls persisted. It was said Joe Sr's old Mafia connections had won the day. Nor were doubters happier when Jack chose brother Bobby as his Attorney-General. It smacked, as Bobby knew, of nepotism.

JFK's presidency did not start well. The disastrous CIA-funded landing of anti-Communist, anti-Castro forces on Cuba in April 1961, which JFK had reluctantly approved, did nothing for his image, even as Vietnam loomed on the horizon. The US military build-up in South-east Asia continued, while in August the East Germans began building the Berlin Wall. Meanwhile, JFK was creating fresh trouble for himself with his affairs. Women were continually being smuggled into the White House. 'Here, would you find who these belong to,' said Jackie disdainfully one day, handing him some panties she had found in her pillow slip. 'They're not my size.'[10]

More dangerous were his affairs with Mary Meyer, who introduced him to marijuana (long before Bill Clinton ever had to deny inhaling!) and joked with him in the White House bedroom about being high when he had to push the nuclear button; and, more importantly, Judith Campbell, who became his mistress in 1960. Unfortunately, she was also the mistress of Chicago Mafia boss Sam Giancana. This was a political, not just a moral disaster. It gave J. Edgar Hoover, the ageing FBI director, more power to blackmail the White House, and threatened public exposure of a CIA plot to use the Mob to murder Cuban dictator Fidel Castro.

But the threat posed by the Giancana–Campbell–Kennedy triangle was sidelined by the Cuban missile crisis of October 1962, eleven months after Joe Sr had suffered a stroke. He could no longer speak nor move. All the Kennedys suddenly felt vulnerable. The maker of their collective destiny could do nothing for them any more.

Yet when the Russians, worried by the secret plot to destroy Castro, began to send troops, tanks, artillery and jet aircraft to Cuba, JFK proved able to act on his own. His ultimatum to Khrushchev to pull out or face all-out war had the world on the edge of its seat for many tense hours before at last the Russians backed down.

This, the climactic hour of the Kennedy presidency, preceded JFK's assassination in Dallas by just over a year.

His premonitions of death had been accurate.

After this, the paralysed Joe Sr 'sort of gave up'. Of the family, a friend said it 'was like a bunch of shipwreck survivors. I don't think they could have made it at all without Bobby.'[11] Yet, though urging the family to keep going, Bobby himself never recovered from Jack's death.

Seven months later, on 19 June 1964, Teddy Kennedy almost died in a plane crash outside Springfield, Massachusetts. The pilot and his friend Ed Moss died. Teddy's lung was punctured, several vertebrae were smashed. 'Someone up there doesn't like us,' said Bobby after visiting his brother in hospital.[12]

Bobby hung on, despite right-wingers circulating a pamphlet entitled 'The Strange Death of Marilyn Monroe', charging that he had been having an affair with the actress and that, when she threatened to expose his dealings in appeasing the Castro regime, he'd had her murdered to shut her up. Her death on 5 August 1962, apparently of a drug overdose, remains a mystery. Involved with both JFK and

Bobby, it seems that both brothers had rejected her. Again, the truth is unlikely ever to be known. Her fate remains part of the Kennedy mystique – and curse.

Like Joe Jr and Jack before him, Bobby now became obsessed with death. 'Sooner or later', he muttered when, during a motorcade, a sudden fusillade of backfiring from a car behind made him flinch. And, as if the threat was not enough, he sought out danger deliberately: climbing the 14,000-foot Mount Kennedy in Alaska, paddling a dugout canoe alone in piranha-infested Latin American waters, out-facing a rhino in Kenya, shooting seven miles of the Salmon River rapids alone in a kayak, when he had never even been in a kayak before. He was daring death to come. And it did.

Persuaded in 1968, against his own better judgement, to run for the Democratic presidential nomination, he was in Los Angeles on 5 June when the news came through: he had won the vital California primary. Leaving a conference in his hotel room, he made his victory statement, then detoured through the hotel kitchen en route to a press conference. A man called Sirhan Sirhan pushed forward with a gun, and fired. So Bobby Kennedy died in the operating theatre at LA's Good Samaritan Hospital. The 'lone assassin' had struck again. Again, it remains a mystery: who set up the killer? Again, it hardly matters, though Bobby, the public friend of minorities and the poor, had made many enemies.

Shattered by this new tragedy, the clan never really recovered. After Bobby died, his father stopped eating and just wasted away, to die at last in November 1969. The family felt cursed.

'It made me wonder what my grandfather could have done for God to do this to him,' said Chris Lawford, one of the many grandchildren (Bobby had fathered ten children himself) who grew up in the shadow of these events.[13]

As for Teddy, the survivor of the four brothers, he tried but failed to accept responsibility for the family legacy. Unshaven, drinking heavily as he moved from one anchorage to the next, he reminded people of the ancient mariner trying to escape a curse. 'They're going to shoot my ass off the way they shot Bobby,' he kept telling people four years later when efforts were made to draft him for the Democratic nomination.[14] So maybe, at some subconscious level, he sought the accident that ruined his political career and made it impossible that he should ever be elected. On 18 July 1972 he drove his 1967 Oldsmobile off Dike Bridge at Chappaquiddick, drowning his passenger, Mary Jo Kopechne. His behaviour thereafter was bizarre. Rather than call the police, he returned to the party he had left and got his cousin to return to the wreck with him. Though their dives to the submerged car proved fruitless, Teddy still delayed telling the police. Swimming over an inlet to Edgartown, he changed his clothes. At 2.30 a.m. he appeared in the lobby of his motel as if to establish an alibi, then from his room made seventeen phone calls, none to the police. Next morning he took the ferry back to Chappaquiddick where, learning that the body had been found, at last he reported to the law. For a week he gave no public explanation. It was a crucial moment in the Kennedy saga. All the old suspicions about the clan's recklessness and ruthlessness came to the fore. At last he made a nationally telecast speech, which did not go down well. Later he publicly wondered if 'some awful curse did actually hang over the Kennedys'.[15]

Perhaps. If so, JFK's widow had already bailed out by remarrying, to Greek shipping magnate Aristotle Onassis. 'I hate this country,' Jackie had snapped at a friend who tried to dissuade her. 'I despise America and I don't want to live here any more. If they're killing Kennedys, my kids are number one targets.'[16] Though castigated by the world's press, she no longer cared. On 10 October 1968, just months after Bobby's assassination, she married Onassis.

That left the children – the third, lost generation. For years nothing went right for them. JFK's daughter Caroline was caught growing marijuana. Edward, Teddy's eldest son, lost a leg to cancer in 1973. Christopher Kennedy Lawford became a heroin addict, as did Robert, Bobby's second son, and his third son, David, who was found dead in a Palm Beach hotel bedroom on 25 April 1984. Joseph, Bobby's eldest son, was prosecuted after a car crash that left a girl friend paralysed. His sister Courtney later married Paul Hill, one of the 'Guildford Four', who spent fifteen years in an English jail for an IRA bombing they did not commit. Others fared little better in the eighties, continuing to hit the headlines for their excesses or accidents. As Chris Lawford put it when in 1983 Bobby Jr was arrested for heroin use: 'If you think of it as one movement from Grandfather's early days to what has happened to Bobby right now, you realise that the Kennedy story is really about karma, about people who broke the rules and were ultimately broken by them.'[17]

Does the doctrine of karma – that every cause (action, deed, word and even thought) must inevitably have its effect – legitimise the idea of a curse? Only in the broad sense, in that Joe Kennedy's children and grandchildren paid a terrible price for his ambition. The old man drove Joe Jr, Jack, Bobby and Teddy so hard that, once Joe Jr was dead – maybe because he could not bear the weight of his father's demands – they had to try for the highest office and so were exposed to the dangers involved in opposing ruthless power groups in a land ruled by money and the gun.

Joe Sr's own insatiable ambition had arisen from his Irish background and his refusal to remain as poor as his ancestors. Yet many other Irish immigrants prospered in the USA without having to fly so high. His ambition was of the sort called hubris in Greek tragedy: challenging the gods usually leads to a disastrous downfall. The basis of his wealth, as created by his father P.J., lay in selling alcohol, in back-room deals to buy votes, and in sharp practice – the very kind of activity that led to Prohibition. And when Prohibition ended, he profited from that too. He had a fleet of ships loaded with Scotch and ready to sail in as soon as the band began playing 'Happy Days Are Here Again'. An anti-Semite who as the US ambassador to Great Britain tried to keep the USA out of the war, if he was not actually pro-Nazi he sailed as close to the wind as possible, meanwhile encouraging his sons to think of themselves as possessing the right to grab whatever they wanted – money, women, power. Faithless and tyrannical, he created in his children a compulsion they could not resist, and lived long enough to see each of the three sons in whom he had placed his hopes die violently. As for the fourth son, Teddy, it took the death of an innocent, Mary Jo Kopechne, to render him politically ineffective.

Yet by the early 1990s there were signs that the younger Kennedys had begun to put the past behind them, turning from hell-raising to good works. By 1993 JFK's son 'John-John', a lawyer still trying to emulate his father by courting Hollywood blondes, was considering a career in politics. Sister Caroline, likewise a lawyer, had co-authored a book on the Bill of Rights. Bobby's eldest son, Joseph, was a Democratic congressman seen as a future high-flyer; his sister Kerry, human rights advocate and lawyer, had married Andrew Cuomo, son of New York governor Mario Cuomo and serving in the Clinton administration; brother Michael, yet another lawyer, worked for an organisation helping the poor to lower their fuel bills; and Robert Jr, his heroin habit overcome, taught environmental law at a New York college while pushing for land conservation. Teddy's son Edward Jr, who lost his leg to cancer as a boy, worked for Facing the Challenge, a non-profit organisation he founded to promote self-help for the disabled.

What had happened to all the ruthless arrogance? It is tempting to think that the old man must be spinning in his grave. As for the curse, if that is what it can be called, it may have been laid to rest at last – but only time will tell.

18   The Curious Case of Carole Compton

One of the oddest criminal cases of modern times was tried in December 1983 in Livorno, Italy, where, despite lack of all but circumstantial evidence, Carole Compton, a twenty-one-year-old Scot, stood charged with arson and attempted murder. Though insisting throughout her trial (which began with her locked behind a steel-barred cage in the courtroom) that she had not laid the five mysterious domestic fires that erupted about her during the short time she worked as a nanny for two Italian families, she was found guilty of arson and attempted arson. The charge that she had tried to murder Agnese, a three-year-old Italian girl placed in her care, was rejected. As she had already spent seventeen months in Italian jails awaiting trial, a thirty-month sentence was suspended and she was deported. Back in Scotland she married, settled down, and had children of her own.

Years later, she recalled with incredulity the nightmarish events that led her to be called *la strega*, 'the witch'; and to be accused of being a pyromaniac possessing the evil eye – in a modern European country.

Absurd superstition? Yet this case is genuinely mysterious. Exciting intense media attention – US horror novelist Stephen King's *Fire-starter* was Italy's bestseller at the time – it drew the interest of authorities on poltergeist phenomena, including English author Guy Lyon Playfair, and Dr Hans Bender of Germany's Freiberg Institute of Paranormal Research. In their opinion, Carole was undoubtedly associated with the fires, but had not physically laid or caused them, nor was she consciously aware of having anything to do with them.

This, then, is not the tale of a curse in the accepted sense. In that there was a curse at all, Carole was its victim, and perhaps its source lay in her own unhappy, confused and turbulent emotions.

So, what *did* happen to Carole Compton? Her story as described here is drawn from her own account, as told to author Gerald Cole – a fact worth keeping in mind.[1]

Carole's family background was insecure. Born in Ayr, in south-west Scotland, to a Catholic mother and often-drunk Irish Protestant father, she grew up amid endless religious argument. She was nine when her mother divorced her father and had a breakdown; eleven when her mother moved to Aberdeen, the oil-boom city on Scotland's north-east coast. Trained as a hairdresser but finding no work in Ayr, in time Carole left her friends and family to join her mother in Aberdeen, to work 'in the fish' – packing wet fish into boxes on a conveyor belt. One day a conveyor belt snapped and she landed in hospital, lucky not to have lost her leg. That decided her. She returned to Ayr to stay with her grandmother and younger brother, and took a job in a day centre looking after old folk, where she enjoyed both the work and the company. One night she went out dancing with her friends and in a disco met a handsome, curly-haired young Italian, Marco Vitulano, a trainee waiter at the famous Turnberry Hotel. He asked her out; and soon they were inseparable. They went steady for two years, but late in 1981 he had to go back to Italy to do his national service. Before he left he gave her a ring. It was understood to be a token of their engagement to be married.

Marco left, and months passed, until one morning in the spring of 1982 Carole got a letter from him, asking her to come out to Italy and meet his family. Starry-eyed, hoping for happiness, and despite her family's doubts and her inability to speak Italian, on 31 May 1982, aged twenty, she flew to Rome.

There she met and stayed with Marco's family. At first, with Marco on leave, all went well. Her doubts began only when at Luna Park, a funfair, another girl came up to Marco and smiled at him. He sent her away but, her fears aroused, Carole asked his sister Marguerite who she was. Marguerite said she was Marco's old girlfriend, and that everyone had assumed that they would marry. Carole, who had never heard about this, felt threatened.

When Marco had to return to army duty, Carole knew she could no longer stay with his parents. Registering with a baby-sitting agency, soon she was hired to look after a two-year-old boy in a house on the Via Margutta, one of Rome's most fashionable areas. The child, Emanuele, was the son of Emanuela Ricci, a wealthy sophisticate who seemed generous and friendly.

The job began on 14 June, just two weeks after Carole's arrival in Italy. Emanuela, apparently unmarried, had several boyfriends and went out a lot, but Carole enjoyed the house and liked Emanuele, and at first, with Marco visiting often, all went well. The only part of the job she did not like was having to feed the stray cats that lurked outside the house; she had already told the Vitulanos that she could not stand cats.

One day, passing the kitchen, she heard a crash behind her. A religious picture had fallen to the floor and broken. She assumed she had brushed against it accidentally, but the middle-aged Sicilian housemaid, Rosa, thought otherwise. She made Carole cross herself and repeat a prayer. To Carole this was crazy, but to keep Rosa happy she went along with it.

She made nothing of this at the time. Then one night she was seized by agonising pain. It was appendicitis. Emanuela paid the hospital bills. As she recovered, Carole continued looking after Emanuele. She and Marco walked him in the Borghese Gardens, where old ladies smiled at them as if the boy were theirs. Carole wondered how long it would be before she and Marco were married, with children of their own. But then the trouble began . . .

The hot season arrived, when the wealthy folk left the city for their holiday homes. One day Emanuela said she was off to Paris, and that her brother Enrico would drive Carole and Emanuele to Ortisei, in the Alto Adige, the Italian Alps, to stay with her parents, the Riccis, 'for a few weeks'. Carole was unhappy about this. It meant being far from Marco, and she would be entirely on her own in a house of strangers who spoke no English.

Emanuela's father had been ill: Nicole, a Mauritian nurse, had been hired to look after him. With her waist-length hair and stunning good looks, Nicole seemed dauntingly glamorous to Carole. Yet at least Nicole, who was ten years older, spoke English. Maybe it would work out. Carole tried to settle in with Emanuele, Nicole, and Emanuela's father, at 10 Via Meisules, a four-storey house on one of the long hillside roads amid lush mountain scenery above the picture-postcard village of Ortisei.

Nicole was good company. But after two weeks there was still no sign of Emanuela's return, and nobody knew when Carole and Emanuele would be going back to Rome, and to Marco. On the evening of 11 July, with the old man watching the World Cup soccer final between Germany and Italy, Carole went for a walk with Nicole and Emanuele. On their return, they saw smoke pouring from a second-floor window at the front of the house. Bursting in, they found Signor Ricci glued to the soccer final on TV, oblivious of the smoke drifting down the staircase. When he realised what was going on, he climbed the stairs, worried about his money. Carole followed him through the smoke, but when he opened the main bedroom door they both flinched back from the heat. She saw a chair and wardrobe blazing. A siren wailed as the fire brigade arrived, and the old man was at last persuaded to get out.

Nobody was hurt, but the second floor of the house was ruined. The cause of the fire was a mystery. The firemen blamed an electrical fault: there had recently been a similar blaze in the house next door.

This was only the start.

Carole moved with Emanuele and the old man into a flat – a third-floor attic conversion above a shop in Ortisei itself. On the Monday, Enrico and his mother came up from Rome, both upset about the fire and worried about the old man. The following morning, still half asleep, Carole heard Signora Ricci shout that she smelled burning. Bursting into the room that Carole shared with Emanuele and Nicole, she found a paper packet smouldering in a refuse bin in a cupboard under a sink. Glaring at Carole, she accused someone of smoking. Carole said she did not smoke. (In her account Carole fails to explain why neither she nor Nicole smelled anything, even if they were half-asleep.)

That afternoon, Emanuela rang from Paris. Signora Ricci took the call. Carole heard her name mentioned several times. She was called to the phone and her heart sank to hear Emanuela say she would be away until September. Two more months without Marco! With Signora Ricci hovering, Carole heard Emanuela say that the fire must have been only a coincidence or careless accident.

The following morning, the grandparents went out with Nicole, leaving Carole in the house with Emanuele and Enrico. She says she was playing with the boy when she heard Enrico shout, 'Al fuoco! Carole! Fire! Fire!' Hurrying out of her room, she saw Enrico rush past her, wearing only a towel. Smoke was curling out of Signora Ricci's bedroom. Hurrying Emanuele past it, Carole saw flames leaping up from the middle of the bed. With Emanuele safely out on the kitchen verandah, she and Enrico doused the fire with saucepans of water. The flames had left a black circle on the mattress, soggy bits of newspapers and magazines lying about it.

'Non senti l'odore del fumo?' Enrico demanded. 'You didn't smell smoke?' Carole said no. Thereafter she felt that everyone was treating her with kid gloves. That evening Emanuela rang again and, though seeming friendly, suggested that Carole return to Rome to stay with Marco's parents while the flat was redecorated. Realising that everyone suspected her of setting the inexplicable fires, back to Rome she went, under a cloud.

Worse was to come.

Marco's parents welcomed her back. She thought she would get back to the job of looking after Emanuele, but not until September. Marco, home on ten days' leave, insisted that she get another job, saying there was no room in his parents' flat, and that she could not wait until September. 'Do you still want to marry me?' she asked. He prevaricated, saying they had plenty of time, and what was the hurry? Though now she wanted to go back to Scotland, Carole kept quiet. She phoned Emanuela to explain that she had to find another job. Emanuela wished her good luck. Marguerita, Marco's sister, recommended her to another nanny agency. In her account, Carole does not say whether this new agency knew what had happened in Ortisei.

Soon a Signora Daniela Tonti contacted the agency. She and her husband Luigi (whose surname was Cecchini) needed a nanny for their three-year-old girl, Agnese, starting at the end of July. Less glamorous and wealthy than Emanuela, Daniela, who spoke good English and seemed friendly, said that she and Luigi worked in television. After an interview at the Vitulanos' flat, Carole got the job, which included teaching Agnese English.

Daniela was keen to take Agnese to the seaside as soon as possible. So, on Saturday, 31 July, Carole found herself being driven from Rome to Elba, an isle sandwiched between Italy's north-west coast and the larger island of Corsica to the west. Here, in this now-popular holiday resort, Napoleon was jailed before escaping to fight his final battle at Waterloo in 1815.

The plan was that Carole, Agnese and Daniela would stay with Luigi's parents on Elba, though Luigi had to return to work in Rome after the weekend.

The day was beautiful, with brilliant blue skies during the hour-long car-ferry crossing to Elba, but Carole felt confused. Why was she rushing off again (and after the last disaster) with yet another family of strangers?

Elba proved to be rugged, with steep verdant mountains sweeping down to one popular beach resort after another. After rounding innumerable headlands the road descended to a broad cove, to a village of dazzling white houses, terraced up to the sun-baked hills. Luigi's parents' house, overlooking the village, was small but pleasant, painted white with green shutters.

When she was introduced to Agnese's grandmother, Carole felt her instant dislike. 'Why have you brought another English girl?' the tiny old woman scolded Daniela, frowning at Carole's bikini top. 'Why not an Italian?' Carole now knew enough Italian to pick up the message. As for grandfather Mario, he ignored her. She sensed Daniela's embarrassment at her mother-in-law's attitude, but felt more isolated than ever.

Inside, Carole learned that the Cecchini grandparents shared one of the two bedrooms, Daniela, Luigi and Agnese the second, and that she had a camp-bed in the living room. Soon it was clear that Grandmother would be a problem. She mumbled when Carole came near her, and if Carole tried doing anything for Agnese, would perform the same chore, in her own way.

Later, down at the beach, Daniela admitted to Carole that her mother-in-law had disliked the last nanny too. 'You must give her time, Carole,' she said, 'Luigi's mother believes in the old way.' Going on to explain how in Italy a special feeling exists between grandparents and grandchildren, Daniela had just revealed that her first child had been born dead, when a scream came from the water. Agnese, on a lilo, had fallen into the sea. Luigi, who was beside her, scooped her up, but came out angrily demanding to know why Carole had not been looking after her. Daniela, so friendly the moment before, supported her husband. Carole realised how afraid they were about Agnese, their second child. Her tension increased. Why was she here? Did Marco really want to marry her? When would she see him again?

The following day, 1 August, proved catastrophic. Told after lunch to clean Agnese up, Carole took her to the bathroom. As she watched the child wash, the door burst open. Daniela stood there, smoke billowing behind her from the mattress of the bed in the grandparents' bedroom. It was not on fire, but one side was scorched. Everyone was yelling as the smouldering mattress was thrown out of the French windows. Carrying Agnese through the kitchen to the dinner table, Carole saw Luigi wave a packet of cigarettes under his father's nose; the old man shook his head. Though remembering Ortisei, she thought Daniela and Luigi blamed the grandparents, both of whom smoked.

Next day she learned how wrong she was.

That evening, as Carole followed grandmother Cecchini into the living-room, a statuette fell from a small table to the floor. The old woman glared at her, though neither of them had been near it. In the morning, Carole was awoken by a loud noise. A silver cake-stand had fallen from its table. Then, as she made up her bed, a glass vase fell from a table behind her and shattered. Carole heard the grandmother mutter '*strega*'. Later she went into Daniela's bedroom, where Agnese was asleep, to put some things away in a drawer allotted for her use. Daniela appeared, bristling, and told her never to enter the room while Agnese was asleep.

Carole went to the toilet but found the old man in it. While she waited outside, she heard a faint crackling sound, either from the living-room or Daniela's bedroom. She called to Daniela: 'Will you come and listen to this?' There was no reply. The old man scowled at her as he left the toilet. The odd noise persisted. It sounded to her like cats trying to get in. Returning to the living-room, she looked out of the French windows. 'Daniela,' she said, 'I think cats are trying to get in.' Just then Daniela and the old man reached the bedroom door. The old man opened it. Smoke billowed out. The edge of the bed was smouldering. Agnese, asleep, lay on the other side of it. Carole, going to snatch up the child, was elbowed aside by Mario. Daniela caught up her daughter; the old man threw the smoking mattress out of the window. Following Daniela and Agnese out of the room, Carole ran into grandmother Cecchini. Enraged, the old woman began prodding her in the chest, screaming: '*E tu! E tu che inizia questi fuochi! E maligna!*' Realising that she was accused of starting the fires, and that she was being called evil, Carole was shaken by the old woman, who called her '*Strega!*' ('Witch!'), then chased her out of the house and into the courtyard. '*Vacca!*' the old woman cried, locking her out.

'*Parti da mia casa! Vacca!*' With the neighbours gathering, asking what had happened, she tried to get back in, but heard herself publicly accused of trying to kill the girl by starting a fire. She hid in a store-room, but the grandfather dragged her out, apparently scared that she would start a fire there too.

Meanwhile, the *carabinieri* (police) had been called. Now also accused of stealing the grandmother's watch, Carole was pushed into the bathroom by Daniela and the grandmother, where she was forced to strip naked. She and her clothes were searched, but nothing was found. Then the police took her away.

Her ordeal had begun. After a night in the local jail she was taken to the mainland, in handcuffs. In Livorno she was locked up in the 'Carcere Domenicani', the 'Dominican Prison'. Here and in another prison Carole was to endure seventeen months before the due process of law brought her into a court at Livorno, to face charges of arson and attempted murder.

This happened in 1982. Even so, in one sense, she was lucky.

It was ironic that Carole should be locked up in an old Dominican monastery. Founded in the 1220s to combat the Cathar heretics of southern France, the militant Dominican friars had established the Inquisition. With the Cathars destroyed, the Dominicans (seeking new reasons to ensure their own survival) had spearheaded the witch-mania. Throughout Europe from the fourteenth to the late seventeenth century, countless numbers of women were burned alive, their confessions of witchcraft extracted by torture. Now, in 1982, Carole Compton found herself accused of trying to kill a child by sorcery. Three centuries earlier, the best she could have hoped for was to be strangled at the stake before the fire was lit – but only if first she had repented of her sins, real or imaginary.

At first Carole thought it all a nightmarish joke. Surely Marco would get her out of this madness! Yet when at last he phoned her, it was to say he was through with her. Moved into a cell with heroin addicts, she was told that the sentence for attempted murder was from seven to twenty-one years, but that if she pleaded insanity she might get off with just two years. An Italian lawyer, Sergio Minervini, despite receiving an anonymous phone call saying that Carole was evil and that he should not take her case, agreed to represent her, but her hopes faded when the British consul told her that legal aid was unavailable to UK citizens abroad. Signor Minervini, however, told her not to worry about the money. Then he asked her how she explained five fires in twenty-three days, with her presence being the only common factor.

She could not. He told her that the prosecution case was that she had been so anxious to get back to Rome to see Marco that she had been willing to do anything. The lawyer made it clear to Carole that she could not really blame people for being suspicious. The fires had happened, after all.

By now there was media interest. In Scotland, a public appeal raised money for Carole's defence. Her mother flew out from Aberdeen to see her, the flight paid for by a local travel agency. A Scots lawyer, Lawrence Nisbet, offered to help, free of charge. The publicity backfired, though. One day Signor Minervini showed her a British newspaper, where, next to her picture, the headline read: THE GIRL THEY CALL A WITCH. She was intimidated by the other prison inmates. On her bed she found an Italian magazine with her photo on the cover, STREGA printed over it, slashed several times. With her psychiatric examination set to start on 17 September, the press stories grew even wilder. Emanuela Ricci, who had seemed so friendly, now claimed that, during the third fire in Ortisei, the corridor had been blocked by flames, Enrico trapped one side, with Carole the other, her bags packed. She also claimed that Emanuele, whenever picked up by Carole, would start crying, saying, 'Mummy, she's burning.'

Carole was deemed sane when examined, and though she passed all lie detector tests, the magistrate in charge of her case refused bail. New reports on the mysterious fires were needed. Lawrence Nisbet withdrew from the case, saying he had done what he could. In December Carole was moved to a women's prison at Trento, near Bolzano. By now she knew some Italian, but Trento proved hard to take. Only her mother's visits, paid for by well-wishers in Scotland, helped to keep her spirits up. Her father, dying of cancer, also visited.

By now the case had come to the notice of parapsychologists. Two British experts on the paranormal, Guy Lyon Playfair and Dr Hugh Pincott, offered to fly to Italy at their own expense. Carole's experiences reminded them of poltergeist cases they had investigated. Insisting that she did not believe any of it, and that she had had nothing to do with any of the fires, she was aghast when Signor Minervini, her lawyer, while admitting that the claims of witchcraft were nonsense, suggested a defence based on the paranormal angle.

'I get off if I say I am a witch?' Carole protested.

Though back in Livorno by spring, her trial seemed as far off as ever. Only in July was a date set – for mid-December. The media circus grew more raucous. On 19 October, UK TV's Channel 4 publicised the case, as part of a series called 'Twenty/Twenty Vision'. The programme suggested that she might need the paranormal angle as part of her defence. More usefully, an expert on fires established that she would have had to have been out of sight for much longer than she had been to have set a fire as severe as the one in Luigi Cecchini's bed. Meanwhile, Italian headlines were full of *La strega*, and *Incendiaria – piromane scozzese! Firestarter*, by US author Stephen King, topped the Italian bestseller list. This novel about fire-raising by paranormal means suggested, as did the Compton case, that three centuries of Science and Reason had not dispelled popular belief in the supernatural.

In the courtroom at Livorno, Carole was locked inside a steel-barred cage. Newsmen surged forward. Reporters held up cassette recorders. 'Carole, do you believe in witches?' 'Carole, what about this witch thing?' It was a madhouse, until the police ejected the media. She was let out of the cage, and the trial began. Witnesses gave evidence. Teodoro Comploi, the chief fire officer in Ortisei, said that in his thirty-eight years as a fireman he had 'never seen fires like those before', and that 'the flames had travelled downward. It was very strange.'

Dr Hans Bender, a well-known German parapsychologist, was also on hand to give evidence, but Carole's defence attorney felt that things were going well and that it was best to avoid the supernatural angle as far as possible. So Dr Bender was not called. Almost all the evidence came from the families concerned, and seemed to go against the defendant. Emanuela Ricci, as glamorous as ever, made a number of disparaging remarks; she said that her maid Rosa had reported several odd incidents – the water boiler had made 'funny noises', and 'the electric meter had been spinning' when Carole stood near it. But Emanuela added: 'Rosa is a Sicilian and very superstitious.'

Even worse, Nicole, grandfather Ricci's Mauritian nursemaid, denied that Carole had been with her on the evening walk in Ortisei on 11 July, when the first fire broke out. She said she had returned from a walk on her own, to find Carole standing outside the smoking house with Emanuele, shouting 'Fire! Fire!' She said that Carole had not told anyone in the house about the fire, not even old grandfather Ricci. Carole lost her temper. '*Bugie, solo bugie!*' she shouted, standing up. 'Lies, all lies!'

The following day, a telegram came from one of Nicole's former employers in Rome, advising the court that she was a 'pathological liar'.

Another expert on fires, Professor Vitolo Nicolo of Pisa University, said he had examined the mattresses on the burned beds in Elba, including Agnese's cot. He had found no trace of suspicious stains, smells or inflammable substances. The mattresses had burned only on the surface, at the same spot, and not on the inside at all. 'Both fires had the same characteristics – great heat but no flames,' he said. 'The fire had also moved downwards rather than up, which I find phenomenal. The burn marks could have been caused by an over-heated iron, but not by a cigarette lighter, a match or any naked flame.' Agreeing with Carole's lawyer that nothing linked her to either of these fires, Professor Nicolo asserted, like Teodoro Comploi before him, that: 'In my forty-five years' experience of this kind of investigation I have never seen fires like these. They were created by an intense source of heat, but not by a flame. I cannot explain what caused them.'

The Cecchini grandparents gave evidence, then Daniela, who described seeing her 'daughter half enveloped in flames'. Asked if at the time of the incident she had the same long hair she had now, she agreed that she had. 'And was this hair also undamaged despite you having to bend over a raging inferno in order to save your daughter?' Daniela answered: 'Yes, but I had to be very quick.' Last of all came evidence from Carole's predecessor as Cecchini nanny, a Scots girl, Teresa Hunter. She said that she, like the au pair before her, had been overworked and resented; that she had invented an excuse to leave after just fifteen days; and that she had never been paid. She thought the fires were caused by short circuits; and that, had they happened while she had been there, she thought she would have been accused, being the only stranger in the house.

But the verdicts proved that the judges believed the evidence of the Riccis and Cecchinis. Carole Compton was found guilty on two charges of arson and one of attempted arson, but not guilty of attempted murder. The sentence of thirty months' imprisonment was suspended due to the time she had already spent in prison. Deported immediately, she returned to Scotland, where in due course she married, to begin the family she wanted so much.

But the mystery remained. What had actually happened?

At least Carole Compton was not burned as a witch, as would probably have been her fate in an earlier age. Yet from her point of view it was bad enough that she had spent a year and a half in prison before being condemned as an arsonist by the Italian legal system, and all this despite there being no clear evidence against her, and though expert testimony asserted that the fires associated with her were abnormal in nature.

Was she unjustly condemned?

Many students of parapsychology, including Guy Lyon Playfair and Dr Hans Bender, continue to insist that the fires associated with her were caused by poltergeist phenomena.

What is a 'poltergeist'? A German term, meaning 'noisy' or 'rattling ghost', it refers to phenomena typically including bangs, raps, levitating furniture and floating domestic objects, showers of pebbles or water that cascade from nowhere . . . and fires lighting without cause. Such phenomena are usually explained as manifestations of unconscious mental disturbance associated with pubertal teenagers. The hauntings cease when the emotional problems triggering them are solved.

Hans Bender, who met Carole and attended her trial, has studied over sixty similar cases. He reports that paranormal combustion is a well-known symptom of what parapsychologists term Recurrent

Spontaneous Psychokinesis (RSPK). He asserts that RSPK victims, like Carole, are wholly unaware of their own part in the fearful phenomena that erupt about them – phenomena that may well arise from personality disorders induced by stress.

Carole Compton had an unhappy childhood. Her mother and father, always arguing, separated when she was eleven. She followed a man to Italy, where he eventually rejected her. She found herself alone among strangers, unable to speak their language. Longing for love and for children of her own, she was hired to nurse the children of parents whose own lives were scarcely stable, and whose parents were suspicious of strangers and, in one case, willing to heed an older body of beliefs.

Carole set no fires, wished no harm, yet domestic objects mysteriously fell to the ground in her presence, and fires erupted, typically in *beds*, in which people make love and procreate. That they occurred around her is undeniable: more dubious is that she was their conscious or sole agent.

'I've never seen fires like those before,' stated Ortisei's chief fire officer, noting that the fires he observed burned *down*, not *up*. Professor Nicolo of Pisa agreed: 'In my forty-five years' experience of this kind of investigation I have never seen fires like these.'

In an Afterword to the tale Carole told the author Gerald Cole, Guy Lyon Playfair suggests that such events, arising from a psychosomatic disorder, are no more 'criminal' than the catching of German measles. Moreover, in his opinion, Carole could not have caused the fires on her own. Perhaps her unhappiness triggered them, but the fears of others contributed to the phenomena. All available evidence suggests that RSPK cannot be produced by one individual; it can develop only via group interaction, as suggested by some other, similar cases which Playfair presents.

In 1978, fire fighters were called seven times to the council flat of a childless couple in Holloway, London, where domestic items including a bed kept catching fire with no apparent cause. In addition, lights switched themselves on and off, doors opened and shut on their own, and books flew off shelves. As in Carole's case, a fireman said of the fires: 'I've never seen anything like it', while the local chief fire prevention officer concluded that: 'There's no explanation at all – no indication of how they started.'

A year later, in the Pyrenean village of Séron, France, during August no fewer than ninety-eight fires broke out before many witnesses, including twenty *gendarmes*. Each fire apparently began with a small charred spot on a bed or piece of clothing. Two young people were jailed, tried and convicted, despite lack of evidence, before later being pardoned or freed.

Playfair notes another recent case, of special interest in that the phenomena were recorded on film. First shown on Brazilian television, the film shows a fire that begins and spreads on a mattress, without apparent cause. A Jesuit priest, on camera, appears to explain the phenomenon away in scientific terms. Blessing the family, he assures them that the problem is solved, then leaves. As soon as he is gone, the fire breaks out again.

Also in Brazil, at Suzano in 1970, sixteen fires broke out for no obvious reason in a small family home. Mattresses, a sofa, clothing and various other objects including a wardrobe were burned. Some of these events were seen at first hand by the local police chief and his forensic expert. The policeman described how a mattress began smouldering in front of his eyes, apparently combusting from within. The forensic expert told Playfair how stones had hurtled round the room even with nobody to throw them.[2]

Another well-known case, investigated by Hans Bender, involves a German girl, Anne-Marie Schaberl. In October 1965 she left her Munich school and began work in the Rosenheim office of lawyer Sigmund Adam. In late 1967 his electrical systems went mad. Strip-lighting failed inexplicably, there were sudden surges in current, his phone bill was absurdly high. A device put in to note each number dialled showed up to six calls a minute to the speaking clock: impossible, as it took at least seventeen seconds to get through to it. The relays were being affected, but how? When a reporter called in to investigate, a bulb fell from its socket and almost hit him. His story of 'the Rosenheim spook' alerted Professor Bender, whose assistant, visiting Adam's office, saw overhead lights begin to swing if Anne-Marie walked under them. Soon it was clear: the current surges occurred only when she was in the office. Tested by Bender she proved to be mistrustful and aggressive. Her rural family background was difficult; she hated town living, and though engaged to marry, she was unhappy. Asked about a year she had spent in plaster because of a tubercular hip, she became disturbed. Tested for ESP, she showed telepathic abilities. She returned to Adam's office: the glitches began again. She was fired, and got another job: again electrical equipment went haywire.

Meanwhile, her fiancé had dropped her. The patron of an electronically controlled ten-pin bowling alley, he was disturbed at how, whenever Anne-Marie walked in, the board registered random scores and the pin-setting equipment went mad. She took a job in a mill: a man died there in an accident. People began to avoid her. Leaving that job, Anne-Marie married, moved outside town, and had three children. The poltergeist activity ceased.[3]

These well-attested cases are but the tip of the iceberg. Alan Gauld, a historian of psychic research, has compiled a list of 500, dating from the sixth century AD, in fifty-three of which 'incendiary effects' are reported. Also, there is the phenomenon of 'spontaneous human combustion', in which it is the depressed victim's own body that burns, often totally, save for arms, legs and head, and often without damaging surrounding furniture or items. In such cases too, the nature of the 'fire from heaven' remains unclear, but appears to be a product of the victim's upset mental condition.

Why include the case of Carole Compton in this book? Because, in the first place, the power of the curse proceeds primarily from the power of the mind – acknowledged or not. The unconscious curse, delivered against the self or against others, may prove quite as potent as a deliberate malediction. Moreover, its functional power springs not just out of the unconscious mind of a particular individual, but out of the interaction between numbers of people, none of them conscious of what is going on or of how the mind works, but all of them scared by the events, and most of them willing to seek out and punish a scapegoat. Thus medieval witch-trials; thus, too, the fate of Carole Compton and others. In one sense, grandmother Cecchini was correct in suspecting witchcraft, but it may be that her own hostility was as potent a factor in triggering the outbreak of paranormal fire as was the fear and loneliness of an innocent young woman far from her home. Such curses are a group phenomenon.

The question remains: how can the law (and common sense) best deal with manifestations of this sort, so long as their extraordinary source remains denied by our incomplete understanding of, or refusal to accept, such events as originating in a realm of natural activity as yet unexplained by science?[4,5]

19   Jinxes and Jewels

There are so many tales of biologically inanimate objects, typically ships, cars and jewels, with which persistent runs of bad luck or disaster are associated, that it becomes hard to avoid talk of a jinx, curse or hex. Such objects appear to be charged, deliberately or accidentally, with a fatal force malignantly influencing the fate of all involved with them (as in the case of the statuette of Ho-Tei: see chapter 12).

In some cases, typically involving buried or mummified human remains, the misfortune may involve a deliberate curse laid at the time of burial on anyone later disturbing the remains; i.e., the curse apparently associated with the mummy of the Egyptian pharaoh Tutankhamen (see chapter 3).

Perhaps similar are the disturbances caused when a dying person's last wishes in regard to their burial are ignored. Typically, in England, such disturbances are associated with a 'screaming skull' (see chapter 10).

Jinxes differ from curses in that the ill-luck is not caused by malign or deliberate intent, but (perhaps) by fatal accident or mischance causing a death-agony so intense as to print itself (as in a haunting) on objects connected with the disaster. Like some ever-replayed recording, the agony persists in the object, adversely affecting all those drawn to it.

In the case of famous jewels whose owners seem unusually prey to bad luck – the Hope, Regent and Koh-i-Noor diamonds among the best-known – it may be that there is a simpler explanation – the consequences of greed. However, occult powers have long been attributed to jewels, especially diamonds, while 'New Age' lore insists that certain crystals and jewels confer powers of healing, clairvoyance, prophecy and protection against evil. Quartz crystal especially was always thought to stimulate altered states of mind; and it is known that crystals can store electricity. Pressure applied hard and fast, as by a hammer, can generate several thousand volts. But what else can crystals store? Bad luck for the greedy? For some gems seem so fated it makes you wonder why anyone would want to own them.

But first, let's take a look at some famous cases of jinxed cars and ships.

★ ★ ★

Every year thousands of people die or are badly injured in road accidents. The carnage is so great it seems as if collectively, and despite attempts to reduce it by drink-driving laws, seat-belts, and so on, unconsciously we accept the slaughter as necessary sacrifice to the God of Convenience and Speed, as bloodthirstily hungry as Moloch or the Aztec Huitzilopochtli.

Usually, when a high-speed crash occurs, the vehicles involved are write-offs, but sometimes vehicles associated with fatal or violent accidents remain in use despite apparently absorbing an unidentified force that causes the injury or death of anyone using them or their parts.

The curse on the Hapsburgs, for so long Europe's premier imperial family (see chapter 11), apparently ended when, on 28 June 1914, the Austrian Archduke Franz Ferdinand and his wife Sophie risked their lives by appearing in the Bosnian city of Sarajevo, then in revolt against Austria. They went ahead with their tour despite a prior appearance by the *Turnfalken*, the ravens which presaged disaster for the Hapsburgs. As their red limousine approached the corner of Rudolph Street, shots were fired by Gavrilo Princip, a student anarchist. Franz Ferdinand and Sophie were both killed, but the car survived the attack unscathed. However, its later history suggests that somehow the horror of that moment remained active in it. All who owned it thereafter had their lives cut short or were injured. It was bought by the Austrian general Potiorek, who died insane after his defeat at the Battle of Valjevo. The next owner died in a crash nine days after buying it. The Governor of Yugoslavia lost his arm in it; the next owner, a doctor, was crushed to death in it; a Serbian farmer was killed as he started it; a Swiss racing driver was thrown out of it over a wall and died; a garage owner driving it (and his four passengers) all died in a crash while overtaking dangerously. Finally the deadly machine ended up in a Vienna museum. Nobody dared drive it any more.

Then there is the red Porsche sports car in which the Hollywood film star James Dean crashed and died in 1955.

Born in Indiana in 1931, this complex, self-destructive young actor had enjoyed a meteoric rise to fame – fame that, however, proved all too brief. In *East of Eden* (1955), and posthumously in *Rebel Without a Cause*, and *Giant* (1956), he projected a moody, smouldering persona that instantly made him the idol of rebellious US youth in a decade that also saw the rise of the 'Beat Generation'.

Pushing the edge too far one bright California day, Dean lost control of the powerful machine and left the road. His sudden death guaranteed his mythic status. As for the Porsche, it was a total write-off.

Yet it proved deadly even after being dismantled.

Bought by garage owner George Barris, it slipped while being unloaded from the breakdown truck, and broke a mechanic's legs. The engine went into another car which crashed in a race, killing the driver. A second car in the same race, equipped with its drive shaft, overturned and injured its driver. Two tyres from it, on a third car, exploded simultaneously without apparent cause. The driver survived: but George Barris found nothing wrong with either tyre. The Porsche's shell, used in a Highway Safety display in Sacramento, fell off its mounting and broke a teenager's hip. Later, the truck carrying the wreck to another display was involved in an accident. The truck driver, thrown out of his cab, was killed when the Porsche rolled off the back of the truck and crushed him. Then another truck carrying it slipped its handbrake and crashed into a store, and in New Orleans in 1959 (so it is said) it broke into eleven pieces while on stationary supports. Finally it vanished while on a train en route to Los Angeles in 1960.

Relating this and many other tales of jinxed cars in their book *Cars of the Stars*, George Barris and Jack Scagnetti tell how James Dean's mechanic Rolf Weutherich, who broke an arm and a leg in the original crash, was in 1968 convicted of murdering his wife; but, as Colin Wilson suggests, it may be going too far to blame this on the Porsche.[1]

Of course, in both these cases the cars were high-powered. Neither, at any time, would be thought a good risk. Both were red, and red, it comes as no surprise, is the car-colour most often associated with accidents and crashes. UK statistical research published in 1993 suggests that yellow, brown and green are the safest colours. Those preferring red, black or white cars are statistically more likely to be involved in accidents.

Yet this does not explain how, in the case of the Porsche, death and injury resulted while it was being used in a Highway Safety Display. Did Dean's tormented spirit, at the moment he died, imbue the killing machine with a destructive energy afflicting all involved with it thereafter?

This, of course, is pure fancy. Of course.

Seamen have always been superstitious. In North Scotland, for example, the old fishermen would not go to sea if, en route to their boats, they were asked where they were going; or if a minister, hare, dog, rabbit or 'ill-footed' man crossed their path; or if certain names like 'Ross' were mentioned. Any such violation was said to curse the proposed voyage: they would turn back rather than risk it. So, no surprise if tales of jinxed ships are as, or more, common even than tales of jinxed cars.

One of the best-known involves the *Great Eastern*.

In November 1857 this fated vessel, at 19,000 tons easily the largest ever built, was about to be launched. Brainchild of the brilliant English engineer Isambard Kingdom Brunel, it was intended to seize control of the lucrative North Atlantic trade route between Europe and America.

Brunel derided the shipowners Cunard and Collins who, since 1840, had vied for commercial supremacy on the route. None of their ships exceeded 3,000 tons gross. He reckoned that a really big ship, say, six times the tonnage of those then operating, would step up the profit margins fourfold.

Moreover, its design and safety features would be revolutionary.

Brunel was a famous man, with the power to command such projects, and his dream rapidly became reality. Registering his company, the Great Eastern Steam Navigation, and guaranteeing shareholders forty per cent dividends, he designed and built a ship that staggered contemporary imagination.

Six hundred and eight feet long and 80 feet in the beam, the *Great Eastern*'s iron hull, divided by transverse bulkheads into ten separate compartments further subdivided into thirty-six, was itself contained within a second, outer hull – Brunel's masterstroke. Even if the outer hull was holed, the inner wall, three feet inside, would remain intact.

Within, ten boilers fed by 112 furnaces (their smoke carried away by five gigantic funnels) produced 15,000 horsepower; more than enough to turn two 58-foot paddle-wheels and an auxiliary 24-foot propellor. In case of engine failure, he rigged up six vast masts able to carry a huge expanse of sail. Ten anchors weighing five tons each guaranteed huge braking power.

Nothing was left to chance. The passenger appointments and fittings were the most luxurious ever seen outside palaces and grand hotels. Walnut, velvet, arabesques, cut glass glittered and glowed in the state-rooms and drawing-rooms. Brunel had achieved his vision.

On 2 November 1857, the *Great Eastern* lay broadside by the Thames, awaiting launch the following noon. Her keel lay across two huge cradles that she'd carry with her into the river. Two hydraulic rams would move her broadside into the water. Heavy chains would control the motion and hold her back, if need be.

The following day the well-wrapped guests took their places on the specially built grandstand. From the shipyard came the men who had built the ship. But at least one was missing – a master shipwright who had been working on the double hull. Nobody knew where he was.

The jinx was about to make itself known.

The launch began. The cradles stuck. The bow moved just three and a half feet; the stern, seven. That was it. During the next few weeks every attempt to free the *Great Eastern* failed. The chains burst. The hydraulic rams fractured the cradles. Nothing worked. Brunel was told that the best thing he could do with his white elephant was leave her where she was and open her up as a public fun-fair.

Three months later, in March 1858, a combination of spring tides and strong easterlies bringing heavy rain succeeded where man had failed. The *Great Eastern* floated at last. 'Gentlemen, I estimated that the cost to launch our ship would be in the region of £14,000,' Brunel told his directors. 'Instead, it has now cost our company nearly £120,000.'

A fortnight later the Great Eastern Steam Company collapsed. The liner was bought for £160,000 by the newly formed Great Ship Company. A year and a half later, on 15 September 1859, the *Great Eastern* at last steamed into the open sea. By then, Brunel was dead. He had collapsed from a stroke on the ship's deck. The day he died the liner's captain had complained to his chief engineer of being 'rudely disturbed by constant hammering from below'.

Disaster struck immediately. Nearing Southampton after four hours at sea, moments after receiving glowing tributes about her seaworthiness from the pilot, one of the smoke-stacks exploded, killing six men in the engine room and ruining the grand saloon.

On 17 June 1860, fitted out at last, she steamed out of Southampton and in eleven days (a new record) reached New York, after a calm crossing.

Yet, though she had accommodation for 4,000 fare-paying passengers, on this maiden voyage she carried just thirty-six. On her second New York voyage, made in ten days, she carried one hundred. The belief in a jinx already existed.

Commissioned as a British government transport to Quebec, on her third voyage she carried 2,125 soldiers and officers, 403 women and children, and forty fare-paying passengers. It seemed a complete vindication. What jinx?

On her fourth voyage she sailed from Liverpool with 400 first-class passengers. As the *Great Eastern* made her way into the teeth of an autumn gale the thud of hammer-blows was heard, coming from below the engine-room plating. Minutes later the ship, caught broadside by huge waves, almost capsized. Both paddle-wheels were torn away; lifeboats were flung into the sea; saloons and cabins were wrecked and scared passengers prayed and sang hymns.

For a night and a day she wallowed helplessly. Late that afternoon the Cunard liner *Scotia* steamed out of the east, circled the stricken ship (six times bigger), then went on without offering help. The fearful passengers and crew endured a second long night. At dawn, a Nova Scotian brig from the west changed course to come alongside. A passenger offered its captain £100 for every day he would stand by them. As the captain refused, the passenger offered to buy the brig and its freight outright so that all passengers could be taken back to England. But, inexplicably, the brig just sailed away. Maybe its mariners felt that such a big boat should be able to look after itself.

Two days later, she was turned, and limped painfully back to port.

She was never again used as a passenger ship. Stripped of her ornate luxury, storm damage and disaster dogged her thereafter. A man was crushed in the paddle wheel, the captain drowned in a boat with a young boy, she was damaged by storm while in port for repairs. Between 1865 and 1866 the *Great Eastern* helped lay part of the North Atlantic telegraph cable but lost it halfway across. She was offered for sale to the highest bidder, but nobody bid, her reputation being so sinister that port authorities round Britain petitioned the government to prohibit her laying-up under their control.

A Liverpool household store hired her as a vast floating billboard; an experiment abandoned after a month. For twenty years she lay derelict. In 1885 a ship breaker, having bought her for £16,000, arranged to have the ship towed to his yards. As tugs began pulling her on her final journey, the watchman on board demanded to be taken off instantly. He had heard the thud of hammer blows. The tug crews laughed, but took him off. Though almost slipping the lines, the empty giant was brought to the breaker's yard.

There she was dismembered. On opening up the double hull above the keel amidships, the breakers found a bag of rusted tools . . . and the skeleton of the shipwright who had vanished before the launch, accidentally buried alive between the double hulls of Brunel's revolutionary new ship.[2]

Another ill-starred ship was the *Hinemoa*, launched three years after the *Great Eastern*, with a different captain for each of its first five voyages. One went mad, another was jailed, a third drank himself into the DTs, the fourth died in his cabin, and the fifth killed himself. On its sixth voyage the ship capsized; and on the seventh two sailors were lost overboard. Written off in 1908 after drifting in a storm, it is said that its disastrous career was due to the fact of its first ballast being gravel from a London graveyard.[3]

Even more ill-fated was the liner *Titanic* which, on her maiden transatlantic voyage, on the night of 14 April 1912, struck an iceberg and sank with the loss of 1,513 lives. To claim a jinx is to stretch the definition of jinx. Yet some odd twists of fate presaged the tragedy, which had been foreseen fourteen years earlier in a novel, *Futility*, by Morgan Robertson. In it a great liner, the *Titan*, thought unsinkable due to its watertight compartments, hits an iceberg during an April voyage, at a speed of twenty-five knots (*Titanic*: twenty-three knots); it has only twenty-four lifeboats (*Titanic*: twenty) for its 3,000 passengers and crew (*Titanic*: 2,207, but it was only two-thirds full); and not only sinks with huge loss of life, but does so in the same part of the North Atlantic as the *Titanic* was lost.

Odder still is the fate of journalist W. T. Stead. In an 1892 article in the London *Review of Reviews*, railing against the inadequacies of marine safety precautions, he had luridly described the fate of a great liner which, hitting an iceberg in the North Atlantic, sank with huge loss of life. Yet twenty years later Stead was on the *Titanic*, and went down with it, despite having been warned by the palmist Cheiro that: 'Very critical and dangerous for you should be April 1912, especially about the middle of the month. So don't travel then by water if you can help it.' Did Stead want to die, or did he feel he had to try to out-bluff what he perceived as superstition?[4]

There is a postscript. In April 1935 a young seaman, William Reeves, stood watch near midnight in the bow of a Canada-bound steamer. The gloom about was impenetrable. Broodingly aware of what had happened in this area twenty-three years earlier, his sense of alarm mounted. He wanted to shout a warning, but there was no obvious cause. Suddenly he remembered the date the *Titanic* had sunk: 14 April 1912. The day of his birth! He shouted a warning. The engines went full astern. The ship stopped just yards from a huge iceberg. Daylight showed icebergs all around. It took nine days for Newfoundland icebreakers to break a way clear for the little tramp steamer. Its name? The *Titanian*.[5]

Finally, the story of the German battle cruiser *Scharnhorst*. Even before completion it rolled over, killing sixty men. The night before its official launch in October 1936, it launched itself, wrecking several barges. In 1939, in its first major action (the bombardment of Danzig), nine seamen died when a gun exploded, and twelve more suffocated when the air-supply system failed. In 1940, hit again and again while bombarding Oslo, it had to be towed away. Entering the River Elbe by night, it hit the liner SS *Bremen*, which sank and was then destroyed by British bombers. Back at sea, British warships closed in on the *Scharnhorst* at dusk. One fired a speculative broadside from a range of 16,000 yards – nearly ten miles away. Directly hit, the *Scharnhorst* sank.[6]

Jinxed cars, ships . . . and objects and places. In *The Werewolf* (1933), the occultist Montague Summers cites the case of a Devon craftsman who married aged twenty-five and moved into a coastal cottage. Two weeks after the honeymoon he came home drunk. This horrified his wife, as he was reputed to be sober and reliable. The following day he swore it would never happen again. When it did, she went to a 'wise woman' who, visiting the house, pointed to a wooden chair and told them to burn it. They did, and the trouble stopped. Later they learned that the chair, a wedding present, had belonged to a drunken butcher who had committed suicide while sitting in it.[7]

On a muggy January day in the early 1960s, the dowser T. C. Lethbridge and his wife Mina visited Ladram Bay on the Devon coast. 'As I stepped on to the beach, I passed into a kind of blanket, or fog, of depression, and, I think, fear,' he writes in *Ghost and Divining Rod*. Mina agreed. 'There's something frightful here,' she said. Her mother had also felt depressed on the beach; her brother said he and his wife had experienced similar feelings in a field near the megalithic centre of Avebury in Wiltshire, again in warm, muggy weather. The next Saturday (once more warm and wet) Lethbridge and Mina went back to Ladram Bay. Again he felt depressed, at the same place, by a brook running on to the beach, Mina indicated the spot where she had felt something '. . . so strong as to make me feel almost giddy'. Later, atop the cliff, she felt someone was urging her to jump. All this made Lethbridge recall the odd recent death of their local 'witch'.

She had told him she meant to curse the cattle of a farmer she was angry with. Ignoring Lethbridge's warning that the curse might rebound, she had died suddenly. Since then he had felt an unpleasant sensation round her house. It had a limit, like a field bounded by a wall, and he could step out of it.

All this, and dowsing experiments he carried out, led him to conclude that such areas of ugly feeling arise from the interaction of negative human emotion with 'terrestrial force-fields' strongest where underground water flows or where damp conditions prevail. The 'ghoul' of Ladram Bay, he believed, may have been caused by someone who had stood on the clifftop contemplating suicide. The tragedy may or may not actually have occurred, but the intention was enough to leave a trace perceptible thereafter to those walking into the 'field' thus impregnated by the gloomy feelings recorded on to it.[8]

After a pleasant family dinner in May 1884 Henry James Sr, father of the American novelist Henry James and the psychologist William James, sat staring into the fire when suddenly 'fear came upon me, and trembling, which made all my bones to shake'. He sensed 'some damned shape squatting invisible to me within the precincts of the room, and raying out from his fetid personality influences fatal to life'. In seconds 'reduced to a wreck', he controlled his fear and sat it out, yet his resulting despair and nervous breakdown lasted two years. Doctors said he had 'overworked his brain'. Researching this tale, the author Colin Wilson learned that this experience had taken place at Frogmore Cottage near Windsor. Associated with the antlered pagan deity Herne the Hunter, who is said to haunt Windsor Great Park, the area is famous for ghostly events. Moreover the cottage lay just a hundred feet from a known ley line (a course of 'earth energy', real or supposed), and the devastating experience occurred on or near Mayday, when such elemental forces are traditionally strongest.[9]

(See Appendix II for the theory of 'thought-forms'.)

The powerful imprint of curse, jinx, or good or ill-luck is also often associated with jewels and precious stones. Valued not only as ornaments implying wealth, status or royalty, gems were anciently used as amulets to ward off evil, in divination (crystal-gazing and lithomancy), and healing. The Egyptians inscribed spells on blue lapis lazuli; Sumerians and Persians used agate, amethyst, jade, carnelian, jasper and onyx as amulets. Diamond was said to dispel poison; agate, to invigorate; jasper, to help pregnant women and prevent witchcraft. Sapphire was said to be good for sweats, eye troubles and ulcers; emerald restrained desire; ruby banished evil spirits; amethyst ensured chastity and (engraved with the head of Bacchus, god of wine) encouraged sobriety. Chalcedony and topaz were said to dispel lunacy: hyacinth, says Marbodius (1037–1125) relieved suspicion, and beryl cured belching. Cleopatra drank dissolved pearls, said to fortify the heart, to honour her lover, Antony. Astrologers held that to wear particular jewels was lucky or unlucky according to one's birth-date. In myth and legend, dragon-guarded jewels symbolise hidden treasure, but also lust, greed and transient wealth. Cut jewels symbolise the soul shaped into a state able to reflect divinity. In the Indian epic *Mahabharata*, a jewel stolen from the Naga (snake) king Vasuka restores the life of the hero Arjuna.

Diamond has always been viewed as the most potent jewel, able to confer curse or blessing. Anciently it was used as a prophylactic against plague. Queen Elizabeth of England wore a diamond to protect her against infection; Queen Isabella of Spain owed her life to a diamond she wore in her girdle: an assassin's knife glanced off it. Napoleon carried the Regent Diamond in the hilt of his sword.

Yet many diamonds, especially the Regent, Koh-i-Noor, and Hope, are said to carry curses. If so, such curses are usually not so much occult curses, but the subtler, more everyday variety invoked by greed and the lust to own entrancing objects.

Thus it is said of the Regent Diamond that the slave who found or stole it near Golconda in Hyderabad, India, fled to Madras where he took a sailor into partnership. The sailor threw him overboard and, selling the diamond for a thousand pounds, went on a long orgy before hanging himself. Next to buy it was Thomas Pitt of the East India Company. Having paid £20,400, he was so scared of theft he never slept in the same bed twice, while his enemies all said he had stolen it. In 1717 he sold it to the Regent of France – from whom it derived its name – for £135,000. Stolen during the Revolution, later it was found with other treasures in a ditch in the Champs Elysées. Set in the pommel of Napoleon's sword, it was captured by the Prussians after Waterloo, and later returned to the French. In its natural state it weighed 410 carats: cutting reduced it to 137.

More famous is a gem called after the alternative name for Mount Ararat, where Noah's Ark came to rest: *Koh-i-Noor*, 'Mountain of Light'. Once the sacred jewel of the Sikh faith, myth says it originated in the time of the Indian god, Krishna. Having passed (usually disastrously) from one dynasty to another, eventually it came into the hands of Ranjit Singh, the 'Lion of the Punjab'. He was so convinced of its powers that, when he died, he bequeathed it to the shrine of Jagannath at Puri in Orissa. However, his heirs refused to give it up and hung on to it, until the British annexed it along with the Punjab and it was gifted to Queen Victoria. Certain that disaster would follow its removal, some Indians pointed to the Crimean War and the Indian Mutiny as evidence. Yet since becoming one of the British Crown Jewels no ill-luck has pursued it. Before it came to Britain it weighed 186 carats; further cutting reduced it to 106.

Darker is the history of the famous blue Hope diamond. The French gem-hunter Jean-Baptiste Tavernier acquired it, probably by theft from an Indian temple, and sold it to Louis XIV in 1668. Ruined by his son's speculations, Tavernier set out for India again aged eighty-four, but died on the way. Cut into the shape of a heart, the diamond was worn at a court ball by the royal mistress, Madame de Montespan, who then fell from grace for her involvement in black masses, where her naked body was used as the altar, and during which infants were sacrificed. The gem's evil reputation grew. A century later it was given by Louis XVI to his Queen, Marie Antoinette, whose involvement with the 'Diamond Necklace Affair' (see below) disgraced her in the public eye and was a contributory cause of the French Revolution. She wore it, and loaned it to her friend, the Princesse de Lamballe who, during the Revolution, was murdered by the mob, her head being paraded on a pike under the windows of the Temple, where Louis XVI and his family awaited execution. Marie Antoinette herself was executed in October 1793.

Along with the other crown jewels, the Hope vanished during the Revolution, but thirty years later emerged in Holland, cut from sixty-seven to forty-four carats. It was now owned by an Amsterdam lapidary named Fals. His son stole the diamond then left Fals to die in poverty. Giving it to a Frenchman, Beaulieu, Fals' son killed himself. Beaulieu brought it to London, where he died mysteriously. London banker Henry Thomas Hope paid £18,000 for it and gave it his name. It stayed in his family seventy years until Lord Francis Hope married an actress. The marriage was a failure; his wife prophesied ill-luck for all who owned the diamond, and died in poverty blaming it. Lord Francis, in dire financial straits, sold the gem to a French broker, Jacques Colot, who went mad and killed himself, having sold it to the Russian Prince Kanitovsi, who lent it to an actress at the Folies Bergère, then shot her from his box the first night she wore it. Kanitovsi was stabbed by revolutionaries, and the gem passed through the hands of a Greek jeweller, Simon Mantharides, who fell, or was thrown, over a precipice; the Turkish sultan Abdul Hamid, who was deposed in 1909, the year after he bought it; and one Abdul Bey, who drowned.

Auctioned in Paris for £16,000, the Hope crossed the Atlantic to New York, where Edward Beale Maclean, owner of the *Washington Post*, paid £60,000 for it. There is also a tale that the New York jewellers sold it to a client who, returning to America to claim it, sailed on the *Titanic*. Maclean's mother died soon after he bought it, as did two servants in his house, and his ten-year-old son Vinson, knocked down and killed by a car. He separated from his wife Evalyn, was ruined by the Teapot Dome scandal, and ended up insane. Evalyn still wore the diamond, dismissing its evil reputation, but when her daughter committed suicide in 1946, it was recalled how she had worn it at the wedding. When Evalyn died in 1947, the New York jeweller Harry Winston bought all her jewels and presented the Hope to the Smithsonian Institute, where it remains on display today.[10]

Marie Antoinette should have kept clear of diamonds. In 1785, the scandal of the so-called Diamond Necklace Affair harmed the monarchy and destroyed the Queen's reputation. Even though she had known nothing about it, Marie Antoinette became known as a vindictive harpy and as '*la putain autrichienne*' (the Austrian whore).

Consisting of 647 brilliants and 2,800 carats, the necklace, a rococo horror of a type called a *rivière* (usually associated with the décolletage of courtesans and actresses), had been made many years earlier by the court jewellers Böhmer and Bassenge for Louis XV's mistress, Madame du Barry, but in 1774 Louis had died before it could be delivered. His son was crowned Louis XVI, with Marie Antoinette as his Queen. Desperate to sell the necklace, Böhmer tried to get the frivolous new Queen to take it off his hands. Her weakness for diamonds was famous, after all. 'Heedless extravagance', her mother Maria Theresa had called it. But Marie Antoinette, warned to avoid conspicuous extravagance and in any case hating the horror, declined to pay the asking price of 1.6 million livres. Hoisting the weeping jeweller off his knees she told him to break it up and get what he could for the stones.

Enter the real villain, Louis, Cardinal de Rohan, a simpleton who craved royal acceptance, was duped by Jeanne de la Motte, an adventuress who, born into poverty, claimed to be a distressed gentlewoman of tattered pedigree. Having convinced the King's sister, Elisabeth, to instal her at Versailles, Jeanne now persuaded de Rohan that she could win him royal favour. She even got a friend, Nicole Le Guay, to impersonate the Queen and meet the amorous Cardinal late at night in the Grove of Venus at Versailles. 'You know what this means,' murmured Le Guay, pressing a single rose into his trembling hand, then hurried away before he saw through the deception.

Dizzy with joy, he gave de la Motte ever larger sums of money. Her greed and ambition grew until, in November 1785, she acquired the necklace.

With the aid of a forged letter, apparently commissioning his purchase of the necklace for the Queen, she told de Rohan the Queen would pay in four instalments. Brought to the Palais du Cardinal, it was transferred to the Queen's supposed courier – in fact Jeanne's lover, De Réteaux. He broke it up and fenced it round Paris. When suspicions were aroused, Jeanne's complicit husband sold the gems in London. As de Rohan waited impatiently for the first sign of royal favour (and the first instalment to pay the jeweller), Jeanne bought an estate and affected a title. She was not looking very far ahead. With no payments forthcoming, the fraud soon collapsed.

Though de Rohan was clearly a dupe, Louis had him arrested and jailed (in luxury) in the Bastille. Yet the Bastille's image was so evil that a torrent of popular broadsheets emerged, representing de Rohan as the martyred victim of absolutist Bourbon tyranny. He was acquitted. And though de la Motte and her confederates were clearly guilty, soon it became clear that in the public mind not they but the detested Bourbons were on trial.

Jeanne's husband was condemned to the galleys. Publicly whipped, she was branded with the letter V (*voleuse*, 'thief'). Two years later she escaped from prison to London, where her attacks on Marie Antoinette met a ready audience – before eventually she killed herself by leaping from a window.

There had been so many rumours about the degeneracy of the royal court that now people were willing to believe anything. It was said the Queen had tried to destroy de Rohan by manipulating de la Motte because he had refused her indecent advances. She was even accused of a lesbian affair with Jeanne. So the credibility of the monarchy was damaged, perhaps fatally, because of a diamond necklace, and though she had known nothing about it, Marie Antoinette's reputation never recovered. Perhaps when she went to the guillotine in October 1793 (with the *Turnfalken* swooping above: see chapter 11) she cursed the affair as the cause of her death.[11]

Among the world's most mysterious objects is the so-called 'Skull of Doom'. Carved out of pure quartz crystal, and weighing 5.19kg (11lb 7oz), with prismatic eyes in which it is said the future may be seen, this object was discovered in 1927 by Anna Mitchell-Hedges, daughter of the British adventurer 'Mike' Mitchell-Hedges, while exploring the Mayan city of Lubaantum. It was on her seventeenth birthday that Anna saw something under an ancient altar – the top half of the skull. Later she also found its detachable lower jaw. Her father gave it to the local Mayans, who told him that 'it was their god, used for healing or to will death'.[12] Later, the Mayans gave it back to him as a parting gift. In 1980 it was still in the possession of his daughter, kept in a velvet cloth on the sideboard in her house.

Its origin and the circumstances of its discovery remain controversial. Some say Mitchell-Hedges acquired it earlier and elsewhere, and planted it for Anna to find on her birthday. She persistently denied this, without ever saying what she knew of it. In 1962 the *Daily Express* journalist Donald Seaman, visiting this formidable woman about another matter (she had been photographed, it turned out innocently enough, with Gordon Lonsdale, the recently convicted spy), was shown the skull. It was the most beautiful yet disquieting object he had ever seen. He asked how much she thought it was worth. 'Probably about a quarter of a million,' she said. Asked if she was not afraid of burglars, Anna Mitchell-Hedges opened her dressing-gown and showed Seaman the Colt .45 revolver strapped to her waist.[13]

As to the skull's origins, in his autobiography *Danger My Ally* (1954), Mitchell-Hedges speculates that it is at least 3,600 years old and must have taken 150 years in the making, and describes how '. . . according to legend [it] was used by the High Priest of the Maya when performing esoteric rites. It is said that when he willed death with the help of the skull, death invariably followed. It has been described as the embodiment of all evil.'[14]

Yet it should be noted that Mitchell-Hedges, who died in 1959, was a man with a sharp sense of humour and a taste for tall tales. The suspicion that he planted it for his daughter to find persists.

A second crystal, similar save that its jaw is not detachable, is in the Museum of Mankind near Piccadilly Circus in London. Cleaners, worried by its stare, insist that it is covered with a black cloth before they will work near it at night. Bought by the British Museum for £120 in 1898 from Tiffany's of New York, the skull is said to be 'possibly of Aztec origin'.

Comparing both skulls, anthropologist Dr G. M. Morant concluded that one was a copy of the other but, since there is no technique for dating crystal, he could not assign it a date. However, French experts date a similar, smaller crystal skull in Paris to the Aztec culture in the fourteenth or fifteenth century, arguing that the Aztecs were obsessed with death, as in the poem:

> Where would we not go to find death?
> For that desire, our heart bleeds.

And so did many other hearts, so far as the Aztecs were concerned. If any civilisation was ever accursed, it was the Aztec, obsessed as it was with human sacrifice. A scant few years before the arrival of Cortes and his *conquistadors* in 1519, the Temple of the Sun at Tenochtitlán was dedicated appropriately. Over a period of three days, seventy thousand victims were pushed up the steep steps of the pyramid to the black basalt altars at its summit, there to have their hearts hacked out by the ceaselessly labouring priests, before the bodies were rolled down the other side to be taken to the kitchens, prepared, roasted and stuffed with peppers.

20 Shakespeare's Scottish Tragedy

One of the oddest beliefs in this collection of oddities must surely be the insistence by actors and others in the thespian trade that one play is so cursed that to mention its name or quote from it inside a theatre is sure to bring bad luck. If it must be discussed at all, then it should be done evasively, by reference to 'that play', or 'the unmentionable', or (a bit close for comfort) 'the Scottish play', or even (far too close for comfort) 'Shakespeare's Scottish Tragedy'.

Yes. *That* play. The one with the three witches, the blasted heath and the walking wood. The one requiring urgent preventive measures if its name is spoken. Some actors will go to extreme lengths to exorcise the danger. Utter it in the hearing of Peter O'Toole, it is rumoured, and you will be lucky to get away with just being told to leave the room, turn round three times, spit, knock on the door three times, then beg to be let back in.

Either that, or you will have to quote a line from *The Merchant of Venice* – 'Fair thoughts and happy hours attend on you' – a play which many actors consider as lucky as *Macbeth* (the name must be spoken) is unlucky.

The bad luck is said to extend to anything ever used for a production of the play. Some actors refuse to wear a particular cloak or helmet if they find out it was once worn in *that* play while, in the old days of travelling repertory companies, the costumes, furniture and sets for *Macbeth* would never be used for *King Lear*, *Othello* or *Hamlet*.

Many in the theatre, however, are sceptical about the alleged curse on this, the most frequently performed Shakespearean play. 'As a young actor I went along with it because the older generation of actors believed in the curse so strongly,' said Richard Eyre, director of a 1993 production at the Royal National Theatre, 'but these days I resolutely refer to the play by its name.' Touching wood, he added: 'I have my private superstitions, but that's not one of them.'[1]

Michael Bogdanov of the English Shakespeare Company had been on the road six months with his production of *Macbeth* without disaster when he told the journalist Nick Smurthwaite that 'If you take any play as popular as *Macbeth*, you'll find a catalogue of disasters attached to its history. I know an actor playing Macbeth was killed on stage once, years ago, but you might as well say all conjurers are cursed because Tommy Cooper died while he was doing his act.'

To be fair, he might have mentioned the Astor Place riot of 1849, in Boston, Massachusetts. Edwin Forrest, the leading American tragedian, had a year earlier toured his *Macbeth* round Britain, but it was rubbished by his English competitor, William Macready. When Macready, on an American tour, in turn brought *Macbeth* to Boston, Forrest took revenge by mounting a rival production in a theatre across the street. Macready came on stage only for patriotic Forrest fans to start pelting him with tomatoes. He ran for cover as the mob outside became so violent that the army was summoned. Ordered to fire over the heads of the rioters (up to 20,000 strong), the soldiers got it wrong and fired into the crowd, killing thirty-one people.

That occasion at least may fairly be said to have been cursed. Yet what evidence is there of a curse and, if there is one, how did it begin?

In his *Supernatural on Stage* (1975; English version, *The Curse of Macbeth*, 1981)[2] actor-director Richard Huggett claims that there is 'overwhelming and indisputable' evidence that, in having his three witches use genuine black magic incantations in the original text, Shakespeare invoked a fatal and irrevocable curse on the play. While agreeing that other Shakespearean plays are also bloody and violent, Huggett suggests that *Macbeth* is the darkest and most despairing of all, a play obsessed with evil and the supernatural, without any light in it at all. Moreover, it was written for a king whose morbid belief in witchcraft and demonology was complete and unquestioning. (We met this king earlier, in chapter 6: *Bothwell and the Witches*.) Born in 1566 and an only child, James VI of Scotland was brought up in a time of violence and cruelty extreme even by Scottish standards. Taken in infancy from his mother, Mary Queen of Scots, he never saw her again. After having numerous lovers stabbed, blown up, or otherwise despatched, Mary ended up in prison in England and had her head chopped off in 1587. A sickly, neurotic homosexual, James was brought up by regents and tutors who crammed Calvinist hell-fire religion into him. Meanwhile, civil war raged, and men and women (mostly the latter) accused of witchcraft fuelled numerous bonfires. Nor did James hang back. In 1593, he was helpful in the torture chamber where the Witches of Berwick, accused of trying to kill him, were 'interrogated' to establish their capacity to fly broomsticks and sail on sieves. In 1595 he published *Daemonologie*, a treatise on black magic.

When Queen Elizabeth died in 1603, he gained the additional title of James I of England. Taking up residence at Hampton Court near London with his queen, Anne of Denmark, this dour, spindly monarch, who had never seen a play in his life – Calvinists hated such frivolities – was instantly captivated by the glories of Shakespearean drama.

He and Anne commanded endless performances. Shakespeare's company had never been kept so busy. Having seen the entire repertoire, James endorsed them as the King's Men and increased their wages for each performance from £10 to £20. The Bard of Avon had to work round the clock, producing enough new plays to meet the royal demand.

Macbeth was written and first performed in 1606. It was a right royal disaster.

It was also wildly inaccurate, historically speaking. But Shakespeare, more concerned with writing a rattling good yarn to please James, knew all about the king's obsession with witchcraft. With only a month to write it, he mixed in various events from Scots history, like the execution of three Forres women in AD 960 for using witchcraft against King Duff. But, claims Huggett, he went too far in his desire for authenticity by using genuine black magic incantations and recipes. The foul ingredients of the witches' brew in Act I, Scene iii were not solely the product of Shakespeare's imagination:

> Scale of dragon, tooth of wolf,
> Witches' mummy, maw and gulf
> Of the ravin'd salt-sea shark.
> Liver of blaspheming Jew,
> Gall of goat, and slips of yew
> Sliver'd in the moon's eclipse,
> Nose of Turk and Tartar's lips,
> Finger of birth-strangled babe
> Ditch-delivered by a drab . . .

Huggett says that, in using real spells for frivolous purposes, the Bard so cursed the play that disaster has dogged it ever since.

This seems, on the face of it, as far-fetched as death-prayers, family curses, jinxed cars and ships, and so on. So why not a jinxed play?

The first performance took place at Hampton Court with Richard Burbage in the lead. The curse struck immediately. Hal Berridge, the boy actor playing Lady Macbeth, was suddenly taken ill: Shakespeare himself had to play the part – or so claims the diarist John Aubrey.

Worse still, James, a coward who hated the sight of cold steel, was so upset by all the blood and guts from the butcher's shop spilled on stage that *Macbeth* was promptly banned for five years. It was performed at the Globe Theatre in 1611, but then vanished from the theatre until 1667. In that year, rewritten by Sir William Davenant for the frivolous tastes of Restoration playgoers as a light-hearted musical complete with dancing and a flying ballet, it was a smash hit.

This version, with three singing witches, was revived in 1703 during a puritan backlash against the theatre led by the reformer Jeremy Collier.

During its run occurred the worst storm in England's history. One and a half thousand seamen died, Bristol was destroyed, and London was severely damaged. Collier announced that the hurricane expressed God's wrath at the iniquitous play. Queen Anne declared a day of fasting. to appease God; the theatres shut for a week. When it was performed in 1721, the cast attacked jeering playgoers with their broadswords, and the army was called in.

In 1744 David Garrick 'improved' the play, rewriting Davenant's version in a vain attempt to restore its tragic stature. In 1775 the actress Mrs Siddons first played Lady Macbeth (in the Garrick version) with only one night to learn the part, and was so overcome by the horror of it that her initial performance was a disaster.

The original text was restored by Kemble at Drury Lane in 1794. With it returned the curse. At one performance, adapted so that Macbeth was slain on stage, the actor sustained a near-fatal stab wound.

Huggett agrees with the sceptics that a play involving so many battles, duels and murders, and taking place mostly at night (meaning dim lighting), is bound to cause accidents. He also accepts that the part of Macbeth is emotionally and physically exhausting, climaxing in four duels fought one after the other, up and down steps and rostrums, so that even with blunted swords, cuts and bruises are only to be expected.

Yet there are many instances of the curse triumphing. Typical was a 1937 Old Vic revival with Laurence Olivier playing the part for the first time. During rehearsals the French director, Michel St Denis, who barely spoke English and could not make himself understood, and Vera Lindsey, playing Lady Macbeth, were badly bruised in a car crash. The following day a dog belonging to Lilian Bayliss, founder and director of the Old Vic, was run over and killed by a car. At the dress rehearsal it was found the sets did not fit. Olivier caught a cold and lost his voice. The opening had to be postponed until the following Friday. Tyrone Guthrie took over from St Denis; the cast worked flat out. Olivier, sitting in the wings, was called on-stage. Just as he left his seat a stage weight crashed down on to it and broke it to pieces. Lilian Bayliss had a heart attack, and died on Friday, night of the first performance. Later a member of the audience, hit by a fragment of Olivier's sword, also had a heart attack and died.

With the press playing up the dreaded curse for all it was worth, the production was transferred to the New Theatre for a three-week run before Christmas, but the West End public stayed away. It was a flop.

Years later, the Old Vic decided to try again. But when the 1954 revival, with Paul Rogers as Macbeth, went on the road, the company manager broke both legs in a car accident, an electrician sustained third-degree burns, there was an attempted suicide, and two of the actresses had abortions.

In 1955 Olivier played *Macbeth* again, with Vivien Leigh as Lady Macbeth and Keith Michell as Macduff. He gave what many who saw it claim to be the greatest modern rendering. A film version was prepared, but the backers got cold feet, deciding that Olivier was not good box-office – this after his film versions of *Henry V*, *Hamlet*, and *Richard III* had all been hits!

In 1967 Peter Hall prepared to direct Paul Scofield as Macbeth at Stratford. He told the company there was no curse. The rehearsals went smoothly, until one day a man employed in the theatre offices collapsed and died of a heart attack. Then Hall himself fell ill with shingles, and for six weeks had to lie still in a dark room. The production was postponed; tickets were refunded. When at last the play opened, it was during an August heatwave. With the actors in heavy plastic costumes it was torture.

In 1970 Anthony Tuckey, of the Liverpool Repertory Theatre, decided to direct the play though other repertory directors warned against it. In the second week of rehearsals the actor playing Macbeth was hit in the eye by a sword. Lady Macbeth caught flu, which spread, so five understudies were needed. Jack Lynn, who had just played Macbeth at Chesterfield, declined to take over. He was suffering from head injuries sustained during his own opening night's final duel with Macduff.

When in 1948 Diana Wynyard played Lady Macbeth, she said after the dress rehearsal she did not believe in the curse. She decided to play the sleepwalking scene with eyes closed, and fell fifteen feet off the rostrum. A real trouper, she completed the scene, though now with her eyes open.

An actress in *Irma La Douce* quoted from *Macbeth* from the wings before going on. That evening her car crashed, and two days later she went down with food poisoning. Actor Martin Jarvis, playing *Hamlet* at Windsor in 1973, remembers how a colleague, quoting from *Macbeth* just before going on, then forgot his entire speech. That same evening, Polonius suffered a stroke, even as Huggett's letter asking Jarvis for *Macbeth* experiences arrived at the theatre. Old Vic actors recall how in the mid-fifties a young sceptic quoted from *Macbeth* during a performance of *The Merchant of Venice*. Minutes later, three actors suffered broken toes and fingers when struck by a piece of mobile scenery, and the young actor, stepping out of the stage door that night, was knocked over by a car and injured, though not fatally.

During the run of *Oliver!* at London's New Theatre an usherette in the lobby, waiting for the show to end, began quoting from *Macbeth* and was severely reprimanded – but too late. Minutes later, in the final scene, the actor Claude Jones fell from a bridge, fractured his skull, and died instantly.

Actors in *Antony and Cleopatra* at the Bankside Theatre in 1973 began to shout a speech from *Macbeth* in the dressing room, just to see what would happen. A storm promptly blew up, producing such a deluge that the canvas roof began to fill up and sag as lightning short-circuited the theatre's power. With the stage now a death trap, the performance was stopped, and the audience got clear just as the roof collapsed. Damage to the theatre was so great that the 1974 season had to be cancelled. What the theatre owner had to say to the errant actors is not known. Probably just as well.

As for fatalities, a wartime production with John Gielgud as Macbeth may hold the record. The rehearsals took place in Manchester's unheated Scala Theatre in January 1942. Beatrice Fielden-Kaye, the Third Witch, fell ill, left the company, and died of a heart attack in her hotel during the final rehearsal, on a Friday. In Edinburgh the actor playing Duncan, Marcus Barron, died of angina. Later at London's Piccadilly Theatre, one of the witches, dancing round the cauldron, could not maintain the tempo of William Walton's music. She collapsed and died on stage. The set-designer John Minton committed suicide in his studio, surrounded by his pre-Raphaelite costumes. The flats used in the production were later used in a light comedy that went on tour. The star was the matinee idol, Owen Nares. He died on the tour.

The most notorious incident occurred in 1947, when the Oldham Repertory Company produced the play. A promising young actor, Harold Norman, played Macbeth. In the final fight scene with Macduff, Norman fell, but instead of dying on stage as rehearsed, he crawled into the wings. 'Douglas, I've been stabbed,' he whispered to Douglas Emery the director, 'I can't take my curtain call.' Taken to hospital, he appeared to recover, but peritonitis set in. Exactly a month later he died. Soon afterwards his baby daughter died of suffocation, and his widow suffered a nervous breakdown. A quarter of a century later it emerged that, in the dressing-room he shared with an older actor before the production, Norman had begun quoting from *Macbeth*, refusing to stop even when warned. Six weeks later he was dead. To this day the Oldham Coliseum refuses to have anything to do with *Macbeth*.

As in the case of the Astor Place riot in 1849, the curse travels well. In South Africa, a passer-by paused outside a Cape Town theatre to watch stage scenery being unloaded. He asked what play it was. '*Macbeth*', a stagehand told him. Promptly, a spear fell out of a bundle being winched into the theatre, plunged into the bystander, and killed him instantly.

The Russian impresario Stanislavski, fascinated by *Macbeth*, spent years preparing and rehearsing it with his Moscow Arts company. After endless delays, at last in the early 1900s the production reached the stage of the dress rehearsal. In the murder scene, Macbeth forgot his lines and turned to the prompter's box for help. There was no reply. He investigated, and found the old man slumped dead over the script. A true Russian fatalist, Stanislavski abandoned the production and never tried it again.

In 1964 Michael Benthall was invited by the Portuguese National Theatre to direct *Macbeth* in translation. It was a splendid production. Two days after the first performance the theatre burned to the ground.

Of a legendary Japanese production it is said that condemned criminals were forced to rehearse and play Macbeth with professional actors, and that Macbeth's decapitation, and the display of his severed head on a pole, was not faked. The production, received with huge enthusiasm, is said to have run until it had exhausted the supply of condemned prisoners. It is not clear how much truth there is in this tale.

As most productions of *Macbeth* outside Britain are mounted in the United States, the curse has done well on the other side of the Atlantic.

Charlton Heston suffered particularly from it. Having played Macbeth several times, in 1953 he took the role in an open-air production at Fort St Catherine, Bermuda. During rehearsals he had a bad motorbike crash and had to take several days off. It was the first time he had ever missed a day's rehearsal. During the first performance, riding his horse bareback in the first scene with Banquo, Heston suddenly rushed off stage, pointing at his tights. 'Get them off me, get them off me!' he demanded, writhing in pain. It later emerged that whoever had laundered the tights had dipped them in kerosene. The sweat of the horses and the heat had caused serious burns on Heston's legs and groin. More accidents dogged the performance, but the climax came when the soldiers storming Macbeth's castle literally burned it down, as planned. Kerosene-soaked logs and wooden structures had been placed all round the open-air set, but a high wind had blown up and the flames and smoke blew straight into the audience, causing a stampede.

At least nobody died in or during this production.

Clayre Ribner, general manager of a Shakespeare Festival at Stratford, Connecticut, remembers how in 1961, during dress rehearsals of *Macbeth*, one actor, on a bike, was knocked over by a car. He was joined in hospital by one of the witches. A stage lift rose too high, she stepped forward, fell, and injured herself badly. After more accidents, in the last month of the season Franklin Cover, playing Macbeth in the White House before JFK (see chapter 17), was injured by a fall then developed a cyst under his left arm. He was operated on, and continued playing in pain, blood seeping through his bandages. Because the dye of his costume worked into his wound, another operation was required. Then Douglas Sherman, a young actor, was found dying of stab wounds near the theatre. The murderer was never found. A week later, the daughter of the actress Colgate Salisbury fell from an apartment window and died. Jack Landau, the company manager, was murdered in his Boston apartment. Two men were charged but released for lack of evidence.

In Minneapolis, a young actor, George Ostroska, collapsed and died of a heart attack while playing his first Macbeth. This happened even as he was talking to the two murderers in the banquet scene, and at the lines:

> There's blood on the face,
> Thou art the best of cut-throats.

There are many more cases. Is there a curse – or not? A radical recent interpretation of the play, by the Odyssey touring company, was based on Balinese customs. While rehearsing in Bali, the company went daily to a local temple to be blessed. 'It was rather comforting, like an insurance policy against evil spirits,' explained the director, Nigel Jameson, saying of the curse that: 'Our culture is so bereft of myth and superstition it seems a pity to pooh-pooh it.'

Which may be a good note (if there is such a thing, given the nature of the subject) on which to end this Book of Curses . . . Except for a new development – the apparent return of an ancient hysteria, in a new form.

21   Afterword: The New Witch-hunts

In Europe the witch-burning craze led to the torture and death of thousands of victims. It ended only when educated folk stopped believing in witches. At last Satan took a back seat – or maybe he was just watching and waiting.

In 1992 in the USA there were over *three million* official reports of child sex abuse, many allegedly involving satanic rites. Whatever the real incident of abuse, in whatever form, mounting numbers of people are being vilified and condemned for activities imagined by those accusing them.

Not every Dominican was a self-deluding hysteric. Nor does every social worker or therapist automatically believe in the sometimes fantastic claims of alleged victims of sexual abuse. Yet some, to validate beliefs of their own, assert that even *dreams* of abuse are *proof* of abuse – and by endlessly questioning bored or scared children, they get the answers they want.

Lives have already been ruined by this new witch-hunting mentality.

In 1989, the staff of the Little Rascals day-care centre in Edenton, North Carolina, were accused of abusing over eighty children, though no visitors had noticed anything suspicious. Of seven people arrested, two were jailed for life, following allegations by the children. Drawn out by parents and therapists over several months (using techniques like refusing meals until the required tale was told), the allegations told of children being microwaved or fed to sharks said to belong to the owner of a video store. Therapists were not asked to testify; doctors found no evidence of abuse; yet the case was tried in 1992, the children being questioned in closed court. Arraigned on 183 charges of satanic paedophilia, Robert Kelly, owner of the day-care centre, received twelve consecutive life sentences. Three jurors complained on a PBS TV documentary that colleagues made them return guilty verdicts.[1]

Awaiting trial as an accomplice, Robert's wife Betsy Kelly noted that the accusations came mostly from non-working mothers. Why? In the *Daily Telegraph*, Claudia Fitzherbert, recognising a new militancy among stay-at-home mothers, observed that: ' "Maternal correctness" involves the banding together of women who have forgone their careers for the sake of their children and are consumed with loathing for their less sacrifical sisters.'[2]

In East Olympia, Washington State, twenty-two-year-old Ericka Ingram broke down at an all-women prayer meeting at her Christian fundamentalist church when another woman said she sensed, via the 'Holy Spirit', that Ericka had been sexually abused by her father, Paul Ingram, a local deputy sheriff and county chairman of the Republican Party. Then Ericka's eighteen-year-old sister Julie began telling of satanic rites involving their family and some of their father's friends. Bullied by prosecuting therapists, their mother Sandy weakened, producing her own memories of satanism and sodomy. At first their brother Chad denied being abused but, worn down, recalled a childhood dream of an obese black witch sitting on him as he lay paralysed in bed – a dream taken to mean that he had been sexually abused by cult members.

When Paul confessed to every charge, a sceptical psychologist *invented* fake charges. Paul not only agreed with but elaborated on them (like Isobel Gowdie in 1662: see chapter 6). The case collapsed too late. Jailed on six counts of third-degree rape, Paul will be eligible for parole in AD 2002.[3]

In New Zealand in April 1993, thirty-five-year-old Peter Ellis, a worker at the Christchurch Civic Childcare Centre, was charged with abusing fifty toddlers between 1986 and 1991. Three female co-workers, accused of helping him to lock up the children in underground mazes or in cages hung from the ceiling, were acquitted. Ellis was jailed for ten years.

It began in November 1991 when a boy told his father he didn't like his teacher's 'black penis' (Ellis is Caucasian). When questioned, he said it was 'just a story', but the worried parents turned to a 'community consultant': the female co-founder of an abuse therapy organisation, START. Her efforts led to Ellis's arrest on forty-five indecency charges, most made by a six-year-old boy who, already in therapy, said that Ellis had abused him, made him eat excrement, and threatened to turn him into a frog. Pushed into a maze, he had met two of Ellis's friends, Spikehead and Boulderhead. He said children were made to stand naked in a circle drawn on the floor of Ellis's house; outside the circle stood slit-eyed guitar-playing white-suited adults holding magic knives. The ritual over, they put the children in ovens and pretended they would eat them. Asked why he had mentioned none of this before, he said: 'Oh, I just remembered today.' During the trial it was said no child could invent such tales. Despite there being no evidence of abuse, and though the charges followed weeks of leading questioning of the children, Ellis was found guilty on sixteen counts. 'I don't blame the children at all,' said Debbie Gillespie on her acquittal. 'They don't think they are actually lying. They are emotionally manipulating their parents. Every time they disclosed [new evidence] they would get these cuddles . . .'[4]

In November 1990, on Scotland's Orkney Isles, eight children from the same 'large and unruly family' were 'uplifted' on the orders of Paul Lee, head of the social services department. Early in 1991 their allegations led Lee to order dawn raids on local homes. 'I was put in a room with a piece of paper and a pen and told to write down what had happened, and if I didn't write it down I wasn't coming out,' said one of the two girls making the allegations. 'I got bribed with a pair of new shoes. I was told that if I said something I could have two pairs.' As a result nine more children were 'uplifted', having allegedly been abused by a satanic coven run by an ageing minister with a weak heart, the Rev Morris Mackenzie. He was said to strip naked on winter nights in an abandoned quarry and there abuse the children. The nine (all from incoming English families) were placed in care. Public outrage led to reunion with their families, but three years later seven of the original eight were still in care. Suspended on full salary, early in 1993 Paul Lee resigned with £57,000 in termination pay. As for the Rev Mackenzie, in May 1993 he left Orkney, his name uncleared. 'As a Christian minister I ought to be able to forgive – but I can't yet,' he admitted.[5]

The term 'False Memory Syndrome' has been coined to deal with such cases. In March 1992, in Philadelphia, the False Memory Syndrome Foundation was set up by parents insisting that they have been wrongly accused of abusing their children, either prosaically or satanically.[6]

Whatever the truth in these cases (it is said there is no smoke without a fire), the vehement literalism leading to their prosecution is as fearful as the eagerness of seemingly sensible people to believe 'evidence' that is often as watertight as the sieves in which witches were once said to sail to sea. And where typically the hysterical accusations were once made by men against women, now it is often the other way round. This may seem no more than poetic justice – but two wrongs never did make a right. Either way, not reason but supernaturalism (Satan's name) is invoked to justify persecution. Sadly, it seems that the accursed ancient mind-set described earlier in this book still persists as the millennium draws to a close.

Appendix I: The Evil Eye

The power of the eye to cast spell or curse is among the oldest, most common of beliefs. Just to be eyed by a person suspected of witchcraft or sorcery is potentially to be cursed. This fear of the 'Evil Eye' persists. Try staring at someone on the bus and see what happens! A tension develops which may lead to an argument or worse. A similar fear is connected with the act of pointing at someone; the suspicion in either case being that the starer (or pointer) is trying to impose their will, to dominate the other, and thus, to curse.

In earlier times it was believed that there is such a thing as an eye-beam; a potent influence emitted from every eye; and that evil-minded folk could manipulate and intensify their eye-beams to wreak havoc and harm. In Egyptian myth the creator-god Atum had a detachable eye, both an agent of his creative power (humanity was formed from its tears) and of his fury. Its power was passed on to the god Horus. A spell from one of the Coffin Texts reads: 'I am the all-seeing Eye of Horus, whose appearance strikes terror.' The eye was associated with Satan, a leader of angels or stars, the 'eyes' of the night sky. So the peacock is connected with Satan due to the 'eyes' on its tail, while in modern occult symbolism the Devil is linked with the Hebrew letter *ayin*, traditionally representing an eye.[1]

The single withering eye of mythical monsters like Balor, King of the demonic Irish Fomorians, the Cyclops, or the Eskimo sea-goddess Sedna represents destructively brute elemental force. The classical case of the demonic evil eye is that of the Gorgon Medusa in Greek myth, her gaze so terrible that anyone meeting it was instantly turned to stone.

Celts thought the 'evil eye' arose from envy or malice on the part of its owner, who might be unaware of the power, and who could cast it at a distance. It was usually attributed to (old) women and those thought to be witches, especially if their eyes were of different colours. If a child (the prettiest) or beast (the finest, and particularly horses or cattle) fell ill, the evil eye was blamed. Horses afflicted would sweat, tremble and weaken daily. It turned ale or milk instantly sour.[2]

In Africa the evil eye is believed to be inheritable. Those born with it cannot remove it. It can cause abortion, make spears break, make rats eat the corn, or sicken cows. In many areas, prolonged staring is taken to be evidence of witchcraft. In many parts of the world the belief remains as persistent now as in the past. 'Eat not thou the bread of him that hath an evil eye!' declared Solomon (Proverbs 23:6), while in Naples even today the cry of *jettatore!* (one who throws or casts the *malocchio*, the evil eye) is enough to send folk scrambling out of the path of the unlucky person who is afflicted or thought to be afflicted with the power.

Particularly feared in Italy is the *jettatore di bambini*, whose gaze is said to bring death to children. Frederick Elworthy, author of the classic work on the subject, *The Evil Eye*, tells of one man in Naples who three times became a godfather: in each case the infant quickly died, so that thereafter mothers who knew him took all sorts of precautions to keep their children out of his sight.

The nineteenth-century Pope Pius IX was said to be a *jettatore*, so that the most devout Catholics, while asking his blessing, would make the *mano cornuta* (see below), pointing two fingers at him to deflect the blight of his eye. It was said whatever he blessed turned into a fiasco. He blessed the Italian campaign against Austria in 1848; battles were promptly lost. He blessed a new column to the Madonna and its workmen: that day a workman fell from the scaffolding and died. And so on. Nobody blamed the Pope; it was not his fault, but precautions against his gaze were necessary.

Many talismans or amulets were designed to protect against *malocchio*, which was believed to work only for the first glance. If this first glance could be deflected, no harm would be done. A potent form of deflection was by means of a grotesque head, such as that of a demon or monster. Elworthy supposes that this is why one class of amulets were called *fascina*, being intended to *fascinate* (from the Latin *fascinare*, 'to bind' or 'to bewitch') the evil glance itself. Such demonic amulets were also known as gorgoneions, grylli or chimerae. Amulets in the form of eyes were painted on ancient pottery, and are still seen on the prows of boats in the Mediterranean. The classic 'deflector' was the shield of Athena, incorporating the head of the Medusa after Perseus used the shield while cutting it from her body. Elworthy also says that most shields were intended to deflect not only arrows and spears, but the evil eye of the enemy, and that, the better to do so, they incorporated striking and colourful heraldic designs.[3]

Other charms against the evil eye included rowan and juniper, burning cloth, iron and horseshoes: and also many hand-signals, most especially in Mediterranean lands. The best-known is the *mano cornuta* – index and little finger extended, middle and ring finger bent back under the thumb, the hand being thrust out against the enemy. Another sign, the *mano fica* (as in the expression

'I don't care a fig!'), consists of the thumb thrust out between first and second fingers, all the fingers being bent back against palm and base of thumb. Often manufactured as an amulet, this sign is identical in purpose with the gesture of 'giving the V-sign'; i.e., making horns against an enemy, usually while speaking a counteracting curse like 'bugger off!'. Likewise, to cross oneself is another form of manual amuletic protection against the evil eye.

Appendix II: Thought-forms

Many occult or pseudo-scientific theories have been advanced in attempts to explain how, if curses or death-prayers act not merely through the victim's suggestibility and terror, they can work at all. It seems plain enough from many tales herein that often the suggestibility or guilty conscience of the victim work to make the prophesied fate self-fulfilling – but many others make it plain that a curse can work even if the victim remains unaware of it. And apart from specific curses, cast by one person on another, there are numerous cases of jinxed cars, ships, jewels, statuettes, houses, etc., in which the ill-luck primarily affects an object or place, and not any specific individual, as in a haunted house, or as in the depression T. C. Lethbridge and his wife Mina experienced at Ladram Bay (see page 208), or as in the fate befalling those associated with James Dean's Porsche or Franz Ferdinand's limousine (pages 202–3).

In such cases it seems as if the horror of violent death has somehow become imprinted on the jinxed machine or haunted house. No curse has been consciously cast, but the effect is as potent as if it had been.

Pursuing such a theory in his book *Design for Destiny*, Edward Russell calls such imprints 'T-fields' (Thought-fields). Observing that in his opinion the conscious projection of such fields is the basis of the ancient custom of blessing or cursing material objects, he writes of the phenomenon that one of its most common forms 'are the thoughts of horror or despair imprinted on the structure of a building in which some murder or tragedy has taken place. These powerful thoughts seem to saturate the building materials and to last indefinitely'.[1]

A common view is that such thought-fields or thought-forms, consciously or otherwise formed, assume their own existence and persona once projected, and that their initiator must take precautions lest they rebound or be cast back. Thus the Kahuna system of capturing subconscious spirits, *Unihipli*, and sending them out to destroy the victim's *mana* (chapter 13). Such spirits are said to have their own distinct, semi-autonomous existence.

Daskalos, the Cypriot 'Magus of Strovolos', claims that 'elemental spirits' consist of thoughts and/or feelings projected by individuals who, by brooding on any powerful desire, create *noetic* (psychic) matter. The elemental is thus initially an inner mental image. He says such images can take on a life of their own and exist independently of their creator. One type is created subconsciously by desire or emotion (might this cause jinx or haunting?); the other is created by controlled thought and projected deliberately (curse?). This more potent type lasts longest, but is less common than unconscious projection, which is often the result of negative emotions like envy and hatred, creating elementals that return to their creator's subconscious, forming habits and obsessions (self-cursing).[2]

In *Magic and Mystery in Tibet*, the renowned French traveller Alexandra David-Neel describes how, doubting tales of the materialisation of thought-forms known as *tulpas*, she visualised and animated such a phantom herself. Choosing for her experiment 'a monk, short and fat, of an innocent and jolly type', after months of intense concentration, 'the phantom monk was formed' and grew 'gradually fixed and *life*like'. This *tulpa* 'became a kind of guest' in her apartment. When she went travelling, 'the monk included himself in the party', and grew independent, performing actions she had not commanded, appearing without her having to think of him, and changing.

'The fat, chubby-cheeked fellow grew leaner, his face assumed a vaguely mocking, sly, malignant look. He became troublesome and bold. In brief, he escaped my control [and] began to prove trying to my nerves . . . I decided to dissolve the phantom. I succeeded, but only after six months of hard struggle. My mind-creature was tenacious of life.'

Noting that a herdsman who saw the *tulpa* in her tent took it for a live lama, she adds: 'There is nothing strange in the fact that I may have created my own hallucination. The interesting point is that in these cases of materialisation, others see the thought-forms that have been created.

'Tibetans disagree in their explanations of such phenomena: some think a material form is really brought into being, others consider the apparition as a mere case of suggestion, the creator's thought impressing others and causing them to see what he himself sees.'[3]

David-Neel makes no comment on what is perhaps the most interesting aspect of her experience: the way in which her mind-creature gradually transformed itself into something sly and malignant. There are two main possibilities. One is that her own subconscious guilt at dabbling in such practices subverted her conscious intention. The other is that, without intending to, she created a puppet which became possessed by a genuine discarnate entity or spirit. Which brings us back to square one: either way, it is all in the mind.

But *what* is all in the mind? The entire created universe?

The English occultist Dion Fortune tells how, while brooding on someone who had hurt her, she 'formulated a werewolf accidentally'.

Lying on her bed thinking of Fenrir, the wolf-monster of Norse myth, she abruptly felt a large grey wolf manifest. In *Psychic Self-Defence* she writes:

'I knew nothing of the art of making elementals at that time, but had accidentally stumbled upon the right method – the brooding highly charged with emotion, the invocation of the appropriate natural force, and the condition between sleeping and waking in which the etheric double readily extrudes.' Elbowing the wolf she told it: 'If you can't behave yourself, you will have to go on the floor.' Pushed off the bed, the beast vanished through the wall. Later another household member said she had seen its eyes in the corner of her room. Summoning the beast back, Dion Fortune saw a thin cord joining it to her. Imagining that she was drawing the life out of the wolf along this cord, she dissolved it, meanwhile resisting the most violent emotional demand to run berserk and destroy 'anything and anybody that came to hand . . .' She concludes: 'It is a curious point that, during the brief twenty-four hours of the thing's life, the opportunity for an effectual revenge presented itself.'[4]

Like Daskalos and David-Neel, she explains such entities in terms of human capacity to create elemental thought-forms that exist independently, their creators too often remaining unaware of what they have done.

In December 1912 a St Petersburg occult group, the Brotherhood of the Rising Sun, invited a Tibetan or Chinese guru to direct an experiment, to create an *egrigor*, an entity similar to David-Neel's *tulpa*. He told them that *egrigors* are created by human thoughts, which consist of electrical energy plus *prana* (alias *mana*, vital force). Ordinary thoughts cannot make *egrigors*, but an accumulation or concentration of good or evil thoughts can create *egrigors* visible to the ordinary physical senses. He continued:

Especially powerful and dangerous emanations are produced by human beings dying violent deaths. Cursing one's murderer or executioner creates a dreadful *egrigor*, which lives in the astralic plane for a long time. Having received, from the healthy, strong body of the murdered or executed person, a lot of *prana*, such an *egrigor* becomes so vital that it can cause trouble even in our physical plane.[5]

Other pertinent instances include the deliberate production during the 1970s by a Toronto group of an imaginary entity, Philip, a ghost from seventeenth-century England. Inventing this wholly fictitious entity, and though they never manifested Philip visibly, they were amazed at the degree of autonomy 'Philip' attained, complete with messages and details of his life on earth. They also generated psychokinetic phenomena. Raps were heard from overhead pipes and the walls; several times the table round which they sat rose off the floor, once chasing one of the group across the room. They duplicated several of these phenomena during a live television show before a studio audience, the table moving about then climbing three steps in the studio.

There's much more going on in the human mind than most of us ever begin to realise. The concept of the thought form may just lie at the very core of the entire strange business of jinx and curse. Not only that, but there is a deeper problem posed by the idea of the *collective* thought-form, and of particular ideas that take root and underlie the behaviour of entire societies – such as dogmas like Original Sin, and beliefs leading to the demonisation of scapegoat groups.

In other words, how far are our individual thoughts our own?

References

1 Introduction

2 Contemporary Curses

1. *America: The Sorcerer's New Apprentice*, Dave Hunt and T. A. McMahon, Harvest House Publishers, New York.
2. 'Doctors Becoming Versed in Curses', Keay Davidson, *San Francisco Examiner*, 2 May 1993.
3. *Arthur C. Clarke's World of Strange Powers*, John Fairley and Simon Welfare, Book Club Associates, London, 1985, pp. 19– 21.
4. *The Occult*, Colin Wilson, Grafton, London, 1979, pp. 82–3.
5. *The White Goddess*, Robert Graves, Faber & Faber, London, 1961 (1946).
6. *The Saturnian Quest*, Wilson Knight, London, 1964.
7. *op. cit.*, 5, pp. 67–8.
8. *op. cit.*, 3, pp. 23–4.
9. *ibid.*, p. 32.
10. *ibid.*, p. 32.
11. *Gypsies of Britain*, Brian Vesey-Fitzgerald, David & Charles, Newton Abbot, 1973 (1944), p. 126.
12. *ibid.*, p. 137.
13. *World of Strange Phenomena*, Charles Berlitz, Sphere, London, 1989, p. 308.
14. *op. cit.*, 8, pp. 28–30.
15. *ibid.*, p. 27.
16. *The Goblin Universe*, Ted Holiday, Llewellyn, St Paul Minnesota, 1986, from the Introduction by Colin Wilson, p. 24.
17. *Experiences of a Present-Day Exorcist*, Donald Omand, Kimber, London, 1970.
18. *op. cit.*, 16, pp. 164–95.
19. *A Witch's Book of Spells, Rituals and Sex Magick*, Diana Dagon, Finbarr, Folkestone, 1983, pp. 37–41.
20. *Blessing or Curse: You Can Choose!*, Derek Prince, Word (UK) Ltd, Milton Keynes, 1990, p. 40.

3 The Curse of King Tut

1. *The Curse of the Pharaohs*, Philipp Vandenberg, Lippincott, New York, 1975, p. 22.

2. *The Tomb of Tut-ankh-amun*, Howard Carter and Arthur C. Mace, 1963 ed., vol. 1, p. 183.
3. *The Search for the Gold of Tutankhamen*, Arnold C. Brackman, Hale, London, 1978, p. 162.
4. *op. cit.*, 1, p. 28.
5. *Pathways to the Gods*, Erich Von Daniken, Berkeley, New York, 1984.
6. *op. cit.*, 1, p. 87.
7. *ibid.*, p. 12.
8. 'Judge rebuts Tut Suit', K. Frazier, *Skeptical Inquirer*, 6 (No. 4), p. 12, USA, 1981–2.
9. 'Mummy's Curse Tut-tutted', K. Frazier, *Skeptical Inquirer*, 5 (No. 1), p. 13, USA, 1980–81.
10. *op. cit.*, 1, p. 20.
11. *op. cit.*, 3, p. 162.
12. *ibid.*, p. 165.
13. *ibid.*, p. 167.
14. 'King Tut's Revenge', J. Randi, *The Humanist*, 28 (No. 2), pp. 44–7, 1978.
15. *op. cit.*, 2, p. 185.
16. *op. cit.*, 3, p. 170.

4   *Ancestral Voices and Original Sin*
1. *Blessing or Curse: You Can Choose!*, Derek Prince, Word (UK) Ltd, Milton Keynes, 1990, p. 23.
2. *Adam, Eve, and the Serpent*, Elaine Pagels, Penguin, London, 1990, p. xxviii.
3. *Starseekers*, Colin Wilson, Book Club Associates, London, 1980, pp. 72–4.
4. *Woman's Mysteries*, M. Esther Harding, Rider, London, 1982 (1955), p. 605.
5. *op. cit.*, 1, pp. 44–5.
6. *Witches and Sorcerers*, Arkon Daraul, Muller, London, 1962, p. 30.
7. *The Comet is Coming*, Nigel Calder, BBC, London, 1980.
8. *The Kennedy Curse*, Arthur Gatti, Regnery, Chicago, 1976, p. 5.
9. *The Pursuit of the Millennium*, Norman Cohn, Paladin, London, 1970, p. 139.

5   *Papal Magicians and the Templar Head*
1. *Pagans and Christians*, Robin Lane Fox, Penguin, London, 1988, p. 615.
2. *Darkness of the Dark Ages*, anon., Morrish, London, *c.* 1890, pp. 12–17.
3. *Witches and Sorcerers*, Arkon Daraul, Muller, London, 1962, pp. 38–42.
4. *Born in Blood*, John J. Robinson, Arrow, London, 1993, p. 60.
5. *Witchcraft Today*, Gerald B. Gardner, Arrow, London, 1975 (1954), p. 79.
6. *Europe's Inner Demons*, Norman Cohn, Paladin, London, 1976, p. 85.
7. *op. cit.*, 4, p. 134.
8. *The Shroud and the Grail*, Noel Currer-Briggs, Weidenfeld & Nicolson, London, 1987, pp. 78–100.

9. *The Sign and the Seal*, Graham Hancock, Heinemann, London, 1992.
10. *op. cit.*, 4, p. 142.

6   Bothwell and the Witches
1. *Witches and Sorcerers*, Arkon Daraul, Muller, London, 1962, p. 60.
2. *ibid.*, pp. 62–5.
3. *Bothwell and the Witches*, Godfrey Watson, Hale, London, 1975, p. 73.
4. *op. cit.*, 1, p. 194.

7   Sister Jeanne and the Devils
1. *The Devils of Loudun*, Aldous Huxley, Penguin, London, 1971.
2. *Witches and Sorcerers*, Arkon Daraul, Muller, London, 1962, pp. 162–77.

8   Celtic Curses
1. *The Magic Arts in Celtic Britain*, Lewis Spence, Rider, 1970, pp. 58–63.
2. *Curses, Lucks and Talismans*, J. G. Lockhart, Geoffrey Bles, London, 1938, pp. 42–3.
3. *Albion*, Jennifer Westwood, Book Club Associates, London, 1986, p. 369.
4. *op. cit.*, 2, p. 54.
5. *op. cit.*, 3, p. 405.
6. *op. cit.*, 2, pp. 44–6.
7. *ibid.*, pp. 48–50
8. *op. cit.*, 3, pp. 406–8.
9. *Strange Spirits*, Pauline Saltzman, Paperback Library, New York, 1967, pp. 98–102.
10. *op. cit.*, 3, p. 406.
11. *Demonology and Witchcraft*, Sir Walter Scott (1830), Bell, New York, 1970, pp. 384–6.

9   The Brahan Seer and the Seaforth Doom
1. *The Prophecies of the Brahan Seer*, Alexander Mackenzie (1877), Constable, London, 1977.
2. *Ravens and Black Rain*, Elizabeth Sutherland, Corgi, London, 1987.

10   English Curses
1. *Religion and the Decline of Magic*, Keith Thomas, Peregrine, London, 1978, p. 602.
2. *ibid.*, p. 605.
3. *ibid.*, p. 605, from *Hereford District Records*.
4. *ibid.*, p. 604.
5. *ibid.*, pp. 115–16.
6. *ibid.*, p. 116.
7. *Curses, Lucks and Talismans*, J. G. Lockhart, Geoffrey Bles, London, 1938, pp. 4–9.
8. *op. cit.*, 1, p. 602.
9. *op. cit.*, 7, pp. 16–17.
10. *op. cit.*, 7, pp. 14–16.

11. *Strange Stories, Amazing Facts*, Reader's Digest Association Ltd, London, 1975, pp. 456–7.
12. *Strange Spirits*, Pauline Saltzman, Paperback Library, New York, 1967, pp. 52–5.
13. *op. cit.*, 11, p. 300.
14. *op. cit.*, 7, pp. 18–20.

11   The Hapsburg Ravens and the Lady in White
1. *The Habsburg Curse*, Hans Holzer, Doubleday, New York, 1973.
2. *Strange Spirits*, Pauline Saltzman, Paperback Library, New York, 1967, pp. 76–84.

12   Boning, Taboo and Oriental Curses
1. *Arthur C. Clarke's World of Strange Powers*, John Fairley and Simon Welfare, Book Club Associates, London, 1985, pp. 15–17.
2. 'The Curse of Uluru', in *Fortean Times*, No. 70 (Aug.–Sept. 1993), p. 17.
3. *Mysteries*, Colin Wilson, Grafton, London, 1979, pp. 456–7.
4. *The Occult in the Orient*, Christopher Dane, Popular Library, New York, 1974, pp. 29–33 (from *A Pattern of Islands*, A. Grimble, Murray, London, 1952.)
5. *ibid.*, pp. 13–21.
6. *Strange Stories, Amazing Facts*, Reader's Digest Association Ltd, London, 1975, p. 374.
7. *The Golden Bough*, Sir James Frazer, Macmillan, London, 1963, pp. 218–21.
8. *ibid.*, pp. 230–34.
9. *ibid.*, pp. 169–70.
10. *ibid.*, p. 224.

13   The Kahuna Death-prayer
1. *The Occult in the Orient*, Christopher Dane, Paperback Library, New York, 1974, pp. 113–19.
2. *Hawaiian Folk Tales*, Thomas G. Thrum, McClurg & Co., Chicago, 1912, p. 25.
3. *The Secret Science Behind Miracles*, Max Freedom Long, De Vorss, Marina del Rey, California, 1991 (1948), p. 8.
4. *ibid.*, p. 11.
5. *op. cit.*, 2, p. 84.
6. *ibid.*, pp. 89–96.
7. *ibid.*, pp. 87–9.
8. *Recovering the Ancient Magic*, Max Freedom Long, Rider & Co., London, 1936.

14   Africa: The Tale of Isaiah Oke
1. *From Witchcraft amongst the Azande*, E. E. Evans-Pritchard (1931), as in *Witchcraft and Sorcery*, ed. Max Marwick, Penguin, London, 1970, p. 29.
2. *Arthur C. Clarke's World of Strange Powers*, John Fairley and Simon

Welfare, Book Club Associates, London, 1985, pp. 17–18.
3. *Blessing or Curse: You Can Choose!*, Derek Prince, Word (UK) Ltd, Milton Keynes, 1990, pp. 124–5.
4. *Strange Stories, Amazing Facts*, Reader's Digest Association Ltd, London, 1975, p. 409.
5. *Blood Secrets*, Isaiah Oke (as told to Joe Wright), Prometheus Books, Buffalo, New York, 1989, p. 191.

15 Voodoo, Fugu and Zombie Resurrection
1. *Voodoo in Haiti*, Alfred Métraux, Andre Deutsch, London, 1959.
2. *Blood Secrets*, Isaiah Oke (as told to Joe Wright), Prometheus Books, Buffalo, New York, 1989, p. 20.
3. 'Constanzo: Voodoo Murders', Frank Smyth, from *Crimes and Victims*, Blitz Editions, Bookmart Ltd, Leicester, 1992.
4. 'Jinxes', Paul Sieveking, in *Fortean Times*, No. 28, Winter 1979, p. 42.
5. *Arthur C. Clarke's World of Strange Powers*, John Fairley and Simon Welfare, Book Club Associates, London, 1985, pp. 32–3.
6. *ibid.*, pp. 21–2.
7. *Divine Horsemen: The Living Gods of Haiti*, Maya Deren, Macpherson & Co.
8. *The Serpent and the Rainbow*, Wade Davis, Warner Books, New York, 1987.
9. 'Possessed by the gods', Francis King, in *The Unexplained* (Orbis partwork, London, 1983), pp. 2490–93.
10. *African Mythology*, Jan Knappert, Aquarian, Wellingborough, 1990, p. 267.

16 Rosalio Moisés: A Yaqui Life
1. *The Teachings of Don Juan: A Yaqui Way of Knowledge*, Carlos Castaneda, Penguin, London, 1970. (And other titles.)
2. *Castaneda's Journey*, Richard De Mille, Capra Press, Santa Barbara, California, 1978; *The Don Juan Papers: Further Castaneda Controversies*, Richard De Mille (ed.), Ross-Erickson Publishers, Santa Barbara, California, 1980.
3. *A Yaqui Life*, Rosalio Moisés, Jane Holden Kelley and William Curry Holden, Bison Books, University of Nebraska, 1977.

17 The Kennedy Curse
1. *Rolling Thunder*, Joey R. Jochmans, Sun Books, Santa Fe, New Mexico, 1980, p. 155.
2. *Premonitions*, Herbert B. Greenhouse, Pan, London, 1975, pp. 81–93.
3. *The Kennedys*, Peter Collier and David Horowitz, Warner, New York, 1984, p. 68.
4. *ibid.*, p. 86.
5. *ibid.*, p. 127.
6. *ibid.*, p. 258.
7. *ibid.*, p. 263.
8. *ibid.*, p. 293.
9. *ibid.*, p. 303.

10. *ibid.*, p. 355.
11. *ibid.*, p. 396.
12. *ibid.*, p. 407.
13. *ibid.*, p. 478.
14. *ibid.*, p. 468.
15. *ibid.*, p. 470.
16. *ibid.*, p. 465.
17. *ibid.*, p. 577.

18 *The Curious Case of Carole Compton*
1. *Superstition*, Carole Compton with Gerald Cole, Ebury Press, London, 1990.
2. *ibid.*, Afterword, Guy Lyon Playfair, pp. 178ff.
3. *Mysteries*, Colin Wilson, Granada, London, 1978, pp. 466ff.
4. *Poltergeist!*, Colin Wilson, New English Library, London, 1981.
5. *Fire From Heaven*, Michael Harrison, Pan, London, 1977.

19 *Jinxes and Jewels*
1. *Mysteries*, Colin Wilson, Granada, London, 1979, pp. 458–60.
2. 'The Hoodoo of the Great Eastern', Warren Armstrong, in *Strange Mysteries from the Sea*, ed. John Canning, Chancellor Press, London, 1992, pp. 285–93.
3. *A Sense of Something Strange*, Archie Roy, Dog & Bone Press, Glasgow, 1990.
4. *Strange Stories, Amazing Facts*, Reader's Digest Association Ltd, London, 1975, pp. 406–7.
5. *ibid.*, pp. 374–5.
6. *op. cit.*, 1, p. 458.
7. *ibid.*, p. 455, from 'Unlucky Possessions', T. C. Bridges, *Occult Review*, March 1927, p. 159.
8. *Ghost and Divining Rod*, T. C. Lethbridge, Routledge and Kegan Paul, London, 1963.
9. *op. cit.*, 1, pp. 477–82.
10. *Curses, Lucks and Talismans*, J. G. Lockhart, Geoffrey Bles, London, 1938, pp. 63–71.
11. *Citizens*, Simon Schama, Vintage Books, New York, 1990, pp. 203–10.
12. *Unsolved Mysteries*, Colin and Damon Wilson, Headline, London, 1993, pp. 358–67.
13. *Arthur C. Clarke's Mysterious World*, ed. Simon Welfare and John Fairley, Fontana, London, 1982, p. 77.
14. *op. cit.*, 12, pp. 358–67.

20 *Shakespeare's Scottish Tragedy*
1. 'The play that dare not speak its name', Nick Smurthwaite, *Sunday Telegraph*, 4 April 1993.
2. *Supernatural on Stage: Ghosts and Superstitions of the Theatre*, Richard Huggett, Taplinger, New York, 1975.

21   Afterword: The New Witch-hunts
1. 'Memories of Hell', Jim Schabel, in *Fortean Times* No. 71 (Oct.–Nov. 1993), pp. 23–34.
2. 'Bedevilled', Mike Dash, in *Fortean Times* No. 72 (Dec. 1993–Jan. 1994), pp. 47–9.
3. *op. cit.*, 1.
4. *op. cit.*, 2.
5. *ibid.*
6. *op. cit.*, 1.

Appendix I: The Evil Eye
1. *The Powers of Evil*, Richard Cavendish, Routledge and Kegan Paul, London, 1975, pp. 166–7.
2. *The Magic Arts in Celtic Britain*, Lewis Spence, Rider, London, 1970.
3. *The Evil Eye*, Frederick Elworthy (1895), Collier Books, New York, 1970.

Appendix II: Thought-forms
1. *Design for Destiny*, Edward W. Russell, Spearman, London, 1971.
2. *The Magus of Strovolus*, Kyriacos C. Markides, Arkana, London, 1985, pp. 34–46.
3. *Magic and Mystery in Tibet*, Alexandra David-Neel, Abacus, London, 1977.
4. *Psychic Self-Defence*, Dion Fortune, Aquarian, Wellingborough, 1977.
5. *Visions, Apparitions, Alien Visitors*, Hilary Evans, Aquarian, Wellingborough, 1984, pp. 216–22.

Free Catalog
of New Age & Occult Books From Carol Publishing Group

For over 30 years, the Citadel Library of the Mystic Arts has been hailed as America's definitive line of works on Wicca and White Magic, Occult Sciences and Personalities, Demonology, Spiritism, Mysticism, Natural Health, Psychic Sciences, Witchcraft, Metaphysics, and Esoterica.

Selected titles include: • The Alexander Technique • Amulets and Talismans • Apparitions and Survival of Death • Astral Projection • At the Heart of Darkness • The Bedside Book of Death • Beyond the Light • The Book of Ceremonial Magic • The Book of Spells, Hexes, and Curses • The Book of the Dead • Buddha and the Gospel of Buddhism • Candlelight Spells • The Candle Magick Workbook • The Case for Reincarnation • Classic Vampire Stories • The Complete Guide to Alternative Cancer Therapies • The Concise Lexicon of the Occult • Cosmic Consciousness • Daily Meditations for Dieters • Deceptions and Myths of the Bible • The Dictionary of Astrology • Dracula Book of Great Horror Stories • Egyptian Magic • Egyptian Religion • An Encyclopedia of Occultism • Encyclopedia of Signs, Omens and Superstitions • The Fairy-Faith in Celtic Countries • From Elsewhere • Future Memory • The Grim Reaper's Book of Days • Gypsy Sorcery and Fortune Telling • A History of Secret Societies • The History of Witchcraft • The Hollow Earth • The Holy Kabbalah • How to Improve Your Psychic Power • How to Interpret Your Dreams From A - Z • How To Make Amulets, Charms and Talismans • Hypnosis • The Kabbalah • Know Your Body Clock • The Lost Language of Symbolism, Vols. 1 & 2 • The Magick of Candle Burning • The Magus • Meaning in Dreams and Dreaming • The Modern Witch's Book of Home Remedies • The Modern Witch's Dreambook • The Modern Witch's Spellbook, 1 & 2 • Moon Madness • Not of This World • Numerology • Our Earth, Our Cure • Out-of-the-Body Experiences • The Pictorial Key to the Tarot • The Practice of Witchcraft Today • Principles of Light and Color • The Roots of Healing • Satanism • Satanism and Witchcraft • The Secrets of Ancient Witchcraft • The Secrets of Love Magick • Shouting at the Wolf • Silent Witness • Stranger Than Science • Strangest of All • Strange World • Study and Practice of Astral Projection • The Symbolism of Color • The Talisman Magick Workbook • Tarot Cards • Teachings of Tibetan Yoga • A Treasury of Witchcraft • The Vampire • The Werewolf of Paris • What Happens When You Die • Where the Ghosts Are • The Wicca Book of Days • Wicca Craft • Wicca Spellbook • Window To the Past • Witchcraft • Witchcraft, Sorcery, and Superstition • You Are All Sanpaku • Zen Macrobiotic Cooking

Ask for these New Age and Occult books at your bookstore. To order direct or to request a brochure, call 1-800-447-BOOK or send your name and address to Carol Publishing Group, 120 Enterprise Avenue, Dept 1675, Secaucus, NJ 07094.